SCIENCE PROVES THE AFTERLIFE:

The Science of Post-Mortem Consciousness Survival

SCIENCE PROVES THE AFTERLIFE:

The Science of Post-Mortem Consciousness Survival

Dr. Alan Ross Hugenot, Engr.SC. D.

Published by New Visions Creatives

ISBN: 979-8-89021-947-3 Paperback
ISBN: 979-8-89021-946-6 Hardback
ISBN: 979-8-89021-945-9 eBook

Amara De Falco
amaradefalco@newvisionscreatives.com
(763) 307-4915

Printed in United States of America

This book is printed on acid- free paper.

Contents

OUTLINE

FORWARD:

"Personally, I would be delighted if there were a life after death, especially if it permitted me to continue tolearn about this world and others, if it gave me a chance to discover how history turns out."

Dr. Carl Sagan **1996**

There is no longer any question, the afterlife is real ….. Objective clinical evidence has now proven *post-mortem consciousness survival* to be a scientific fact.

Objective evidence is the gold standard for scientific proofs, and now we have unequivocal objective clinical data proving that *Post Mortem Consciousness Survival* is real. Indeed, **The individual consciousness (spirit, soul) has been proven to survive the death of the physical body,** and movieson to occupy an alternative dimension.

While we can not say "where" that alternative dimension is located in the spacial sense of 3-D, yet, thefact that consciousness continues to operate in an undiscerned "location", while the brain is not functioning and the heart is stopped, proves that a functioning brain is not required to support consciousness.

Also, the discovery of Dark Energy and Dark Matter proves that **Classical Materialist science is currently unable to discern 96% of the universe.** String theory postulates that this undiscerned Dark Energy and Dark Matter must contain eight additional dimensions. … This leaves a lot of "room" and great deal of cosmic energy for surviving consciousnesses to persist within.

Finally, **real *After Death Communications-ADC* has been proven to occur** between individual post mortem surviving consciousnesses and consciousnesses still living in the physical, through the parallel phenomenon of Evidential Mediumship and poltergeist activities.

Part 1 of this book (chapters 1-5), describes the objective clinical evidence which proves each of these scientific facts, and also discusses what this all means for our existential perception of eternity.

Part 2 (chapters 6-8), explores beyond the the Event Horizon at the far reaches of the Near-Death experience, describing what we have so far been able to discern about the various dimensions of the afterlife from information received through *After Death Communications-ADC* (Evidential Mediumship) coming from surviving consciousnesses still alive on the other side.

Also, I will often quote Dr. Carl Sagan who is one of the most deep thinking cosmologists of the 20th century, a well respected scientist he realized that he was not an atheist, but was instead an agnostic. One of his favorite quotes about many aspects of science was **"We just don't know"**.

THE EVENT HORIZON: I have been trying to articulate this truth all of my adult life, yet have found it difficult to separate it from my own story.

As a young adult, I was killed in a motorcycle wreck, fell into a coma and then left my physical body behind. In an out-of-body journey which would later be termed a *Near-Death experience* I moved through an alternate dimension traveling to the edge of the etheric. Arriving at a borderland, which if crossed would be the end of this physical reality,

Today, astro-physicists call this border *"the Event Horizon"* and what lies beyond it a *"Dark Hole"*. Thisis the place where light disappears entirely. But, as I arrived there I was waylaid by a *Being of Light*. This being wanted to know if I was truly ready to cross into the further dimensions of the energy within thatdark hole. ... *Was I finished with my physical life? ... Had I accomplished my destiny? ... Or, did I still have unfinished business in the physical dimension of space-time?*

Shortly the *Being of Light* answered the question for me saying ***"You must return to the physical foryet a little while, in order to complete your destiny before you can move on into the dimensions beyond."***

In the half century since that day, much has been learned by science about the Near-Death experienceas frontier scientists have studied it extensively. And, I personally have worked closely with some ofthose scientists. Yet, while they now know much about the terrain between our dissolution from the physical cadaver and this etheric boundary; not much has been learned about what lies just beyond., because every Near-Death experiencer did not cross over but instead came back. Indeed, the actual existence of the *Event Horizon* was only recently discerned by frontier astro-physicists. Yet, much has been communicated back to us by those consciousnesses who die cross over.

In this book I will first present the latest objective clinical evidence which has recently proven that *post- mortem consciousness survival* is a scientific fact. and I will then go on to collate what we do knowabout those alternate dimensions which lie beyond, as discovered in the research of frontier scientists over the last century. Describing what it will be like when you pass on and make your transition into the afterlife. And, I will tell the story of my own experience with all of this. For the full story of my Near-

Death experience see *Appendix 4. - My Near-Death Experience.*

WHERE SCIENCE IS NOW: Today, frontier scientists have established, and replicated the following scientific facts:

1. **Clinical Evidence proving Post-Mortem Consciousness Survival** continues to be replicated daily in the world's hospitals.

2. **Astrophysics has proven that 96% of the universe is undiscerned**, and *String Theory* postulatesthat there are eight additional undiscerned dimensions.

3. **Scientific study of the Near Death Experience**, has shown us the out-of-body terrain leading up of theportal of death at the event horizon.

4. **The undiscovered country just beyond the Near-Death experience has been described in After Death Communications-ADC** received from surviving consciousnesses who are alive and occupying those indiscernible dimensions just beyond the event horizon, where I stood in my Near-Death experience.

Current medical practice has scientifically verified, and replicated *Post-Mortem Consciousness Survival,* proving that this was never a mere religious superstition, but has always been a true scientific fact. The truth is that we all survive the transition called death as we move into the next dimension. Indeed, as Dutch cardiologist and Near-Death researcher Dr. Pim von Lommel, MD quotes what one NDE survivor said in his book *Consciousness Beyond Life: The Science of the Near-Death experience (c) 2007…..*

"Dead turned out not to be dead".

Not surprisingly, the collected scientific evidence also indicates that:

1. **EVERYONE'S CONSCIOUSNESS WILL SURVIVE PHYSICAL DEATH:** It is apparent from the best science that NO ONE IS GOING TO ESCAPE ETERNAL LIFE. This is exactly whatSaint Paul states throughout his epistles **"Heaven is a free gift, it is not earned or deserved, but is the gift of God, lest any man should boast."** Each of our consciousnesses will continue in alternative dimensions of existence (i.e. located in what we currently perceive as dark energy and dark matter). And, that is what Part 2 of this book imperfectly describes.

2. **ALSO, IT IS APPARENT FROM BOTH STUDY OF THE NDE, AND THROUGH THE AFTERDEATH COMMUNICATIONS RECEIVED THAT THERE IS NO AFTER DEATH**

RETRIBUTION, as was previously forecast by the Roman Catholic church in collusion with the secular Roman Emperors Constantine and Justinian. That falsehood was fabricated in order to utilize the church to control the masses, through fear of hell to pay.

Indeed, the only afterlife "punishment" for our previously errant ways, will be our own deep and heartfelt remorse for those actions, as we do our own life review and compare what we could have done with what we actually did.

THE NEXT STAGE: Hopefully, all this information will help you to perceive that your own approaching death will not be the end of consciousness. … But, instead you can begin to perceive it merely the end of this chapter and a transition to the next stage of your continuing life in eternity.

CHAPTER 1
OBJECTIVE CLINICAL EVIDENCE PROVES THEAFTERLIFE

"How is it that hardly any major religion has looked at science and concluded, "This is better than we thought! The Universe is much bigger than our prophets said, grander,more subtle, more elegant?" Instead they say, "No, no, no! My god is a little god, and I want him to stay that way." A religion, old or new, that stressed the magnificence of the Universe as revealed by modern science might be able to draw forth reserves of reverenceand awe hardly tapped by the conventional faiths."

— Dr. Carl Sagan, <u>Pale Blue Dot: A Vision of the Human Future in Space</u>

"I would like to suggest that superstition is very simple: it is merely belief without anyevidence."

Dr. Carl Sagan, Gifford Lecture No. 1, 1985[1]

1. SO WHAT EXACTLY CONSTITUTES A SCIENTIFIC FACT? When you start to talk about the science of Post-Mortem Consciousness Survival most people will immediately ask, "Didn't science already prove that there was no afterlife survival?

And, that presumptive rumor has been carefully spread for the last couple of centuries, so it is widely believed. But, to be honest there is no scientific evidence proving that there is no *Post- Mortem Consciousness Survival*. Instead, there is a great deal of objective evidence for it.

First, it will be helpful to consider just what kind of evidence is required for a scientific proof?

Some of the world's greatest scientists have been unsuccessfully attempting to demonstrate *Post-Mortem Consciousness Survival* to be a scientific fact for the last 140 years, but they lacked the gold standard of objective evidence.

Beginning with the formation of the *Society for Psychical Research-SPR* in London in 1882, some of the worlds greatest minds have worked on this existential question including:

- **Dr. William James** of Harvard,

- **Sir Oliver Lodge,** Inventor along with Tesla of the Radio , and

- (Author's note: Marconi, stole the idea losing the patent lawsuit in US Supreme Court in 1947),

- Nobel Laureates like **Dr. Charles Robert Richet**, Nobel Prize for Medicine, 1913;

They collectively worked at collating and publishing an overwhelming quantity of ***subjective anecdotal evidence*** attempting to prove "scientifically" that *post-mortem consciousness survival* is a fact .

Unfortunately, these frontier scientists were never able to develop any *objective clinical or laboratory evidence* to prove their hypothesis of *Post-Mortem Consciousness Survival.* Instead, for centuries they relied on the ***"preponderance of evidence"*** theory, which always wins in court, but does not count at all when proving scientific facts.

Indeed, a century ago, back in 1893 *The National Spiritualist Association,* in the USA, whose members have lots of subjective personal evidence for *Post-Mortem Consciousness Survival,* adopted as one of their principles, the following definition:

> ***"We affirm that communication with the so-called dead is a fact, scientifically proven by the phenomena of Spiritualism (Mediumship)."***

But, again that affirmation/definition relies on ***subjective anecdotal evidence,*** which can not be used to prove something scientifically. This is because Spiritualist mediumship, which is discussed in Chapter 3, only provides subjective anecdotal evidence to the participating individuals but does not provide any ***objective and replicable laboratory or clinical evidence.***

Consequently, while Spiritualist Evidential Mediums and research scientists may personally know from their own subjective experience that consciousness survival is true; it is nearly impossible to convince someone else who has not experienced the phenomena themselves of this fact.

Science, in order to be "science", must be based entirely on reason, and therefore must disallow *subjective* anecdotal evidence which is based on personal experience and personal feelings. **This harsh scientific rigor prevents personal superstitions from being claimed as scientific truths.**

2. THE GOLD STANDARD: Yet, any hypothesis which can be proven ***objectively*** using laboratory or clinical evidence which can be replicated by another scientist is considered to be a proven scientific fact. This is demonstrated by proving the following three things using unequivocal, and replicable *objective* evidence:

1. The fact hypothesized must be a logical possibility,

2. There must be evidence for this fact, and

3. There must be no evidence against this fact.

Further, the gold standard of acceptable objective evidence includes only two forms of data:

1. **Laboratory data** resulting from carefully controlled experiments, and/or

2. **Clinical data** collected from controlled and monitored medical practice.

On the other hand, once something can be proven objectively, and is therefore established as a scientific fact; then all subjective evidence proving the same hypothesis becomes a validsecondary replication.

This means that when *Post-Mortem Consciousness Survival,* is finally proven with objective evidence, suddenly all the previously collected *subjective anecdotal evidence*, which has been amassed over the last 140 years, by frontier scientist at the SPR, IANDS, IONS, the Rhine Research Center, and DPS at the University of Virginia, will immediately become valuable data as a secondary form of replicating evidence for the already scientifically proven fact of *Post- Mortem Consciousness Survival.* This automatically happens just as soon as someone providesreal objective proof.

3. BUT, OBJECTIVE CLINICAL EVIDENCE ALREADY EXISTS: The inconvenient fact that materialists are trying to ignore is that 21st century medical practice has providentially provided that "gold standard" of **objective clinical evidence** required for such scientific proof ofpost-mortem consciousness survival.

Medical doctors have repeatedly proven that numerous patients, under controlled and monitored conditions, have actually:

1. DIED,

2. STAYED DEAD, even several hours or longer, with no respiration and no bloodcirculation. being just "stone cold dead". Then

3. WHEN SUBSEQUENTLY REVIVED, their consciousness resumed a normal physical life, with no psychological or mental losses.

Consider that while their physical body was "stone cold dead" their consciousness was surviving"somewhere". and that "somewhere" although still undefined qualifies as an "afterlife".

This phenomenal evidence of survival has been replicated many times at several major hospitals, over the last 32 years and has always been accomplished under carefully monitored and controlled conditions. In these cases the patients were actually dead by all our standard definitions. Most often they suffered a cardiac arrest while in the ICU while fully monitored.During the time that they were "stone cold dead" they had:

- No brain wave (EEG),

- No heart beat (EKG),

- Were not breathing, and

- Had a declining body temperature.

Additionally, in all these cases no life-saving or resuscitative measures like *Cardio Pulmonary Resuscitation - CPR* were in use with the patient during the extended time (up to several hours) that they were observed to be completely *"stone cold dead"*.

4. CLINICAL DEATH & RESUSCITATION: Today, standard medical practice is to monitor hospital patients suspected of a pending cardiac arrest, by placing them in an *Intensive Care status,* hooked up to all the modern sensors. Then, if they do have a spontaneous heart attack itwill all be recorded on the computers. When their electro-cardiogram-EKG flat lines because their heart stopped, their brain loses oxygen and ceases to function so their electro- encephalogram-EEG also flat lines. But, the timeline of the entire sequence of events is also officially recorded.

At the point of having no EKG and no EEG and no respiration they are, by all out standard definitions, *"stone cold dead"*. Previously, medical science **presumed** (but with no clinical proof)that this was the end of consciousness, and the end of life.

However, with the advent of *cardiopulmonary resuscitation-CPR,* it became standard practice toattempt reviving the patient using CPR and defibrillation paddles. But, these so-called "heroic" techniques have historically had only a 15% success rate, and of those only 11% finally leave the hospital to resume normal lives.

This extremely poor rate of success is because CPR attempts to force the broken heart pump, which has just failed (cardiac arrest) to continue working even though it is completely defunct.

But, recently, a better resuscitation technique has come into common use. Known as *Hypothermic Cardiac Arrest Therapy-HCA,* it has replaced CPR and defibrillation in many hospitals. The increased success rate of this newer resuscitation technique has changed medical terminology, and the terminal conditions that used to be considered "physical death" are now defined as ***"clinical death".*** ....

Also, *Hypothermic Cardiac Arrest-HCA* therapy has been successfully bringing people back from *"clinical death"* even as much as several hours later....

5. HOW HYPOTHERMIC CARDIAC ARREST THERAPY WORKS:

At normal body temperature of 98.6°F (37°C) when circulation and respiration suddenly cease due to cardiac arrest, the brain cells immediately start to deteriorate within 3 to 10 seconds. Shortly the cells of the physical body will also begin to "spoil". Unfortunately, after sufficient deterioration the consciousness can not be recalled back into that cadaver because the cells are no longer viable.

The body's high temperature is the main problem. If a deceased cadaver is left as is, then the temperature will only drop at about 2°F every hour. So if the deceased person had a normal temperature of 98.6°F (37°C), at the time of cardiac arrest, then it will take three hours for the cadaver to get down below the critical hypothermic temperature of 93°F (34°C), where the cells won't spoil. Unfortunately, in three hours the cells will have "spoiled" to the point that they are no longer viable.

On the other hand, by rapidly cooling the cadaver down below 93°F (34°C), within 30 to 40 minutes post cardiac arrest, their cells will stop spoiling..... Most hospitals now cool the body down to 86°F to allow a 6°F margin of safety.

At these safe temperatures the cadaver can then be kept in "cold storage" for severals hours without the need for respiration or blood circulation to prevent spoilage. During this time in "cold storage" the physical body is completely dead by all our definitions, with no blood circulation, no respiration, and no activity in the brain.

Yet, this cold storage pause allows surgeons extra time to repair the damaged heart with a bypass or whatever else it needs to allow full circulation to the heart muscle when they later restart the heart. When the surgery is complete they can re-warm the cadaver, and as it approaches normal temperatures they apply the defibrillation paddles to re-start the heart beat. At that point, the out-of-body consciousness will be coaxed back to this dimension (our normally observed physical reality), where it re-occupies the cadaver and returns to life in this reality.

Not surprisingly, these re-enlivened cadavers return from cold storage to active life as the same personalities they were before with no noticeable physiological or mental losses....

This literal "re-incarnating" of the consciousness back into the same physical body occurs easily when these careful hypothermic therapies are utilized to keep the physical body from deteriorating (spoiling).

Many of these formerly *"stone cold dead"* patients also retain clear memories of what thedoctors were doing during the extended time period that they were physically dead. Their physical brains were not functioning to support their consciousness, but they were still conscious, and witnessing activities from a perspective *outside their bodies,* usually watching from near the top of the room.....

Their consciousness was apparently out-of-body (literally "on the other side"), in another dimension where their consciousness was indiscernible to the medical personnel. That "other dimension" where their consciousness was hanging out (sometimes for several hours) whilethey physical body was "stone cold dead", fully qualifies as an "afterlife".

Also, when those clear memories of what the doctors were doing can be verified by theattending medical staff, it becomes all too obvious that while their cadaver was completely dead and flat-lining the consciousness associated with that cadaver was observing actual events entirely without support from a functioning brain.... And, also that it was doing this observing from a location outside our normally observed physical reality; an alternative dimension.

A. **STONE COLD DEAD FOR AT LEAST 45 MINUTES:** This technique of *Hypothermic CardiacArrest Therapy* was first used 32 years ago, back in August of 1991. At the Barrow Neurological Center in Phoenix, Arizona.

Interestingly, the patient, Pam Reynolds, also had a Near-Death experience during the time thatshe was completely dead. Later, both she and her doctor were interviewed on CBS television's news show *48 Hours.*

Dr. Robert Spetzler MD's surgical team had placed Pam Reynolds[1,2]into full *HypothermicCardiac Arrest-HCA.* Dropping her core temperature down to 60oF (16oC) they then completely drained all the blood from her head and left her with no measurable breathing, no heart beat (EKG) and no brain wave (EEG). Pam was completely "stone cold dead", by all our standard definitions for a little under one hour.

During this procedure she was hooked up to every medical measuring device available, measuring blood pressure, blood flow, oxygen level in her blood, core body temperature, and cordial brain activity, all of which verified that she was actually *dead* by every definition we have for death. Indeed, they actually drained all her blood out of her head while they worked to repair an aneurism in the vessels of her brain, and there was no blood in her head for over 20 minutes.So, there is no possible way that her brain was getting any oxygen, her EEG was flatlined and her physical brain was not functioning to support her consciousness. Yet, she was still recordingmemories.

Dr. Sabom discusses Pam Reynolds case in at this URL:[3] https://youtu.be/ GleW0qLQUtY

But, here is the chronology. Pam Reynold's heart was stopped with massive doses of potassiumchloride at 11:05 am. And, 20 minutes later, by 11:25 her body temperature had been lowered to60°F (16°C), she had no EEG brain stem activity, despite having 110 decibel clicks in both ears.Then the cardio-pulmonary bypass machine was shut down and her blood was completely drained out. She was literally *stone cold dead* from her heart stopping at 11:05 am until at least 11:52 am a period of over 45 minutes.

The aneurysm was removed and the vessel repaired by the surgeons so that by 12 noon they were again circulating her re-warmed blood using the cardio-pulmonary bypass machine. Yet,by this time she had been without any circulating blood for over 55 minutes.

Her EEG was now coming back and by 12:32 pm her temperature was back up to 89.6°F(32°C). So the cardio-pulmonary bypass machine was turned off, and Pam was officially alive again. Consequently, depending on how you define death, Pam had been completely "stonecold dead" for between 45 and 87 minutes.

Interestingly, while Pam was officially "stone cold dead", she progressed through a typical Near-Death experience, her consciousness was watching the surgeons from the top of the room, before she moved through a tunnel into the light where she met with her deceased relatives. When it was time to return to her cadaver she went back through the tunnel and reincarnated into that previously completely "dead" cadaver.

She had these NDE experiences and memories while her brain was not functioning to support her consciousness, and yet she was still conscious and having memories of actual experiences......

So, obviously even 32 years ago, any scientist whose mind was open far enough and who was willing to do the research could easily discover from this published objective clinical evidence that,

"a functioning brain is not necessary for consciousness to continue to exist".

B. **COMPLETELY DEAD FOR SEVERAL HOURS:** More recently, Dr. Sam Parnia, MD[4] often performs a similar procedure regularly in New York and London, during cardiac arrests. He improved on the technique used with Pam Reynolds so that the deceased only needs cooling to a temperature below 93∘F (34∘C). Dr. Parnia has found that he can leave the patient in this "coldstorage" for as long as four hours, while attending physicians use modern diagnostics to find outwhat is causing the problem with this patient's heart.

Dr. Parnia often brings patients back to life who have been literally dead for three or four hours, having been kept in "cold storage" with no respiration and no heart beat. So, it becomes obviousthat the rapid cooling by artificial means to hypothermic levels is the critical event, which retains the physical body in a useable condition for the associated consciousness.

Further, the consciousnesses of around 20% of these patients will continue to observe what is going on, while they are *"stone cold dead"* . Apparently, their consciousnesses are still recordingmemories with out any support from a functioning brain.

Dr. Parnia discusses all this in 2019 at this URL:[5] https://youtu.be/ Hz_4FGdWVF8

> *Author's note: Dr Parnia's work should not be confused with* **Hypothermic "AFTER" Cardiac Arrest Therapy** *as described by Johns Hopkins, which has a nearly identical name, and uses some of the same cooling techniques, except that during this procedure described by Johns Hopkins the patient's heart is artificially kept beating. Dr. Parnia is not using such artificial resuscitation techniques while the patient remainsdead, but only later to re-activate the cadaver.*

6. WHAT HAVING ACHIEVED THIS OBJECTIVE CLINICAL EVIDENCE MEANS: Simply put, the following facts have finally been "scientifically proven" by the unequivocal clinical evidence acceptable to science which has been produced by Dr. Robert Spetzler & Dr. Sam Parnia, and also replicated by other hospitals:

1. **Consciousness does not require a functioning brain** in order to think and record memories (i.e. the brain is just a receiver like a radio or television).

2. Survival of the individual consciousness after the associated physical bodyhas clearly died, can last for <u>at least several hours.</u>

3. While having an NDE during the time that their cadavers were clinically dead the associated consciousness appears to have become entirely discarnate and was **operating from a perspective entirely outside the normally observed physical reality** (i.e, on the other side).

4. Such ***Post-Mortem Consciousness Survival* is apparently "normal"**, and

5. **Consciousness can also re-incarnate**, that is return back in to the observed physical reality (i.e. come back to this side).

While Dr. Parnia provides many additional examples in his 2013 book *Erasing Death*[6], the following are two additional case studies recently reported in the popular news media that illustrate extended time frames for *post-mortem consciousness survival:* after cardiac arrest outside the hospital:

HIKER SURVIVES AFTER GOING INTO CARDIAC ARREST FOR SIX HOURS[7]:

A British woman whose heart stopped beating for six hours has been brought back to life inwhat doctors have described as an "exceptional case". Audrey Schoeman developed severe hypothermia when she was caught in a snowstorm while hiking in the Spanish Pyrenees with her husband in November of 2019.

Doctors say it is the longest cardiac arrest ever recorded in Spain. Mrs Schoeman, who has made a near-full recovery after the ordeal, says she hopes to be hiking again by spring. The 34-year-old, who lives in Barcelona, began having trouble speaking and moving during severe weather in the Pyrenees, later falling unconscious. Her condition worsened while waiting for emergency services and her husband Rohan believed she was dead.

At a press conference on Thursday, Mr Schoeman told Catalan channel TV3: *"I was trying to feel a pulse... I couldn't feel a breath, I couldn't feel a heartbeat."* When the rescue team arrived two hours later, Mrs. Schoeman's body temperature had fallen to 18°C (64.4°F). Upon arrival at Barcelona's Vall d'Hebron Hospital, she had no vital signs.

But, the low mountain temperatures which made Mrs Schoeman ill, also helped to save her life, her doctor Eduard Argudo has said. *She looked as though she was dead,…. But we knew that, in the context of hypothermia, Audrey had a chance of surviving."*

Hypothermia had protected her body and brain from deteriorating while unconscious, Dr Argudosaid, despite also bringing her to the brink of death. He added: "If she had been in cardiac arrestfor this long at a normal body temperature, she would be dead." In a race against time, doctors treating Mrs Schoeman turned to a specialized machine capable of removing blood, infusing it with oxygen and reintroducing it to the patient.

Once her body temperature had reached 30oC (86oF), they used a defibrillator to jump-start her heart some six hours after emergency services were contacted. Mrs. Schoeman was released from hospital 12 days later, with only some lingering issues with the mobility and sensitivity of her hands due to the hypothermia.

Watch the video describing this on[8] https://youtu.be/ayyLpOtkzW8

NORWEGIAN WOMAN SURVIVED LOWEST BODY TEMPERATURE EVER RECORDED[9]

In May 1999, 29-year-old radiologist Anna Bågenholm and two other young doctors set out for aday of skiing in the Kjolen Mountains of Norway. All experienced skiers, they headed off track toenjoy the fresh powder, but Bågenholm took a fall and slid downhill, landing head-first through the ice of a frozen stream.

Her friends quickly grabbed hold of her skis and tried to pull her out, but the ice was too thick and she was jammed between rocks. They called for help, but in the meantime, Bågenholm wasstuck upside down, in heavy gear, and being pulled in by icy cold water - pretty much a worst- case scenario.

Thankfully, she managed to find a pocket of air, and struggled to stay conscious waiting for help to arrive, but after 40 minutes, she stopped moving. By the time the rescue team arrived, she had been under the ice for 80 minutes, and was frozen solid.

Her heart wasn't beating, she wasn't breathing. She was clinically dead. No one had ever been brought back from such a low temperature before, but her friends immediately started CPR on her, hoping that she might be able to be revived after being air-lifted to the University Hospital ofNorth Norway in Tromsø.

By the time she reached the operating room at the hospital, it had been more than 2.5 hours since she first fell in the ice, and her temperature was still an unprecedented 13.7 degrees Celsius (56.7 Fahrenheit).

"She has completely dilated pupils. She is ashen, flaxen white. She's wet. She's ice cold when I touch her skin, and she looks absolutely dead," head of the emergency medical department, Mads Gilbert, told CNN a decade later.

"On the ECG [electrocardiogram], which the doctor on the helicopter had connected her to, there is a completely flat line. Like you could have drawn it with a ruler. No signs of life whatsoever." But, he made an important decision. "We will not declare her dead until she is warm and dead," said Gilbert.

Gilbert's hope was that Bågenholm was so cold that her brain would have begun to slow down before she died, protecting it from damage. Our bodies' preferred temperature of 37.5ºC (99.5ºF), our brains can only go for around 20 minutes without oxygen before irreversible damage sets in. But, as we cool down, the body's metabolism also slows way down in order to keep us alive, which means the brain can get by with far less oxygen.

Given how unprecedentedly cold Bågenholm was, Gilbert thought that perhaps the continuous CPR she'd received since being pulled out of the frozen river might have been enough to keep her brain functioning properly. His team hooked Bågenholm up to a heart-lung machine, and they pumped her blood out of her body to warm up before circulating it through her again - very gradually, over several hours, her temperature began to rise.

The heart monitor blipped a few times, but continued to flatline. The team waited. At around 4 pm the next day, almost a day (24 hours) after Bågenholm had fallen into the river, her heart restarted, and began pumping the blood on its own again.

Gradually the rest of her body began to heal, too. After 12 days, she opened her eyes, but it took more than a year for her to be able to move and walk again due to nerve damage. She's now fully recovered, and works at the same hospital that saved her life. Her case didn't only make the record books, and a study in The Lancet journal - it also changed the way doctors approached hypothermia deaths.

"In a victim of very deep accidental hypothermia, nine hours of resuscitation and stabilization led to good physical and mental recovery. This potential outcome should be borne in mind for all such victims," concluded The Lancet study. Before 1999, no patient had survived being frozen to death at the University Hospital of North Norway. But between 1999 and 2013, nine out of 24 patients survived hypothermic cardiac arrest, a 2014 study led by Gilbert found. Doctors at the University of Pittsburgh Medical Centre hospital are now actually inducing hypothermia in critical patients, to prolong the window in which they can stop their bleeding and save their lives.

"We think of death as being a moment in time," physiologist Kevin Fong told NPR back in 2014, "but actually, it is a process." When we're warm, that process happens in minutes, but when we're cold it slows down - and, occasionally, that can work in our favor. Check this out at:

- https://www.rd.com/list/people-who-froze-came-back-to-life/ [10]

- https://www.sciencealert.com/this-woman-survived-the-lowest-body-temperature- ever-recorded [11]

INESCAPABLE CONCLUSIONS:

This objective evidential data amassed in clinical practice and also being reported in the popular media articles above clearly prove scientifically and unequivocally that:

Post-Mortem Consciousness Survival continues after complete physical death.

In the examples given above consciousness can apparently survive, without the support of a functioning physical body for as long as 3, 4, 6, or even 24 hours….. And, that individual surviving consciousness associated with the deceased cadaver can also be summoned back into the observed physical reality (literally re-incarnation) even several hours after the cadaver has been completely dead, so long as the cadaver has been kept in cold storage and not allowed topsoil or decay.

Of course, many serious scientists may have difficulty accepting this recent objective evidence, because it contradicts the prior speculations and presumptions of science, which they previously understood to be fact.

For example, it has been commonly thought for several centuries that consciousness required a functioning brain. But, this presumption conflicts with this latest objective clinical evidence, and so it is now time to re-examine the underlying basis of such presumed facts.

Unfortunately, instead of accepting the objective clinical data for consciousness survival, many scientists and physicians are hiding behind superficial explanations like ***"Somehow the brain got oxygen"***. These are feeble statements trying to change the facts so they can cling to their previously perceived world view. But, it is obvious from the objective clinical data that there was absolutely no blood circulation to bring that oxygen to the brain, and no signal from the EEG or the EKG, showing no activity in the brain or the heart.

On the other hand, some serious scientists have raised a valid question:

"If people are actually surviving death and later returning to life, then it would seem that this should be occurring fairly often and not just be limited to one or two isolated cases?".

But, here again the truth is simply obscure….. Literary studies conducted by the *International Association for Near-Death Studies (iands.org)* since 1978 have documented anecdotal accounts of thousands of cases like this recorded in the literature of the last 2,400 years beginning with Plato around 400 BCE.[12] Plato describes what the skeptics have dubbed **The Myth of Er,"** but which is clearly a description of a Near-Death experience survived by Er, so it is not a myth at all.

REPLICATING OBJECTIVE CLINICAL EVIDENCE:

Dr. Spetzler's and Dr. Parnia's pioneering work and findings that the consciousness continues entirely without a functioning brain using *Hypothermic Cardiac Arrest therapy* have also been replicated independently by a Cardiac Surgeon in the Netherlands.

Dr. Pin Van Lommel, MD, living near Amsterdam has documented hundreds of cardiac arrest cases, which occurred while the patient was in the *Intensive Care Unit-ICU* with all their vital signs being monitored including EKG and EEG. He has carefully culled and analyzed those specific cases in which the patient also remembered a Near-Death experience occurring during the period of cardiac arrest.

Of course, not everyone who had a cardiac arrest remembers an NDE, but between 19 and 20% do remember having NDE's. Out of the 850 cardiac arrest cases studied, Dr. Van Lommel interviewed nearly all who did remember a Near-Death experience during the time of their cardiac arrest. These patients reported memories of what occurred during the same times whenthe ICU monitors verified that they were officially brain dead (i.e. their EEG was flatlined) and they had no brain function. Yet, their consciousness, without any support from a functioning brain, was still recorded vivid memories of verifiable details. Details which medical personnel were able to authenticate.

Dr. Van Lommel's objective clinical evidence again replicates and verifies everything that Dr.s Spetzler and Parnia have also scientifically proven. Dr. Van Lommel, first published his findings in the Dec 15, 2001 in *Lancet*,[13] one of Europe's most respected medical journals.

Dr. Van Lommel also discusses all this in his 2011 book *Consciousness Beyond Life*[14], where he summarizes the current state of theory among scientists on *post-mortem consciousness survival*, while collating this with quantum physics and the NDE as:

> *"Most people still believe that death is the end of everything that used to be my own belief. But, after many years of critical research into the stories of NDErs, and after careful exploration of current knowledge about brain function, consciousness, and some basic principles of quantum physics, my views have undergone a complete transformation. I found the most significant finding to be the conclusion of one NDEr: "DEAD TURNED OUT NOT TO BE DEAD". I now see the continuity of our consciousness after the death of our physical body as a very real possibility."*

Dr. Pim van Lommel, Cardiac Surgeon

Dr. Van Lommel, with whom I have become personally acquainted, is interviewed in a video at this URL:https://youtu.be/RkF4KzWTrKA[15]

So now we have overwhelming replication by both hypothermic cardiac physicians and traditional cardiac physicians, with objective clinical evidence, of the scientific facts that:

1. **Consciousness does not require a functioning brain** in order to think and record memories (i.e. the brain is just a receiver like a radio or television).

2. This survival of the consciousness after the physical body has clearly died, can last for at least several hours.

3. While having an NDE during the time that their cadavers were clinically dead the associated consciousness appears to have become **entirely discarnate andwas operating from a perspective entirely outside the normally observed physical reality** (i.e, on the other side).

4. Such *Post-Mortem Consciousness Survival* **is apparently "normal"**, and

5. **Consciousness can also re-incarnate**, that is return back in to the observed physical reality (i.e. this side).

Of course, for *post mortem consciousness survival* to fully qualify as a proven "scientific fact" there also has to be no evidence against the hypothesis.

And, despite the fact that many self proclaimed experts have told us that, **"Science has long ago proven there is no afterlife",** none of these so-called experts are ever able to cite any specific scientific data which disproves *Post-Mortem Consciousness Survival......* and while none of them has taken the time to research and find this imagined underlying science backing up their presumptions; yet they often remain adamant that *Post-Mortem Consciousness Survival*must be impossible.

Frankly, because there never has been any evidence showing that *Post-Mortem Consciousness Survival* is impossible, their presumption of it's impossibility becomes no more than a *religious superstition.*

Again, one of the purposes of science rigorously requiring **objective evidence is that itprevents personal superstitions from being claimed as truths.**

Consequently, we now have everything necessary to demonstrate that: *Post mortemconsciousness survival* **is a "scientific fact":**

1. The hypothesis is a **logical possibility,**

2. There is much replicated **evidence for it,** and

3. There is **no evidence against it.**

TWO LOGICAL QUESTIONS: Now, because our habitual perspective on the normally observed physical reality is restricted to space-time (i.e. three dimensions of space and one of time), we are driven to ask the next two questions:

1. **WHERE** (space) do these *Post-Mortem Consciousnesses* survive?, and

2. **HOW LONG** (time) do these consciousnesses survive post-mortem?

The answer to the first question WHERE? is easy.

Although Materialist scientists like to pretend that science already knows everything, with many of them attempting to discover the "*Theory of Everything*",.... Yet, a gaping hole in our presumed complete scientific knowledge accidentally appeared in 1998, showing that our limited knowledge does not begin to approach "everything".

Astronomers and Astrophysicists observing through the Hubble Telescope noticed that the expansion of our universe was accelerating, rather than slowing down due to gravity as had been presumptively speculated for the previous 350 years…. These scientists have since determined that this acceleration is being caused by hidden forces which they named *Dark Energy* and *Dark Matter,* and they also calculated that together these two undiscerned entities make up roughly 96% of the universe.

This gaping hole of not being able to discern 96% of what's out there within the limitedviewfinder of our standard model for space-time, illustrates the monumental hubris of thearchaic Materialist perspective, which habitually defines our normally observed physical reality.

Trying to limit the universe to the 4% which our five senses can discern as our normally observed physical reality within the limited perspective of of space-time looks very foolish in hindsight. It is like saying ***"If I can't see it, then it can not exist"***. But, if science had taken that perspective with the invisible forces of electricity and magnetism where would our industrial world be today?

Yet, if our perceptive box of three dimensional space-time misses more than 96% of everything, then there is plenty of "left over" reality, which according to string theory includes 8 more dimensions. And, that leaves plenty of room where consciousness can hang out after it leaves our familiar 4% (i.e. this side). So the answer to that WHERE question, will be found is in one of the eight alternative dimensions which are outside of our normally observed reality of 3D plus time.

Further, with *Post-Mortem Consciousness Survival* now a proven scientific fact, it is up to dedicated parapsychological scientists to discover all the additional dimensions predicted by string theory which exist in that other 96%, but which the backward looking Materialist believers prefer to deny could even exist.

Additionally, parapsychologists are also now allowed to incorporate as valid secondary replication, all the overwhelming *subjective* anecdotal evidence which agrees with that now proven premise.

Of course, when working with *subjective* evidence scientific rigor requires that double and triple blind conditions should be maintained in all our work in order to decrease the chance of mis- interpretation or personal emotional bias coloring the data. And in fact, leading parapsychological scientists have been utilizing double and triple blind laboratory techniques forall of their studies since the early 1970's.

The answer to the second question HOW LONG is more complicated.

Determining "HOW LONG does the consciousness survive post-mortem?" will take a bit more scientific research because it necessitates answering several additional existential questions at the same time, as follows:

1. **If, consciousnesses can depart from the physical and return easily to the same cadaver, then "What would prevent that consciousness from returning to a different cadaver?"**

2. What proof do we have that an individual consciousness is permanently "attached" to a specific physical cadaver?

3. How long can consciousness survive when not associated with the normally observed physical reality (i.e. this side), or with a particular physical cadaver manifesting in this reality?

4. Finally, What would prevent reincarnation of a prior consciousness into adifferent cadaver later, or even many years later?

The answers to these additional existential questions are now being found in several areas of scientific research, where to date only *subjective* evidence was yet available. But, the subjectiveevidence in all of these areas of research is now validated by *Post-Mortem Consciousness Survival* now a proven scientific fact. Those areas of research are discussed in the following chapters.

CHAPTER 2
OBJECTIVE PROOF VALIDATES PRIORSUBJECTIVE ANECDOTAL EVIDENCE

"I would love to believe that when I die I will live again, that some thinking, feeling, rememberingpart of me will continue. But as much as I want to believe that, and despite the ancient andworldwide cultural traditions that assert an afterlife, I know of nothing to suggest that it is morethan wishful thinking."

— Carl Sagan, <u>Billions & Billions: Thoughts on Life and Death at the Brink of the Millennium</u>

"There are claims in the parapsychology field which, in my opinion, deserve serious study," with [one] being *"that young children sometimes report details of a previous life, which upon checking turn out to be accurate and which they could not have known about in any other way than reincarnation."* Carl Sagan

Unfortunately, Dr. Carl Sagan died at the end of the 20th century, just as the objective clinical evidence for *Post Mortem Consciousness Survival* was coming to light. The Pam Reynolds caseoccurred in August 1991, but replication by Dr. Parnia & Dr. von Lommel would not occur until the 21st century, and Dr. Sagan crossed over died on Dec 20, 1996.

But, replication now established that *Post-Mortem Consciousness Survival* was in fact real, and qualified as a scientific fact using the "Gold Standard" of objective clinical evidence. This unequivocal proof legitimizes the overwhelming subjective evidence for *Post-Mortem Consciousness Survival*, which has been developed by frontier scientist over the last 140 years,which now become replication for the objective clinical evidence. Some of that overwhelming subjective evidence is listed below.

1. EVIDENCE FROM MEMORIES OF PAST LIVES: At the University of Virginia, *Department ofPerceptual Studies-DPS*. The late Dr. Ian Stevenson, MD, carried out lengthy investigations of over 2400 cases of children remembering past lives, by interviewing the actual participants. His studies took place over 50 years, traveling and working in both Eastern and Western cultures. And since Dr. Stevenson's transition his colleagues, Bruce Greyson MD, and Jim Tucker, MD, as well as others, are continuing his work of examining individual cases of children whoremember past lives.

This research has all been carefully documented using rigorous science to weigh the subjective evidence, as reported in Stevenson's books; *Twenty Cases Suggestive of Re-incarnation* ©1974[16] and *Children Who Remember Previous Lives* ©2001[17]. Jim B. Tucker M.D. published on this same subject his book *Life Before Life* ©2005[18]

This research is all discussed in the February 2017 YouTube video *Is There Life After Death? 50 years of Research at UVA* at URL:[19] https://youtu.be/0AtTM9hgCDw, which has had overa million views since posted.

Typically, children between three and five years old, begin relating memories of an earlier life to their parents in the present life. These children often have detailed accounts of their wives, husbands, mistresses, and children from the previous life.

Often children will have graphic memories of how they died and/or who killed them. They can even recognize former friends and family members still living when the child is taken to the vicinity where the previous life took place.

In a few cases, they can also remember and replicate the dialect of the prior home event hough they have had no exposure to this dialect in this current physical life. In other cases, they may even carry a physical birthmark or physical deformity that corresponds with an injury received in the previous life. Stevenson published another book, *Where Reincarnation and Biology Intersect*[20], which shows photographically these corresponding deformities which match the prior remembered incarnation.

Yet, by the time these children reach age 8-10 years old, they will begin forgetting the prior life as they assimilate into their current physical life. When they are surrounded by a culture that encourages these types of prior life memories then the memories may continue well intoadulthood. But, of =cource in Western culture, which does not subscribe to reincarnation, such memories are not typically appreciated by Mom and Dad, so children merely put them aside andquickly forget them.

Following are a three representative examples of the cases Dr. Stevenson has verified, followed by two additional cases, added more recently. My favorite case is this first one about Marta Lorenz, for two reasons; first, it began with a prediction during the prior life stating that the soul would reincarnate and return as a friend's daughter, and the narrative is underlaid with a powerful love story.

A. MARTA LORENZ CASE[21]***:*** The parents had been given the prediction ***"I will return as yourdaughter"***, before that first life ended, and prior to their later pregnancy. So, before the birth of this child they wisely chose to observe the daughter's life under strict single-blind laboratory conditions.

The results of this decision to single blind the "experiment" provide amazing evidence. Here are the details as carefully documented by Dr. Ian

Stevenson who interviewed all the players exceptthe original Sinha, who had died in 1917. The following is my shortened paraphrase of thatstory:

Maria Januaria de Olivero, nicknamed Sinha or Sinhazinha, was born about 1890, in the village of Dom Feliciano, about 100 miles SW of Puerto Alegre in the province of Rio Grande de Sul, the westernmost state of Brazil. After Sinha's father disapproved of one of her suitors, the youngman committed suicide. Sinha, who loved the young man, was distraught and therefore exposed herself to the elements and to tuberculosis, acquired an infection of the lungs and larynx, and then, a few months later, she also died.

However, on her deathbed she acknowledged to her dear friend, **Ida Lorenz,** that she wanted todie and had tried to become infected with TB. She also promised Ida that she would returnagain and be born as Ida's daughter. Sinha further predicted that:

> **"When reborn ,and at an age when I can speak on the mystery of rebirth in the body of the little girl who will be your daughter, I SHALL RELATE MANY THINGS OF MY PRESENT LIFE, AND THUS YOU WILL RECOGNIZE THE TRUTH".**

In October 1917, Sinha died the day after her declaration to later return as Ida's daughter. Atthat time she was about 28-years-old.

Ten months later, on August 14, 1918, Ida Lorenz gave birth to a daughter, whom she named Marta. This child would have been conceived about a month after Sinha had died.

Ida and her husband had agreed to maintain the single-blind conditions and never spoke of Sinha's prediction to Marta, to their other children, nor to the neighbors, or to anyone who might ever come in contact with any future daughters. They also never told her anything about Sinha,It was to be the parents' personal secret.

But, when Marta was two-and-a-half, she began to speak, exactly as predicted by Sinha saying **"...when she had been big before"**. She volunteered to her parents that she had been **nicknamed Sinha** in her prior life, and also that her real name in that prior life had been **Maria**.

Marta said all this despite the fact that the names Sinha and Maria had never once been utteredin their household. Marta made no less than *120 separate declarations over the next few years about details of Sinha's life,* carefully recorded by her parents.

Although, her home from the former life was only 12 miles away, her father, in order to keep the single-blind conditions, never took Marta there until she was 12-years-old, although she had asked numerous times to go to her former home. And, it was not until the time of this visit, atage 12, that the parents from the prior life heard anything about Marta being the reborn Sinha.

When Marta was a child of 3 or 4, and bereaved adults would suffer from grief, Marta would comfort them by saying,

"I died, and I am living again"[22]

And another time, during a rainstorm, when one of her sisters expressed regret that their dead sister Emilia would get wet in the grave, the child Marta said,

"Don't say that, Emilia is not in the cemetery. She is in a safer and better place than weare; her soul never can be wet". [23]

So, although Marta's memories have faded since the vivid days of her childhood, it is apparent from what she said in early childhood that as a child she also remembered her ten months of lifeon the other side between the two lives here.

I highly recommend reading this particular case in Dr. Stevenson's book "Twenty Cases Suggestive of Reincarnation"[24]. The narrative runs 20 pages and is heavily documented and researched. Check it out also at this URL:[25] https://psi-encyclopedia.spr.ac.uk/articles/marta-lorenz. If the file won't link copy the address to your browser.

B. BISHEN CHAND CASE: [26],[27],[28] Bishen Chand Kapoor was born into the Gulham family in 1921 in Barielly, India. At the age of one-and-a-half, he began asking questions about a town called Pilibhit, which was located about 50 miles away, a place no one in his family knew much about and did not know anyone who lived there. Bishen asked his parents to take him there,and it was obvious to them that he believed he had lived there in a prior life. By the time Bishen was five-years-old, he could clearly articulate memories of his former life and from that village where he and his present family had never visited.

By 1926, he was stating that in the former life had been named Laxmi Narain, was the son of a wealthy landowner, and claimed to remember an uncle named Har Narain. Later, it would be discovered that this "uncle" was actually the father of Chand's remembered self with that same name of Laxmi. The young Chand described the house of Laxmi Narain, including various features of the layout, as well as a neighbor's house with a green gate, and how he had enjoyedthe singing and dancing of the young women who entertained men in bars. He often spoke and could even read words of Urdu, a language written in Arabic script, even though Hindi was the language spoken in Chand's home and **no one had taught him Urdu or how to read it.**

> *Note These two items are remarkable, a mere five-year-old child remembering how he enjoyed watching the dancing girls in adult bars during his past life, and also speaking and reading a foreign language that he had not been taught.*

A local attorney, K.K.N. Sahay, heard about Chand's memories and came to the house to recordstatements from the boy and other family members. In one of those most surprising memories, the boy recounted killing a suitor of his mistress, **showing surprising awareness for a five- year-old of the difference between a wife and a mistress.** None of the family nor the attorneyhad ever heard of the real Laxmi Narain. It is important to know that the attorney wrote down Chand's complete narrative at this time *before the attorney or Chand ever traveled to Pilibhit.*

When the attorney, along with the young Chand and Chand's father, traveled the 50 miles to Pilibhit, it was immediately confirmed that a man named Laxmi Narain had indeed shot andkilled a rival lover of a prostitute who was still in the town. Narain had avoided prosecution because of his wealth, but had died two years later at age 32. By the time Chand was five, not quite eight years had elapsed since the death of the adult Laxmi Narain.

When taken to Laxmi's old school, the boy ran to the classroom, described the teacher, andfrom an old photograph, identified and named classmates, one of whom was in the crowd that had gathered. Chand, had a heartwarming reunion with Laxmi's mother, whom he greatly preferred over his own biological mother. The green gate was seen as described, and when given Laxmi's tabla drums, he was reported to have played them with great skill. Before leaving the house, Chand revealed where he had, during the past life as the adult Laxmi Narain, hidden some gold coins, which were recovered the following day.

This story clearly suggests that the consciousness survives in a very real form. The facts of Chand's language and musical skills, the adult emotions this toddler displayed, his identification of people by name from a photograph, even though he had never met them in this life, all are irrefutable proof that the consciousness survives. This case has been carefully verified and documented by the researchers at the University of Virginia. Check this out at this URL:[29] https://psi-encyclopedia.spr.ac.uk/articles/

bishen-chand-kapoor. If the file won't link copy the address to your browser.

C. SHANTI DEVI CASE:[30] Shanti Devi was born in 1926 in old Delhi. At about the age of three, she began to tell her parents stories regarding a former life, in which she was married to a man named Kedar Nath, who lived in the nearby town of Muttra. In that prior life she also had two children, and she had apparently died in childbirth bearing a third child in 1925. She described in detail her home in Muttra where she had lived with her husband and children.

When her parents tired of trying to stop her from telling these stories, her grand-uncle, Kishen Chand, sent a letter to Muttra to see how much, if any, of the little girl's story was true. He mailed it to an address that Shanti herself remembered and gave to him. That letter was received by a widower named Kedar Nath. His wife Lugdi had died in childbirth in 1925, the year before Shanti was born. Quite naturally, Kedar Nath suspected this was all a fraud. So he sent his cousin, Mr. Lal, who lived in Delhi to visit Shanti at her home in Delhi. The cousin would know if she were an imposter.

Mr. Lal went to Shanti's home without announcing his relationship and pretending to be on business. But, when Shanti answered the door, she screamed and jumped into his arms. Her mother then came to the door. Before Mr. Lal could speak, the nine-year-old Shanti said, ***"Mother this is a cousin of my Husband! He lived not far from us in Muttra and then moved to Delhi. I am so happy to see him. He must come in, I want to know about my husband and my sons."***

Mr. Lal confirmed for Shanti's parents all the facts she had told them over the years. Soon they reached the consensus that Kedar and his son should come to Delhi to meet Shanti. Later, when Kedar arrived Shanti, although only nine-years-old, treated him as a normal adult wife would do. She kissed him and called him by pet names. Shanti served him biscuits and tea. And then when Kedar's eyes began to fill with tears, she comforted him using personal phrases and endearments known only to Kedar and his late wife Lugdi Nath.

News reporters decided to sponsor Shanti on a trip to Muttra. They thought that she should be able to lead them to her former home. But, as the train arrived in Muttra, Shanti saw her relatives from her prior life on the platform (relatives who had not been to Dehli, and whom she had not seen in this life). She yelled and waved at them as the train slowed at the platform. Before getting to meet the relatives she told the reporters that they were the mother and brother of her husband. On the platform, she began to speak with them. The reporters noted that she had correctly named them.

Then, the reporters realized that nine-year-old Shanti was not speaking Hindustani, the language she spoke at home in Delhi, but was instead speaking coherently in a dialect specific to Muttra. Shanti had never learned - nor been exposed to - this strange dialect, but according to the news reporters, she spoke it fluently, and if she actually was the deceased Lugdi's reincarnated consciousness, then she would easily know this local language.

> *Note: this use of the dialect was reported in the news accounts, but could not later be verified by any eye-witnesses for Ian Stevenson during his research some decades later.*

Next, as the reporters had requested, Shanti lead them to the Nath house. Although, she had never been in Muttra during her current life, she lead them directly to the Nath house. On the way, she told them things that only Lugdi could have known. Lugdi's husband Kedar asked her specifically where she had hidden some rings that Lugdi had owned before she died. Shanti told him that they were hidden in a pot that she had buried (during her former life) in a location at their prior home where they had lived together before moving to this house. Later, the investigators were able to dig up the rings where she had said they were buried. The records also indicate that everyone who had previously known Lugdi in Muttra now accepted Shanti as being Lugdi's reincarnated consciousness.

Shanti's case has been investigated by numerous researchers over the years. Clearly, cases like this, with remembered foreign language, remembered buried objects, and spontaneously recognized faces from the prior life, are indeed rare. Yet, many of them do exist. And, just one such case, with so many facts revealed which were unknowable to anyone except the departed's consciousness from the prior life, would seem to be all that is required as compelling proof that reincarnation actually happens. Check this out at:[31] https://www.carolbowman.com/dr-ian-stevenson/case-shanti-devi If the file won't link copy the address to your browser.

As our Western Culture has slowly shaken-off the restrictive *single lifetime theory* more people have recognized that children are remembering their past lives.

D. JAMES LINEGAR CASE:[32] a 2-year-old in Lafayette, Louisiana, remembered his prior life as James Houston and recalled being shot down during World War II on March 3, 1945, while flying his Navy Corsair over Chi Chi Jima. Houston was a pilot flying from the Aircraft Carrier, *USS*

Natoma Bay CVE-62, and the child James Linegar remembered Houston's friend, Jack Larson, a fellow pilot on the ship.

Jack Larson is still living. The child remembered that his plane was hit near the engine and crashed in flames. Eyewitnesses of his crash have verified the fact that his plane was hit in the engine. James Houston's sister is still living, and has now come to believe that James Linegar isactually her brother reincarnated. She believes this simply because of all the things little James knows that only her deceased brother could have known. His parents published their story, *Soul Survivor,* in 2010.[33]

A video discussing this is found at this URL[34] https://youtu.be/h82PwADicl8

E. BARBO KARLEN CASE: Barbo was born to Christian parents in Sweden in 1954. When shewas less than 3-years-old, she told her parents that her name was not Barbro, but was Anne Frank. This was less than ten years after Anne Frank had died in the Bergen-Belsen concentration camp in 1945. At that time Barbro's parents had no knowledge of who Anne Frank might have been. The book, *Anne Frank: Diary of a Young Girl*, also known as *The Diary of Anne Frank,* had not yet been translated or published in Swedish.

Barbro stated how her parents desired that she call them "Ma" and "Pa," but she knew that they were not her real parents. Barbro instead said that her "real parents" would soon come to gether and take her away to her "real home". While still a child, Barbro told her parents details of her life as Anne. Barbro also had nightmares as a child, in which men ran up the stairs and kicked in the door to her family's attic hiding place. All of this with no knowledge of the story of Anne Frank.

Both James Linnegar's and Barbro Karlan's cases are discussed at this URL[35] https://youtu.be/9w2MCpzE8u0 For those who are interested here is a URL that lists 61 children who have past life memories,[36] https://psi-encyclopedia.spr.ac.uk/articles/children-whoremember-previous-life

CONCLUSIONS FROM SUBJECTIVE ANECDOTAL EVIDENCE OF PAST LIVES: Careful checking the facts with all participants in both the remembered past life and the current life, in many cases provides double and triple blind conditions. University of Virginia has replicated this level of research for thousands of cases. This impressive collection of scientific anecdotal evidence of memories of actual past lives lived points to the fact that either the consciousness telling the story actually lived that prior life, or they have a deep level of access in the present moment to the consciousness that did live that life in the past. Either case it is evidence of *Post-mortem consciousness survival.*

Further, this anecdotal evidence replicated from thousands of *Children Remembering Past Lives* simply agrees with the prior listed clinical evidence of *post-mortem consciousness survival:*

2. EVIDENCE FROM PAST LIFE REGRESSION THERAPY:

Another field of research into past lives where MD's have developed clinical evidence is *Past Life Regression Therapy* where people are put under hypnosis and their subconscious memories of past lives are accessed.

Unfortunately, like psychic mediumship this is an area which is ripe with fraudulent practitioners So, parapsychological scientists must be extremely careful in who they work with here and mustalso verify all the data, which is why I choose to believe only therapists who were already economically successful before they discovered this past life hypnotherapy.

As discussed earlier, Dr. Ian Stevenson in his work with children's past life memories, found that while children could remember their past lives between the ages of four to seven years old, if their memories were not openly discussed in those early years, and continued to be discussedin later years, then the memories would fade and would not be remembered in later life. This is appears to be true for all of us, which is the reason why you and I as adults can not remember any past lives.

Apparently, as we each become accustomed to this current life, those memories of prior lives are suppressed from our conscious mind. But, our subconscious still retains those past life memories and can be accessed using hypnotherapy.

A. CATHERINE & Dr. BRIAN WEISS: One prominent MD psychiatrist, Dr. Brian Weiss, a nationally-recognized expert in pharma-psychology before he accidentally discovered these sub-conscious past life memories in one of his patients; has delved deeply into this controversialarea of *Past Life Regression Therapy.*

A recognized professional and formerly *Chief of Psychiatry* at the hospital affiliated with the *University of Miami.* Dr. Weiss is convinced that reincarnation is real. He describes the problem this way,

> **"I have encountered some extremely talented people—psychics, mediums, healers and others.... and I have encountered even more who have limited talent or skill and are mostly**

opportunists…. But, I have also been careful not to throw out the baby with the bathwater….. One person or one experience might be disappointing, but the next might be truly extraordinary and should not be discounted because of previous events."[37]

Dr. Weiss was always a disciplined, conservative scientist and physician who distrusted anything that could not be proven by the traditional scientific method. Graduating Phi Beta Kappa, magna Cum Laude at Columbia University in 1966, he received his M.D. at Yale University in 1970. Following internship at New York University-Bellevue Medical Center he completed residency in Psychiatry at Yale. Next, he taught at The University of Pittsburg and The University of Miami where he lead the pharmaceutical division. He became Associate Professor of Psychiatry at the University of Miami medical school, and Chief of Psychiatry at the University affiliated hospital, by which time he had already published 37 scientific papers and book chapters in his specialty field. Obviously, Dr. Weiss is not the type of recognized professional who would lightly espouse fringe ideas……

But, in 1980, he met a new patient named Catherine….. For 18 months, Dr. Weiss used conventional methods of therapy attempting to overcome Catherine's symptoms, but when nothing else worked, he tried using hypnosis. It was during a series of trance states that Catherine began to continually recall her "past-life" memories. It also became apparent that she could not remember these past lives at all during her waking state.

In hypnotic trance, Catherine also spoke of the time between lives. It was during one of these sessions while Catherine was in a trance state that Dr. Weiss was contacted by beings other than Catherine,….. These beings called themselves, "Masters". These were separate beings on the other side, who were in charge of Catherine's "curriculum" who spoke through Catherine to Dr. Weiss….

Further, to show Dr. Weiss that they were separate beings from Catherine, these "Masters" told Dr. Weiss private things about himself that Catherine could not have known…. One of these Masters told Dr. Weiss that he (the Master) had been incarnate in the flesh 86 different times…..Catherine, while in a trance state, could recall some of what had taken place in her past lives, but *even in trance she could not recall any of the things these "Masters" had said* to Dr. Weiss through her.

After considerable contemplation, especially about how it would affect his professional status Dr.Weiss courageously decided that:

"I knew that no possible consequence I might face could prove to be as devastating as not sharing the knowledge I had gained about immortality and the true meaning of life." [38] *Dr. Brian Weiss*

So, in spite of any damage to his own standing in the medical community, he decided to go public with what he had learned.

In the 2013 video at this URL Ophra interviews Dr. Weiss; on the subject of Catherine:[39] https:// youtu.be/WMlLoPYwZ5w. If the file won't link copy the address to your browser.

In his numerous books published since 1980, among which are *Many Lives, Many Masters*[40], *Messages from the Masters,*[41] and *Same Soul Many Bodies*[42]; Dr. Weiss tells his story in great detail and I recommend reading all these books.

Basically, Weiss' books tell the same story as Dr. Ian Stevenson's books on reincarnation. Using regressive hypnotic therapy merely bypasses our forgetfulness and allows those of us who can't consciously remember our prior lives to access the information that is dormant in our subconscious. After reading Dr. Stevenson's and Dr. Weiss' books, it becomes easy to see that reincarnation and having past lives is quite *normal.*

"I believe that each of us possesses a soul that exists after the death of thephysical body and that it returns time and again to other bodies in a progressive effort to reach a higher plane."[43] *Brian Weiss, M.D.*

I have been privileged to hear Dr. Brian Weiss speak in San Francisco in February, 2002, and again in Long Beach in October 2015. During his 2002 presentation Dr Weiss mentionedseveral additional cases that had recently come to his attention and I looked up one of them.....Jenny Cockell

B. *JENNY COCKELL / MARY SUTTON:*[44] This story is a great read and Jenny's book is available from Amazon.com. Jenny, is an English housewife with two children, who, like Dr. Ian Stevenson's subjects, spontaneously remembered, beginning in early childhood, that she had lived a prior life in Ireland, where she had eight children, but that she had died before those children were fully grown.

From childhood on, Jenny drew pictures of her house and a map of the shoreline and her church, which had an unusual façade. She researched Irish maps looking for the town of *Malaheit*. After she found it, she traveled there and felt that it was the place where she had livedbefore. Jenny found both the church and her former home. The home had become a ruin and had been empty since the 1950's. But, she believed she had lived there in the 1920's or 30's, and that she had been named Mary Sutton. She also believed that she had died from the complications of childbirth, leaving behind her children. So, she kept inquiring.

Today, Jenny has managed to reunite with five of Mary Sutton's eight children who are stillliving, and she has also found the room in a Dublin hospital where Mary (her former self) died. Four of the children (all older than Jenny is today), now believe that Jenny is their deceased mother Mary, reincarnated. This belief is because of all the things she can remember about theirlives together. The fifth child prefers to believe that the consciousness of his deceased mother Mary speaks to Jenny from another dimension, telling details to Jenny. But, Jenny emphatically tells that child of Mary's, ***"No, I am actually Mary"***.

A video discussing this case is found at this URL:[45] https://youtu.be/snnmlqz_UCc If the file won't link copy the address to your browser

3. REPLICATION FROM ADDITIONAL PAST LIFE REGRESSIONS: Another clinical psychologist Peter Ramster, of Sydney Australia, independently replicated Dr. Weiss' results. Hamster also decided to make a documentary film (The URL for the film is listed below)Ramster published his first book[46] "*The Truth About Reincarnation*" in 1980. In 1981 he videoed his past-life hypnosis sessions with four women in Sydney, Australia, all of whom remembered past lives in Europe. Dr. Ramster then instructed each patient while under hypnosis that they should when re-awakened remember everything they had told him. Then, he visited the locations in Europe which had been described by the four women and carefully researched with local historians the names dates and details they have given while under hypnotic regression. Village and hamlets names given where difficult to validate a century or two later, but withfurther research some of the names appeared on old maps.

Then, in late 1981 and 1982, he brought the four women to England and France where they revisited the scenes of their past lives with a film crew. Everyone, especially the women, was amazed as each patient found confirmation of things they had recalled out of their sub- conscious minds during hypnotic trance about prior lives in Europe while being videoed 8,000 miles away in Sydney, Australia. Ramster produced the film in 1983 which was televised in Australia and the UK. And, the story of each patient is best told in the video he produced.

On this first video, is Ramster's televised documentary film ***Reincarnation - 1981***[47]

- **Case 1 - Cynthia Henderson** as Amélie de Cheville in Normandy, France.

- **Case 2 - Helen Pickering** life as Doctor James (Archibald) Burns, Scotland.

- **Case 3 - Jenny Green** life as Dorothe Halman, of Düsseldorf a Jewish teen girl in NaziGermany during the Holocaust.

- **Case 4 - Gwen McDonald** life as Rose Duncan, born in 1765, whose house was RoseCottage in Somerset, England.

Watch the Entire Film at: https://youtu.be/TrXtkYV9sk8

On this second video URL Ramster is interviewed recently regarding his documentary film:[48] https://www.youtube.com/watch?v=tCmsuvbfI1E

CONCLUSIONS FROM CLINICAL EVIDENCE OF PAST LIVES: Obviously, both children and adults do retain sub-conscious memories of prior lives…. But, scientifically what does this actually mean?….

There are a couple of alternatives: It could be something similar to what is hypothesized by some scientists regarding mediums, that they are not receiving the communication from a surviving consciousness, but have instead "somehow" tapped into the information through some unexplained means of *anomalous cognition.* Similar to what one of Mary Sutton (Jenny Cockell)'s children wants to believe.

But again, the simplest and most elegant explanation using Occam's razor is that *"somesurviving consciousnesses have reincarnated many years later."*

And, this replicated clinical evidence from *Past Life Regression Therapy* agrees with the prior listed clinical evidence of *post-mortem consciousness survival.*

Further, since *post mortem consciousness survival* is a scientific fact, is there evidence that wecan communicate with theses surviving consciousnesses?

CHAPTER 3
ADDITIONAL EVIDENCE FROM VERIDICAlMEDIUMSHIP

1. EVIDENCE OF AFTER-DEATH COMMUNICATION, THROUGH THE ANOMALOUS COGNITION OF VERIDICAL EVIDENTIAL MEDIUMSHIP

A valid *After-Death Communication-ADC,* received with veridical substantial evidence that the medium could not have known or guessed, can be one of the strongest proofs of *post-mortem consciousness survival* ,which is easily accessible to the average reader. And, while it may only qualify as personal *subjective* evidence, yet it can be very powerful emotionally and philosophically.

DISCLAIMER: While I am one of the first to admit that there are a lot of fake psychic mediums, and also many very kind and loving, but absolutely mediocre mediums out there, if you want to communicate with your deceased relatives then do search out a trained *Evidential Medium:* who will probably have several of the following characteristics:

- *FIRST:* **They will usually be successful in a secular career as a non-medium**, and do not need to make their living from psychic mediumship…. *THIS IS BIG*….. Unfortunately, commercial mediums are under a great deal of pressure to "perform" for their clients….. But, when a medium does not need income from their mediumship, and has never-the-lessachieved renown, the chances are much greater that they provide outstanding evidence and are not mediocre.

- *SECOND:* Because they take their mediumship seriously they will have taken the personal trouble and expense to attend courses on Evidential Mediumship at *Arthur FindlayCollege of Psychic Science* in Stansted, UK, a week there with travel costs from theUSA, etc. is an investment of over $4,000. But the best evidential mediums like the true professionals that they are, will have gone there multiple times….. As I myself have donein my own research.

- *THIRD:* **They may not even charge for their readings** (because they are successful in their prior careers, they don't need to make their living as a medium and are actually doingit for their personal love of the craft and to provide service to their fellows). Normally they will continue in their prior professions and do not see mediumship as a career change.

Receiving a personal communication from the surviving consciousness of a discarnate loved one through a trained *evidential medium,* who is a complete stranger to you, when accompanied with substantial veridical evidence (i.e. details the medium could not have known, including the departed's personality, name, relationship, cause of death, etc.,) provides one of the best demonstrations of *post-mortem consciousness survival* that is easily accessible for most of us. And, I have personally received several communications from discarnate friends as well as relatives with undeniable evidential details through evidential mediums to whom I was a complete stranger. There is nothing like having your own personal communication from the departed.

2. INVESTIGATIONS BY SIR OLIVER LODGE FOR SPR 1883-1909: The British physicist Sir Oliver Lodge, is one of Great Britain's foremost scientists..... Lodge holds patents along with Tesla in the development of wireless telegraphy which we call radio (Marconi stole his ideas from Lodge and Tesla, and Marconi lost the intellectual property lawsuit in the US Supreme Court in 1947). Lodge was elected as a *Fellow* of the Royal Society in 1887 and was Knighted in 1902, all for his scientific achievements.

Lodge, also undertook the scientific investigation of mediumship in 1883-1884 for the *Society of Psychical Research (SPR)* and continued this investigation until his death in 1940. Working with Dr. William James of Harvard and other respected scientists, Lodge scientifically investigated all the great mediums including Eusapia Palladino, Lenora Piper and Gladys Osborne Leonard.

Based on the research of the SPR, Lodge then wrote about the scientific actuality of *Post- Mortem Consciousness Survival* and *After-Death Communication-ADC* in his 1909 book entitled *The Survival of Man,* saying:

"The first thing we learn, is continuity (i.e. life continues). **There is no such break in the conditions of existence as may have been anticipated; and no break at all in the continuous and conscious identity of genuine character and personality. Essential belongings, such as memory, culture, education, habits, character and affection. All these, and to a certain extent, tastes and interests... are retained** (in the next life).

"Meanwhile, it would appear that knowledge is not suddenly advanced, we are not suddenly flooded with new information, nor do we at all change our identity; but powers and faculties are enlarged, and the scope of our outlook on the universe may be widened and deepened. If effort here has rendered the acquisition

of such extra insight legitimate and possible".[49] taken from Lodge's book *The Survival of Man* (©1909)

Lodge, has here stated that *Post Mortem Consciousness Survival* (or as he terms it "continuity")is a fact, as proven by all the research done by the *Society for Psychical Research-SPR*. But soon thereafter he would be gifted with personal knowledge of these facts.

3. ***SIR OLIVER LODGE'S ULTIMATE VERIFICATION 1915:*** Six years after publishing that book confirming that science had *proven post-mortem consciousness survival*, and *After-Death Communication,* Sir Oliver Lodge had a unique confirmation of his scientific findings.

One of his three sons, Second Lieutenant Raymond Lodge, was killed-in-action in Flanders on September 14, 1915…. Tragic though a death is, this provided the Lodge family with the unique opportunity to personally verify the reality of *After-Death communications,* which his science at the SPR had already verified.

Eleven days after making his transition to the afterlife, on September 25, 2015; Raymond Lodge began communicating with Sir Oliver and Lady Lodge through the mediumship of both *Gladys Osborne Leonard* and *Alfred Lord Peters*. Raymond also communicated with his brothersthrough a number of mediums to whom the brothers were strangers using false names. Raymond even began communicating directly at family circles at home, even coming through at family meal times.

By the end of April, 1916, a preponderance of evidence that Raymond had been communicatingwith them had been accumulated by the Lodge family. So, Sir Oliver Lodge then published a second book entitled Raymond, or Life and Death ©1916, in which he said:

> ***"The number of more or less convincing proofs which we have obtained is by this time very great,… I am as convinced of continued existence on the other side of death as I am of existence here,…*** (this statement is from one of the world's foremost physicists).

He goes on to discuss the merits of objective verses subjective evidence:

> **"It may be said, you cannot be as sure as you are of sensory experience** (objective). **I say I can. A physicist is never limited to direct sensory impressions; he has to deal with a multitude of conceptions and things for which he has no physical organ – the dynamical theory of heat, for instance, and of gases, the theories of electricity, of magnetism, of chemical affinity, of cohesion,**

aye, and hisapprehension of the ether (i.e. dark energy) **itself, lead him into regions where sightand hearing and touch are impotent as direct witnesses, where they** (objective senses) **are no longer efficient guides"**[50] from Raymond or Life and Death (©1916)

This is the finest and most documented scientific confirmation of *post-mortem consciousness survival,* and is coming from one of the greatest scientists of all time...... While Lodge's two books may today seem antiquated, taken together they are a very convincing read.

Further, Dr. Frederick H.W. Myers (see the cross correspondences below), prior to his death in 1901, had been a colleague of Oliver Lodge's working in the SPR, and Raymond communicatedback from the other side that the reason that he was able to come through so quickly (within twoweeks after his death) was because Dr. Myers, who's surviving consciousness was alive and well on the other side (14 years after his own transition) went looking for Raymond among all the new souls arriving from the trenches of the Western Front. Dr. Myers helped Raymond realize where he was and what had happened, and Raymond reported this back to his father through the mediums.

Normally, it takes newly deceased souls up to six months or longer to figure out what has happened and where they are, when not met on that side by a friend or relative. Unfortunately, such "confusion" about the new situation is especially troubling when the newly deceased soul did not believe in *post-mortem conscious survival.* ... Arriving in the afterlife their first thought is, ***"If I am still alive, then I could not have died".*** ... ... They can actually stay in that confused state for a very long time, and may even become "earthbound" which is where we get poltergeists.

Besides, Dr. Myers help, Raymond also was fully aware of his father's research with the SPR, and so Raymond himself believed in *post-mortem consciousness survival,* and was fully expecting to be alive after his physical death. All of this allowed him to begin coming through in just 11 days.

4. THE NEED TO KNOW YOU WILL STILL BE ALIVE AFTER YOU ARE DEAD:

Indeed, this prior knowledge of consciousness survival and the need to have someone to greet you when you arrive on the other side was repeated to me personally when I received a message with significant evidential details from a friend named Barbara fully two years after her death. This occurred during a Spiritualist service at *Arthur Findlay College of Psychic Science* in Stansted-Monfitchet, UK, where the medium delivering the messages was a complete stranger to me and also had no idea who I was or that I was in the audience of approximately 120 people.

The medium identified me as the recipient of the communication from the details provided bythe discarnate communicator, and at the end of the message the medium said:

"The communicator wants to thank you specifically for telling her that she wouldn't be dead when she passed on……

"Because that knowledge saved her so much time in the new life…….

"She said that she is already assisting new arrivals in their adjustment to the same facts, and to help them awake to their new lives there."…..."

"She also says, and with much emotion, that WHEN SHE COULD NO LONGEREVEN HAND YOU A COOKIE, STILL YOU CAME IN ORDER TO TELL HER THE MESSAGE THAT SHE WOULD STILL BE ALIVE……

She says THAT she loves you, and to thank you again for having the courage togive her that important message"

Message delivered to author by Simone Key at Arthur Findlay College Dec 2014

Those cookies were on the counter between us in the kitchen on the night that I told Barbarathat I knew for sure that she would still be alive after she died.

But, my point is that it is vitally important for the dying to know as 2nd Lt. Raymond Lodge didknow and as Barbara knew, that they will still be alive after the change called death.

5. ***DOUBLE BLIND DEMONSTRATIONS - BY Dr. FREDRICK H.W. MYERS* THE CROSS CORRESPONDENCES:**[51],[52] This is one of the most famous of all After-Death Communications because it was accomplished posthumously by one of the great minds of psychical research, Dr. Fredrick H.W. Myers (d.1901). Widely known as the "Cross Correspondences", Myers' devised this double-blind proof, which he actually conducted from theother side as a *Post-Mortem Surviving Consciousness*.

Beginning this double blind proof six years after his own death, Myers chose to send messages back from the other side to five separate mediums living on three continents. Dr. Myers sent each medium disconnected fragments of the message (often in obscure Greek or Latin) with instructions to send their fragments to the SPR in London.

Later De. Myers recruited two other deceased SPR colleagues to work with him, Dr. Henry Sedgwick (d.1900), & Dr. Edmund Gurney (d.1888) both of whom had pre-deceased him. Thesethree discarnate consciousnesses worked together and continued doing these transmissions from the other side for over 30 years,….. providing double blind evidence for **long term** *post- mortem consciousness survival.*

The fragments were purposefully delivered in foreign languages not familiar to the mediums. Further, these scraps would only make sense if all were collected and pieced together by the SPR.

> ***To each automatist*** *(a medium who does automatic writing)* **the information would be so fragmentary and strange as to be meaningless; but when pieced together, it could carry information of a kind that only could have come from Myers himself…"**

This double-blind demonstration was purposefully transmitted so disjointedly in order to providea double-blind communication that would silence all the Materialist skeptics simply by showing that it *could not* have been one medium's idea, but that it was actually Dr. Myers' surviving consciousness communicating back from the afterlife through the different mediums.

To prevent the skeptic's criticism, Myers set it up where no single medium would know what the other was doing. What Myers and his colleagues did was no easy task: to orchestrate the activities of five mediums on three continents, while doing it all through the power of *anomalous cognition.* But, do it they did.

To read all about this Google *"Cross Correspondences"* and here are two videos that summarizeit well.

The Cross-Correspondences are discussed by Russel Targ and Jeffery Mishlove on thevideo at this URL. [53] https://youtu.be/to7NEq0A9to

And also in a short video at the URL [54] https://youtu.be/eZbWIdkirck

6. *"DROP IN" COMMUNICATORS:* While the evidence produced by the careful science of William James, Sir Oliver Lodge studying mediums, and what Dr. Fredrick Myers provided from the other side is excellent, the drama of drop-in communicators offers anecdotal evidence that iseven more convincing of *post mortem consciousness survival* for most non-scientists.

In the world of Evidential Mediumship the majority of seance circles are held with the intention ofcommunicating with specific individuals on the other side. Usually the sitters want to hear from departed relatives like Mom, Dad or Grandma.

Occasionally however, a seance will be visited instead by an uninvited spirit. When the details ofwho and what regarding the "drop in" can later be verified it unequivocally proves that the medium was not merely reading the minds of the participants...... Here are a couple of examples of verifiable "drop-ins"

A. SINKING OF HMS BARNUM:[55] AND HELEN DUNCAN During World War II, in 1944, an English medium, Mrs. Helen Duncan, was conducting one of her regular séances for a group of women in Birmingham, England. During one séance, she was spontaneously interrupted by the disincarnate consciousness of a recently drowned man who claimed to have been a sailor from the crew of HMS Barnum (a British warship). He contacted Mrs. Duncan at this séance becausehis mother was in attendance that same evening that he was drowned and he wanted to report to her that his ship had just then been sunk by the Germans and that he was safely on the otherside. Speaking through the medium, he told his mother that everyone aboard, including himself, had drowned.

Unfortunately, British Naval Intelligence did not want this classified information about the ship's sinking to get out, and so arrested Mrs. Duncan accusing her of the crime of *"Witchcraft"* undera law dating back over 200 years to 1735. Unfortunately, the Navy continued the prosecution and Mrs. Duncan was actually convicted in 1944 of this ancient crime of W*itchcraft*, and was sent to prison.

Now, it is apparent from the facts of the case that Helen Duncan's only *crime* was that shesomehow knew the truth, which Naval Intelligence did not want to have publicized. She merely told the truth being related to her by the disincarnate spirit of the drowned sailor. So, Helen Duncan was literally jailed for the "crime" of telling the truth.

British Prime Minister, Sir Winston Churchill was adamant at the time that Mrs. Duncan had not committed any crime whatsoever and should be immediately released. However, being that it was wartime, British Naval Intelligence won the day and kept Mrs. Duncan in prison until the warwas over the following year.

Winston Churchill was so moved by this travesty of justice, (jailing someone for telling the truth) that he bothered to have all the "Anti-Witch" laws in Great Britain repealed in 1951, so that todayin the United Kingdom, "witches" (mediums) have the same rights and freedoms as any religious clergy. And subsequently the Anglican Church has also accepted mediumship as beingcompletely valid.

Finally, in 1998, 54 years later, according to a news story reported by Reuters, a full pardon wasfinally being processed for Mrs. Duncan (who died in 1956).

Check it out on this video[56]: https://youtu.be/yJX1hmkGgg8 The skeptic investigators comeup with several "probable" ways Helen could have "known" about the sinking of the HMSBarnum in advance,….. but then they also dig up another earlier seance when she knew the HMS Hood had been sunk before the Admiralty even heard about it, and that one could nothave been faked…..

B. CRASH OF AIRSHIP R-101 and EILEEN GARRETT: October 7, 1930, Apparently, Eileen Garrett, a well known trance medium, was holding a seance at the National Laboratory of Psychical Research which had been set up four years earlier by Harry Price, Price, and three others had arranged a sitting with Eileen Garrett to attempt a spirit contact with deceased writer Sir Arthur Conan Doyle who was a Spiritualist.

But instead a drop in visitor came through claiming to be the Captain of the R-101 airship which had crashed two days earlier. The voice described the crash and included a great deal of technical information. The accuracy of which was confirmed six months later during the official inquiry into the crash. While the verbatim transcript of the seance was published in the newspaper the following day it is still under copyright. But, the drop-in communicator who claimed to be the airship's commander Flight Lieutenant H.C. Irwin made two statements which there is no possible way that the medium could have found out about except through communication with the deceased.

First, the communicator stating that "This exorbitant scheme of carbon and hydrogen is entirely and absolutely wrong." This was entirely insider information….. The R-101 had been contemplating a series of experiments which would burn a mixture of hydrogen and diesel (fuel oil) with the hydrogen obtained from the airships gas bags. While no experiments had been carried out, a gas main had been installed from the gas plant to the engine test house. And the communicator was making reference to this….

Second, the communicator stated that "We almost scraped the roof at Achy", because Achy is asmall village which was not mentioned in any press reports of the airship crash, and it is not named in any guide books and is not on any local French maps, but does appear on the large- scale ordnance flying maps which Lieutenant Irwin would have been using. And two French officers later stated at the inquiry that when the airship passed over Poix near Achy that the airship was only three hundred feet from the ground, which verified the seance report.

A reporter who had attended the seance to hear from Arthur Conan Doyle, instead published thestory and the details. His account was read by a Mr. Charlton, who had been involved in the R101's construction, who acquired a copy of the report from Harry Price. Charlton and his associates said the report was "an astounding document," because it contained more than 40 highly technical and confidential details of what occurred on the airship's fatal flight. ***It appeared very evident,*** said Charlton, ***that for anyone present at the seance to have obtained information beforehand was grotesquely absurd.***

The only hypothesis Charlton had to explain all the evidence was that ***"Irwin did actually communicate with those present at the seance, after his physical death."*** Based on this Charlton later became a Spiritualist.

Prior to the official inquiry into the crash, which took place six months later, Major Oliver Villiers of the Ministry of Civil Aviation participated in a series of seven seances with Eileen Garrett.And, heard the testimony of four other officers who had lost their lives in the disaster, who identified themselves by name.

In one of those seances a deceased officer from the Airship, Lt. Commander Noel Atherstone communicated that he had kept two diaries attesting to the lack of airworthiness of the airship. The diaries were finally located in 1967 (nearly 40 years later), where the following statement was found:

> ***"There is a mad rush and panic to complete the ship. It is grossly unfair to expect the officers to take out a novel vessel of this size... The airship has no lift worth talking about and is obviously tail heavy.".***

Six months after the crash, the Court of Inquiry report showed that practically every one of the statements received by Eileen Garrett was correct; none were incorrect. To check this all out here are several URL's:

- Here is a video URL which discusses R-101: [57] https://youtu.be/ yfTK_qjl_5Y?list=PLLB-82YMhiPFPKSm2Ke69aK0DKTftpvo0
- EILENE GARRETT & R-101:[58] http://www.euro-tongil.org/

swedish/english/er101.htm

- A video discussing the engineering of the R-101 and its crash is located here [59] youtu.be/ixxXhZVFXxQ with no mention of Eileen Garrett, or any mediumship.

- The best description of the seance is on this site with verbatim transcript [60] http://www.harrypricewebsite.co.uk/Seance/Garrett/leaves-r101.htm

7. OTHER INTERESTING 20TH CENTURY AFTER DEATH COMMUNICATIONS: Following are two cases which have been fully documented by ADC researchers, and which you can look up online for yourself.

GEORGE PELLEW'S ADC:[61],[62] A very famous trance medium in Boston, MA, Mrs. Lenora Piper, who was carefully studied by Dr. William James, Sir Oliver Lodge, and other members of both the British SPR and the American SPR, channeled the surviving consciousness of GeorgePellew, who had died previously. Mr. Pellew spoke with over 150 different people who attended various séances conducted by Mrs. Piper. 30 of those people had actually known Pellew before he died. Mrs. Piper, however, had never met Pellew while he was living. Pellew had alwaysbeen skeptical of mediumship and post-mortem consciousness survival. But, he had made a pact with one of the SPR investigators Dr. Richard Hodgson that ***"If I ever die and find out the afterlife is real and mediumship is valid, I will come through to you"***.

The discarnate Pellew, speaking through Mrs. Piper, was able to identify 29 of the 30 people attending her seances who knew him before he died, but none of whom were known to the medium. The only person Mr. Pellew could not properly identify was a childhood friend whom Pellew had not seen in decades. The 29 people he identified easily and correctly were convinced by the mannerisms Pellew exhibited (through the medium) that they had in fact spoken with George Pellew, still living in the afterlife. Many were willing to testify that they had communicated with a disembodied, surviving consciousness that appeared to be George Pellew. This case is wonderfully told in Deborah Blum's 2006 book, *Ghost Hunters*[63] and also in Michael Tymn's 2013 book, *Resurrecting Lenora Piper.*[64] Or check it out at https://psi-encyclopedia.spr.ac.uk/articles/leonora-piper[65]

This brings us to the following which is one of the best-documented double-blind experimentswhich was invented and carried out entirely by deceased SPR investigators on the other side.

B. MONTAGUE KEEN's ADC:[66] Montague (Monty) Keen, aged 79, one of Britain's more prominent researchers in psychic phenomena, and a member of the SPR, died of a heart attack while speaking at the podium on January 15, 2004, during a public debate with a skeptic, at the Royal Society for the Arts, in London.

A few weeks later, his wife Veronica contacted University of Arizona Scientist Dr. Gary Swartz Ph.D., and reported that she had received messages from her deceased husband through several different mediums, all stating that Monty wanted to conduct some research with Dr. Swartz, whom he had met several years earlier..

Dr. Swartz and his research associate, Julie Beischel, then designed a two-part double-blind research project involving several mediums. One of the mediums they used was Allison DuBois,whose career as a psychic legal investigator is what the NBC program "Medium" is based on. During the session DuBois did not know anything about the subject of the reading, but Monty, speaking through DuBois, described his death as, "falling at the podium", and then Monty referred to an upcoming event which was dedicated to his memory, an event which had been scheduled only after his death.

So, here we have the deceased spirit speaking about events which were not on any calendar before he died and which were also unknown to the medium. Further, Monty said, speaking through the medium, that this event was a, ***"somewhat flattering surprise"***. He also said, that their communication in this way would be an excellent "White Crow". This speaking about things that were not part of his memories before he dies proves that mediums are in fact, communicating with a living, surviving consciousness. This entire séance was video taped at theUniversity of Arizona Research Laboratory.

Monty had been a member of the British Society of Psychical Research for over 55 years. Ihave read the published transcript of that DuBois reading. It is clear that Monty just replicated the type of proof from the other side that Fredric H.W. Myers had provided in the famous Cross Correspondence work 100 years earlier. Monty communicated that:

> ***"...The thing about the after-life that stood out for him, and that made him so happy is howhe could still be here so much after his passing, and, how he would feel energy-wise, like he did when he was younger instead of with the issues he had accumulated as he got older." 8*** Monty Keen, from the other side

The researchers concluded that the medium was definitely receiving information related to the designated deceased, which was outside the possibility of telepathy. And they further stated:

"…These kinds of observations provide compelling evidence, if not convincing evidence, that intention, choice and intelligence, and hence some sort of personal consciousness, survive bodily death".[67]

Gary E. Swartz, Ph.D. & Julie Beischel, Ph.D., University of Arizona 2005

Check this out at: [68] https://anomalien.com/has-montague-keen-really-returned-from-the-dead/

8. FINAL CONCLUSIONS: SO WHERE DOES THIS LEAVE US?

We have scientifically proven with objective clinical data, the following facts:

A. Our individual consciousness is not dependent on support from the functioning of a physical brain, and can operate entirely independent of the normally observed physical reality (i.e., this side)

B. This survival of the consciousness without a functioning brain has been observed to last, at least for several hours.

C. Such post mortem consciousness survival is apparently "normal".

D. Consciousnesses associated with deceased physical bodies recorded memories during the time that their cadavers were clinically dead, which could only have been observed from spatial locations outside the cadaver. Indicating that the consciousness was at the time discarnate and operating entirely outside the normally observed physical reality (i.e., on the other side).

E. Later, these apparently discarnate consciousnesses returned to the normally observed physical reality by reincarnating back into their previously associated cadavers.

Using the overwhelming subjective anecdotal evidence of societies like the SPR, IANDS, IONS and DPS at University of Virginia, and others; which have often been collected under single, double and triple blind conditions, we have also scientifically proven these additional facts:

F. It is apparent that individual consciousnesses surviving outside the observed physical reality have repeatedly found ways, usually through anomalous cognition (After-Death Communication-ADC), to send information to persons who are still alive here within the normally observed physical reality (i.e., on this side)

G. **It is apparent that individual memories observed previously by human consciousnesses can continue for centuries, retained somewhere outside the observed physical reality. And, those memories can be carried back into this observed physical reality by new-born consciousnesses** (which may or may not be the same consciousness which had the original memories).

H. **It is apparent that individuals retain in their sub-conscious memories of prior life times, or can at least tap into such memories when under hypnotic trance** (They may or may not be the same consciousness which had the original memories, but it is likely that they are).

Above Items A-E are all now proven scientific facts, while items F-H are "apparent" facts based on A-E being true. Yet, all these above observed facts A-H can be supported by the single hypothesis that:

OUR INDIVIDUAL CONSCIOUSNESS DOES SURVIVE POST MORTEM, AND CONTINUES LIVING FOR AN UNDETERMINED LENGTH OF TIME.

*Therefore, at a minimum it should be clear that **"post mortem consciousness survival is a fully proven scientific fact"**.*

CHAPTER 4
SCIENCE OF HOW EVIDENTIAL MEDIUMSHIPWORKS:

"Until we understand….. how limited our normal perceptions are, it is useless even to attempt to get an intelligent understanding of the phenomena which occur in the seance"

"Until we clearly understand that our senses here only respond to a very limited range of vibrations, namely those we term "physical matter" (and) that outside these there is a universe full of life, which responds to a higher range of vibrations, unreal to us, but more real than physical matter, we can not grasp or understand in all its' fullness the psychical phenomena which develop through mediumship".

"To refuse to examine the (data) of Psychic Science…. because the phenomena are contrary to what is thought "should be", is blind stupidity due to ignorance and prejudice." Psychic Scientist Arthur Findlay (1924)

1. THE SCIENCE OF MEDIUMSHIP:

A. WE THOUGHT WE KNEW "ALMOST" EVERYTHING:

Although, it is childishly comforting to believe that, ***"Science has already solved everything"***, that just is not true, and never has been true. …..

Further, honest scientists have always known that we can discern only a very small fraction of reality, while the limited intellect pseudo-scientists want to believe instead that ***"We already know everything"***.

The spectrum of electromagnetic radiation shown in the graph to the right illustrates how little wecan discern. When considering the spectrum if we think of it as being a mile long, then mankind's visible range (that small portion of reality that we can actually visually discern) is only an inch long within that mile, or 1/63,000 of the photon energy (electro-magnetic forces) in the universe, which is itself pretty small.

Also, that mile long spectrum represents only 4% of the energy in the universe….. What we can visually see, and what we can otherwise discern of that entire radiation spectrum is only 4%.

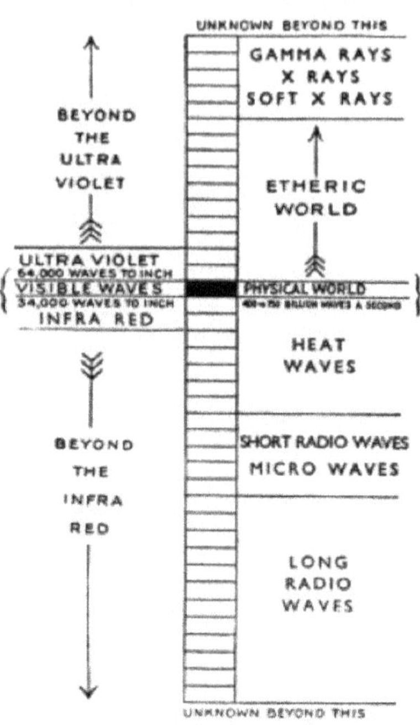

The other 96% which we can not even discern, and only know of, due to its observed effects, is what astro-physicists have termed, *"Dark Energy"* and *"Dark Matter"*. But contemplating these factsit shortly becomes clearly obvious that we humans can only discern an infinitesimal fraction of the universe….Just as Arthur Findlay said in the above quotation, although Dark Energy was not discovered until 74 years later.

But, before we go into the full explanation of the 96% of the universe that we can not discern known aa *Dark Energy* and *Dark Matter*, we need a little background information on how this strange contradiction between the Materialist's perspective and reality (as proven by *Quantum Electro-dynamics-QED*) came into being.

In the late 19th century and the early 20th century, most leading edge scientists believed in the reality of an as yet undiscerned **luminiferous aether**. In the 1860's & 70"s, the genius of James Clerk Maxwell had mathematically consolidated the anomalies of electricity and magnetism with "Maxwell's Equations", and Maxwell had also pointed out that there had to be some invisible and undiscerned medium for the electro-magnetic forces (shown in that spectrum of radiation) to propagate through. Without such a medium electro-magnetic waves including light photons would simply have no way to propagate. At the time all the leading scientists knew that although we could not discern this aether, still it must exist.

This undiscerned aether was literally required to hold the wave function of potentiality as later described by *Quantum Electro-dynamics-QED*. and to propagate the light radiation shown in the spectrum. Consequently, although it appears empty, **the truth was known that space could not be empty.** And, the greatest minds of the time had concluded that this unseen medium must be the ether (or aether).

Incidentally, when demonstrating as an Evidential Medium and communicating with the other side James Maxwell occasionally comes through. Uninvited by me he just drops in when the need arises. He has often come through to me both in my 3:00 AM daily journaling with Helen and also when I get readings from other mediums. He usually shares an answer I have been looking for in the science of electro- magnetic resonance.

One of the supporters of the concept of the aether was Sir Oliver Lodge, the British Physicist, and one of Great Britain's foremost scientists, who also holds patents in the development of wireless telegraphy, and who along with Tesla is credited as the inventors of the radio[1]. Lodge was elected as a *Fellow* of the Royal Society in 1887, and was Knighted in 1902).

> *1 **Technical Note:** many people believe that Marconi invented the radio, but he did not. He borrowed the ideas of Tesla and Lodge and engineered his "wireless" radio. However, Marconi lost the patent suit filed by Lodge and Testla against him, Unfortunately, the case was finally decided in 1947, after all three men were deceased. Marconi merely utilized his t=stolen idea and created a huge monopoly.

Sir, Oliver Lodge stated in his book **Ether and Reality** where he commented on the Ether which was first described by James Clerk Maxwell.

"We can summarize briefly what we know, The two oppositely charged particles, the negative and the positive, are respectively an electron and a proton. They are both exceedingly minute; and there is a sense in which there size has been measured. They are far smaller than atoms, incomparably smaller, the smallest things (yet) known; even if there were a hundred thousand of them in the atom, they would not be in the least crowded, there would be plenty of empty space. Different atoms are now known to be composed of a different number of electrons, and by their different number and grouping they constitute the different chemical elements. The atoms of all chemical elements are built of electrons and protons and of nothing else*2. .....

> *2 **Technical Note:** Of course, in the century since Lodge wrote this, sub-atomic particle physics has advanced to knowing about quarks and gluons by the late 1990's. But the understanding of the ether (i.e. dark energy) has only made slow progress.

"Physical matter is in reality an open network of electrons and protons, and the distance between the electrons and protons in an individual atom, in relation to its size is immense. If we consider the nucleus as commanding the same position in an atom as the sun does in our solar system, then the relative distance the electrons are apart from one another and the protons might betaken as the equivalent to the distance the planets are from the sun. If we consider the atom as something the size of a village church, then the pin head would represent the relative size of one of the electrons of which it is composed. These protons and electrons in the atoms are thus far asunder, moving at enormous speed and they are linked together by this invisible ether which occupies much the greater space within the atom. **Matter is thus constructed of minute electric charges, both positive and negative, not moving haphazardly, but freely and orderly, and connected together by**

the invisible aether, *which is now believed to be the basicsubstance of the universe"* James Clerk Maxwell.

Of course, as history has shown, during the 1940's through the 1990's *Materialist* physicists got the upper hand, and idea of the luminiferous aether was discounted. To Materialists it remains simply obvious, ***"As anyone can see space is empty"***...... Unfortunately, then in 1887 when the faulty Michelson–Morley experiment seemed to show that there was no aether the Materialists assumed they even had "proof".that there was no luminiferous aether. On the other hand, savvy scientists today know that theseexperiments by Michelson & Morley were severely flawed and later proven completely wrong, and had not proved there was no aether. Yet, even today skeptical materialists seem not to have gotten that inconvenient memo about Michelson & Morley's failures. So, they adamantly maintain there is no luminiferous aether, and continue to die-believe the idea in 2023.

Yet, after holding back scientific progress for nearly a century with their closed minded thinking, the *Materialists* came up against a blank wall, when *"Dark Energy"* and *"Dark Matter* "entered the picture.

Over a century after the Michelson–Morley debacle alleging to disprove the aether. In 1998 astronomers deployed the Hubble space telescope and were able to look into deep space, they shortly discovered that the Universe is expanding faster and faster, speeding up due to some previously undiscerned force ratherthan slowing down due to the forces of gravity as supposed. for the previous 300 years.

Further, this *"Dark Energy"* force was overcoming gravitation and causing the universe to expand more rapidly... Mathematically, the only viable explanation so far, is that this force is *"Dark Energy"* and *"Dark Matter"*. Not so surprisingly, this Dark Energy theory also explains and agrees with the late 19th century concept of "the luminiferous aether", and what we perceive as "space" is not empty, but filled with invisiblewave function energies.

So now, entering the third decade of the 21st century Astrophysics and astronomers realize that our extremely limited Materialist paradigm (of only believing those things that the five senses perceive can be real) takes in only the 4% of the Universe which is made of light energy, and completely overlooks 96% ofthe universe (24% Dark Matter and 72% Dark Energy). And, this inability to discern these forces is simply because it is outside the limited range of humanity's 5 senses......

Open minded scientists, with sufficient intellect to see beyond superficial appearances have known for over a hundred years that materialism is not true, as Dr. Max Planck (who gave us the quantum) said in 1900:

"Mind is the matrix of matter".

Planck also said that,

"Science advances one funeral at a time."

And those same open minded scientists are busily seeking to explain the Universe, instead of hidingbehind the stupidly comforting thought of **"We already know almost everything".**

So lets review a little scientific history regarding **After Death Communications-ADC** *(or mediumship)* between those of us still living and those post mortem surviving consciousnesses who have passed on.

1883-1916, INVESTIGATIONS BY SIR OLIVER LODGE FOR SPR:

Sir Oliver Lodge, was elected as a *Fellow* of the Royal Society in 1887, and Knighted in 1902) for his outstanding work. Lodge began investigating After-Death Communications (mediumship) and Post- Mortem Consciousness Survival in 1883-1884 for the **Society of Psychical Research-SPR,** and continued this investigation until his death in 1940.

Lodge, as head of the *SPR* scientifically investigated the work of all the great mediums including; Eusapia Palladino, Alta Lenora Piper and Gladys Osborne Leonard.

He published a summary for 30 years of the SPR's research on *After-death Communications* and *Post- mortem Consciousness Survival* and Mediumship in his book __*The Survival of Man*__ (in 1909), in his conclusions p. 341 - 343, he makes the following statement:

"What we have to announce, then, is no striking novelty, no new mode of communication, but only the reception, by old but developing methods, of carefully constructed evidence of identity (Evidential Mediumship) more exact and more nearly complete than perhaps ever before. Carefully constructed evidence, I say. The constructive ingenuity exists quite s much on the other side of the partition as on our side; there has been distinct co-operation between those on the material and those on the immaterial side; and we are at liberty, not indeed to announce any definite, but to adopt as a working hypothesis the ancient doctrine of a possible intercourse of intelligence between the material and some other, perhaps immaterial, order of existence.

"But let us not jump to the conclusion that the idea of space no longer means anything to persons removed from the planet. They are no longer in such with MATTER truly, and therefore can no longer appeal to our organs of sense, as they did when they had bodies for that express purpose; but, for all we know, they may exist in the ether and be as aware of space and the truths of geometry, thoughnot of geography, as we are. Let us not jump to the conclusion that their condition and surroundingsare altogether and utterly different…That is one of the things we may gradually find out not to be true.

"The first thing we learn, perhaps the only thing we clearly learn in the first instance, is continuity (consciousness survival) There is no such sudden break in the conditions of existence as may have been anticipated; and no break at all in the continuous and conscious identity of genuine character and personality. Essential belongings, such as memory, culture, education, habits, character, and affection — all these,, and to a certain extent tastes and interests — for better for worse are retained. Terrestrial accretions, such as world possessions, bodily pain and disabilities, these for the most part naturally drop away.

"Meanwhile it would appear that knowledge is not suddenly advanced — it would be unnatural if it were — we are not suddenly flooded with new information — nor do we at all change our identity'but powers and faculties are enlarged, and the scope of our outlook on the universe may be widened and deepened, if effort here has rendered the acquisition of such extra insight legitimate andpossible.

"On the other hand, there are doubtless some whom the removal of temporary accretion and accidents of existence will leave in a feeble and impoverished condition; for the things are gone in which they trusted, and the are left poor indeed There is a general consistency in the doctrines that have thus been taught through various sensitives (mediums and prophets),, and all I do is add my testimony to the rational character of the general survey of the universe indicated by FWH Myers in his great and eloquent work. " Sir Oliver Lodge

This was published 1909, five years prior to the outbreak of the "Great War" (World War I), which was six years before Lodge's son, Lt. Raymond Lodge, was killed by shrapnel, near Ypres, in Flanders in September 1915. So as a scientist he had already published the fact that the afterlife was real, before he was given a personal example of it.

While losing one of his three sons was not a happy event for the Oliver Lodge and his family, on the otherRaymond's death in 1915 gave Lodge the opportunity to personally verify the reality of consciousness survival.

Raymond, knowing his father was entirely receptive to such things, reported back in a series of readings and seances, which allowed Lodge to personally test his earlier findings at the SPR.

Further, Dr. Fredrick H.W. Myers, a colleague of Lodge in the SPR, who had passed over in 1901, was there on the other side to greet Raymond when he arrived. Myers assisted Rayjmond in communicating back with this side.

Consequently, just eleven days after making his transition, on September 25, 1915 Raymond Lodge began communicating with Sir Oliver and Lady Lodge through the Evidential Mediumship of Gladys Osborne Leonard and Alfred Lord Peters.

Soon Raymond and his siblings began to communicate at home through table tipping. Both Raymond's living brothers sought out mediums where they obtained readings as anonymous sitters. In all these avenues Raymond came through extensively.

Raymond or Life and Death.

By the end of April, 1916, a preponderance of evidence that Raymond had actually been communicating with them had been accumulated by all the Lodge family members, and Sir Oliver Lodge then published a second book ***Raymond or Life and Death* (c)1916.** in which he said:

"The number of more or less convincing proofs which we have obtained is by this time very great,... I am as convinced of continued existence on the other side of death as I amof existence here,... It may be said, you cannot be as sure as you are of sensory experience. I say I can. A physicist is never limited to direct sensory impressions; he has to deal with a multitude of conceptions and things for which he has no physical organ –the dynamical theory of heat, for instance, and of gases, the theories of electricity, of magnetism, of chemical affinity, of cohesion, aye, and his apprehension of the ether itself, lead him into regions where sight

and hearing and touch are impotent as direct witnesses, where they are no longer efficient guides". quoted from *Raymond or Life and Death* (c)1916.

Unfortunately, pseudo-scientist materialist skeptics usually ignore Lodge's 1909 book, and instead portray Lodge as so grief stricken over Raymond's death that it affected his interpretation of the data, unaware that he published his scientific findings six years before Raymond died.

But, this bald faced fabricated lie is only so much m*aterialist skeptic "horse shit",* which only a die-hard pseudo-scientist idiot would choose to voluntarily ingest. Honestly, how stupid and ignorant must they be to lie about this obvious chronology?

Yet, the truth not so cleverly obscured by this "stinking" materialist subterfuge is that Lodge had actually published his scientific opinions that *Post-mortem consciousness survival was real SIX YEARS PRIOR TO HIS SON"S DEATH.* And had stated that in his scientific opinion, unbiased by any grief and entirely based on the findings of the SPR, that **SCIENCE SUPPORTS POST MORTEM CONSCIOUSNESS SURVIVAL,** and then six year later acknowledged that his son's subsequent death and reporting back had only proved his earlier unemotional scientific conclusions.

HOW MEDIUMSHIP WORKS: Here is Oliver Lodge's definition of mediumship from his second book

Raymond or Life and Death (c)1916, which is the clearest description I have ever found.

> *"Suffice it to say that the kind of medium chiefly dealt with in this book is one who, by waiting quietly, goes more or less into a trance, and is then subject to what is called "control" — speaking or writing in a manner quite different from the medium's own normal or customary manner, under the guidance of a separate intelligence technically known as "a control", which some think must be a secondary personality — which indeed certainly is a secondary personality of the medium, whatever that phrase may really signify — the transition being effected in most cases quite easily and naturally. In this secondary state, a degree of clairvoyance or lucidity is attained quite beyond the medium's normal consciousness, and facts are referred to which must be outside his or her normal knowledge. The control, or second personality which speaks during the trance, appears to be more closely in touch with what is popularly spoken of as "the next*

world" than with customary human existence, and accordingly is able to et messages through from people deceased; transmitting them through the speech or writing of the medium, usually with some obscurity and misunderstanding, and with mannerisms belonging either to the medium or to the control. The amount of sophistication varies according to the quality of t medium, and to the state of the same medium at different times; it must be attributed in the best cases physiologically to the medium, intellectually to the control. The confusion is no greater than might be expected from a pair of operators, connected by a telephone of rather delicate and uncertain quality, who were engaged in transmitting messages between two stranger communicators, one of who was anxious to get messages through but perhaps not bey skilled at wording them, while the other was nearly silent and anxious not to give any information or assistance at all; being, indeed more or less suspicious that the communicator was not really there . Under such circumstances the effort of the distant communicator would be chiefly directed to sending such natural and appropriate messages as should gradually break down the inevitable skepticism ofhis friend."

While, Lodge is speaking of the trance mediumship he observed in Lenora Piper and Gladys Osborne Leonard, most of what he says is also equally applicable to mental mediumship, even including the secondary personality, which I personally experience, even though I am only partially (1/4) in trance whenI demonstrate before a congregation, at a seance.

B. CURRENT SCIENCE OF AFTER-DEATH COMMUNICATIONS:

Please also realize that all of the science on *Post-Mortem Consciousness Survival* and mediumship did not take place a century ago. There are many para-psychologist scientists working on these phenomena today, and in the following I will briefly describe how I have often personally been the scientist's guineapig at three different venues.

2012-PRESENT, INVESTIGATIONS BY INSTITUTE OF NOETIC SCIENCES (IONS):

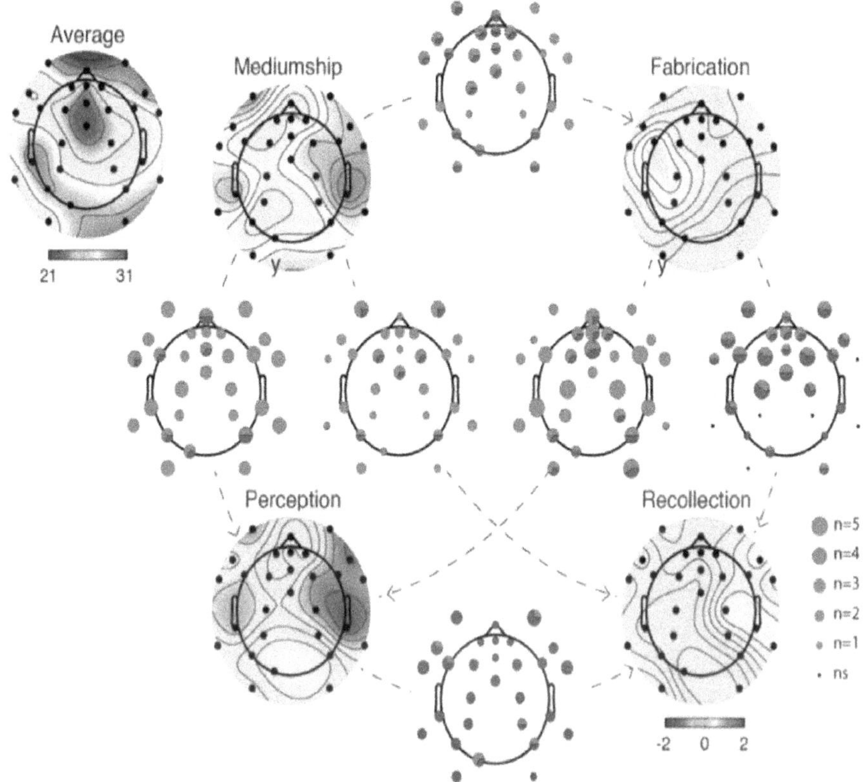

TESTING MEDIUMS: A recent *Institute of Noetic Sciences-IONS* study published in 2012[69], investigated the correlations between the accuracy of mediums' statements and their brain electrical activity, and also differences in mediums' brain activity between four subjective states were studied, including: PERCEPTION, RECOLLECTION, FABRICATION and MEDIUMSHIP communication, as shown above in the graphic printouts from the 2012 IONS report utilizing the 32 point EEG measurements. And, as you can see MEDIUMSHIP is different from all the others.

This study has since been replicated by a second study, also conducted at *IONS* but involving different mediums, in 2014 & 2015. I participated in that second study as one of the test mediums. So, I am intimate with the triple blind conditions, doing my mediumship while isolated in a faraday cage. and wired for 32 point EEG. etc.

In both studies, It was found that the ***mediumship communication*** mental state differed from the ***perceptive, fabrication & reflection*** mental states in the fact that larger amplitude, high power gamma waves were observed being generated by the brain during the *mediumship communication* mental state.

This rise in gamma waves seems to be from eye, ear or muscular activity….. In other words, the mediumswere receiving information through eyes, ears and feelings, rather than imagining or fabricating them. Thereport concluded that:

> ***"The study's findings suggest that the experience of communicating with the deceased may be a distinct mental state that is not consistent with brain activity during ordinary thinking or imagination".***

This is important scientific verification of the fact that as ***mediums we are actually <u>receiving</u> outside information*** during *medium communication* mental activities. The mediums all propose that they are communications being received from the deceased. Although, the data is insufficient to confirm scientifically that the source of the communications is actually surviving consciousness, yet it does show that the source is outside the medium. This also tends to show that the brain is in fact merely a limiting filter which reduces our total perception of consciousness, while there is actually a great deal more that our minds know, but of which we are unconscious.

The next step is to figure out experiments that can isolate data under test conditions that will explain where that information being received by the mediums is actually coming from. We mediums may "know" that it is coming directly from deceased loved ones, but, science asks the question, "How do we provethat it did not happen some other way; like ESP from living minds?"

I was personally involved in the replication study as an IONS test medium in November, 2014, and February 2015. Where I worked with Dr. Dean Radin and Dr. Arnaud Delorme, to verify what mediums arecapable of, and I am currently involved as a sponsor of this ongoing work

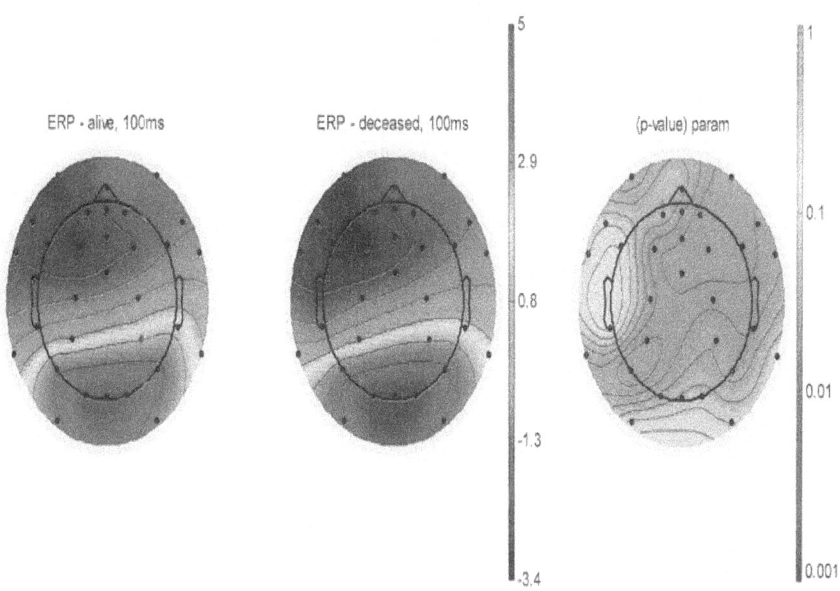

ALIVE   DEAD   ENERGY

The above diagrams are print outs of my own 32 point EEG,, when I am choosing between photos of people answering the question. *"**Is the person pictured in the photo, currently alive or dead?**"* Certainly, not normal mediumship work. But, it allows a triple blind experiment. These were generated in November 2014.

Dr. Arnaud Delorme's program for analyzing mediums and meditators 32 point EEG. Each circle shows my head. My nose is the triangle at the top, my ears are also shown on each side, and the back of my head is on the bottom. At the far left is a diagram when I am observing a photo of a person who is still living. in the middle is a diagram of my head when I am observing a photo of a person who is deceased.

Notice, at the back of my head (bottom of each image) which is where the visual cortex is located, howthe diagram on the left is dark red, but the diagram in the middle is a darker red. These are thedifferences in cognition between **"Dead"** and **"Alive"** images. Order these concise laboratory conditions My accuracy was only about 64% correct

The green diagram shows where energy is concentrated in my brain. Notice yellow at my left ear, and yellow at the back of my head. This indicates that my visual cortex is registering the image shown on the computer screen in front of me and the "answer", whether the person in the photo is alive or dead, isbeing received in my left ear. Of course, that is where I already know "Helen" hangs out.

But, looking back at my own p-value images, my mind appeared to me to be drifting somewhere between FABRICATION, RECOLLECTION, & PERCEPTION. Until the scientists pointed out there is no "turquoise"in my p-values, which appears in those other three and said that this similar appearance was merely coincidental, as I transitioned from PERCEPTION to MEDIUMSHIP

ISOLATION CHAMBER OR CABINET ?

Dr. Dean Radin, Ph.D. Chief Scientist at *IONS* took the photo of me appearing to the left, just after they had wetted the electrodes on my head, for the 32- point EEG The towel on my shoulders is to catch the drips. This is all just before placing me in the Electro- Magnetic Isolation Chamber (Faraday cage).

HELEN'S HUMOR: Back in the 1890's, it was common for mediums to sit in "cabinets" in order to concentrate their energy. Of course, the skeptics always suspecting fraud wondered what themediums were doing in those "cabinets". So mediums figured out how to work without cabinets…

Yet, even today, at Arthur Findlay College of Psychic Science we mediums still sit in three sided cabinets when we do trance mediumship and partial materializations, under red lighting. But there were so many fraudulent mediums in the 1890's and early 20th Century that this practice was discouraged.

Yet, as we (myself and the departed Helen) entered this Friday cage "Isolation Chamber" at *IONS* to do this experiment, and after *we* got inside they closed the door so that I was supposedly "isolated".... But, Helen whispered in my left ear. ***"Alan, what are theythinking? I'm right here in the 'cabinet' with you….This is not an isolation chamber……it is anold fashioned "cabinet".***

2015 TO 2018 – PERSONAL WORK WITH LACH AT UNIVERSITY OF ARIZONA: In the Fall of 2015, I also began working as a research Medium with Dr. Gary Swartz, Ph.D, Director of the Laboratory for Advances in Consciousness and Health (LACH) at the University of Arizona. (Lach.web.arizona.edu). While I had been reading Dr. Schwartz's work for over 10 years we had never had occasion to meet formally until June 2015, when we were both speakers at at convention of the Academy of Spiritual and Consciousness Studies, and I met both he and his wife Rhonda, who also spoke at the conference. Subsequently, we have since done significant research together, with me traveling to Tucson and Dr. Schwartz traveling to San Francisco.

Previously, Dr. Schwartz had been studying Mediumship for over 30 years. And, as a part of an extended research project looking at the controls and accuracy of mediumship experiments including double and triple blinding and published in several papers in 2002, 2005 and 2011, Dr. Schwartz found that:

*"**The totality of the experiments effectively rules out potential conventional psychological explanations of (1) Fraud, (2) "cold reading" techniques used by fake mediums (psychic entertainers) to coax information from sitters, (3) visual, auditory and olfactory cues, (4) sitter rater bias, (5) vague, general information, (6) statistical guessing, and (7) experimenter effects. "***

*"**The totality of the experiments also essentially rules out one potential anomalous (i.e. paranormal) explanation: the possibility of telepathy (or mind reading) by the medium of the sitter's mind. For example, in numerous experiments research mediums obtained information that the sitter did not know, which was subsequently confirmed by relatives or friends living hundreds or thousands of miles from the sitter and the medium. And in triple blinded experiments, the experimenter (the proxy"sitter") was blind to the information about the sitter; hence the medium could not have been reading the mind of the proxy sitter (experimenter) to obtain the accurate information they received about the sitter's deceased loved ones."***

One of Dr. Swartz's studies, which he undertook with Dr. Julie Beischel in 2007, published in *EXPLOREthe journal of Science and Healing* [3(1),23-27] in 2007. This paper concludes that:

"The results suggest that certain mediums can anomalously receive accurate information about deceased individuals. The study design effectively eliminates conventional mechanisms as well as telepathy as explanations for the information reception, but the results cannot distinguish among alternative paranormal hypotheses, such as survival of consciousness (the continued existence, separate from the body, of an individual's consciousness or personality after physical death) and super-psi (or super-ESP; retrieval of information via a psychic channel or quantum field)."

That paper also suggested the best triple blinding methods for Mediumship studies.

Consequently, these were the control conditions that Dr. Delorme and I had adopted for the Second Experiment in my personal research work at the Consciousness Research Lab for the Institute of Noetic Sciences. Using triple blind conditions in February of 2015, I did readings for 32 individuals (all employees of IONS) in two days, with spectacular accuracy, which replicated Dr. Schwartz' prior findings with other mediums at LACH in 2007.

Although, I can never find out the precise results of the 2015 IONS readings due to the triple blinding. I dooccasionally bump into one of the 32 employees to whom I gave readings, at *IONS*. And to date I have confronted more than 10% of those 32 sitters, most of whom I did not know before the readings.

Typically, they come running up to me anxious to tell me about the reading. But, I quickly tell them to hushand not tell me anything because it will, "un-blind the triple blind study", which would allow skeptics to sayI pre-cognitively found the information I had given them. This is a silly argument when though those same skeptics also do not believe in pre-cognition. But, I tell the excited sitter that they can tell me if it was goodor bad without being specific about the details. and they have invariably said**.... "OMG, It was a really great and very evidential reading"**, but without telling me the specific details and so not un-blinding the experiment.

These readings were probably so good because, under these triple blind conditions, my analytical mind could not possibly get involved in any of the methods controlled against. And, so with no analysis or guessing possible, this leaves only one place to find the information, entirely from intuition (which means from Spirits on the other side).

2016 - PSYCHICAL RESEARCH FOUNDATION-PRF: In January of 2016, I also became a paid research medium for the Psychical Research Foundation, working with their Bryan Williams Director of Research (psychicalresearchfoundation.com). This work was double blind but involved Bryan making a drawing of what I described using standard police likeness reproduction techniques. However, to keep it blinded I was not allowed to review the completed sketch. PRF then asked the "sitter", to judge whether Brian's sketch matched the deceased target. So, this meant that Brian interpreted what I said into his ownvision of what had come through from Spirit.

Frankly, adding that one extra step of Brian's sketch, brought the accuracy down to 50% out of two trials. Basically, the first sitter said yes Brian and I had depicted the correct person, the second sitter said that we had not. I believe this experimental technique needs some refinement to get rid of the need to have Brian's vision super-imposed on top of mine A better method would be to have the medium create the sketch using the police likeness techniques. …. For example I am personally a fantastic portrait artist. While even 50% correct is still a 500 batting average which would be hot stuff if this was baseball, at the same time adding a second non-medium analytical mind in the loop often destroys mediumship.

C. CONCLUSION:

So what I have to report is that real science, indeed our most proven science of the 20th and 21st century ***Quantum-Electodynamics-QED, Entanglement*** and ***Non-locality*** not only allows, but indeed requires consciousness outside of body. Further, *Post-Mortem Consciousness Survival* is consistent with our best science, and matches our laboratory results which have proven that psychic phenomena are all valid, andthose same principles of *QED* and *Non-Locality* also prove that that classical *Materialism* is simply comatose, as a rational explanation for reality.

EVIDENTIAL MEDIUMSHIP TAKES DEDICATION: My personal experience of mediumship necessary to communicate with surviving consciousnesses is that it is not a gift, indeed the only "gift" is knowing you can do it. Some people would hold out that they were "given" this unusual "gift", and that it was probably "given" me during my NDE. But, if death in a motorcycle accident is a "gift" then I suppose that idea could be true. Yet, my experience, both in conducting developmental circles training mediums and at *Arthur Findlay College of Psychic Science* is that ***anyone can learn to have this "gift" and channel spirits from the other side, if they will only practice long enough.***

Personally, I did not start working as a medium on the platform at Spiritualist churches until my 8th year ofstudying mediumship. Spectacular *Evidential Mediumship* like accurately getting names of the deceased relatives for strangers takes refinement of your ability to surrender and get into flow, very much like the technique of a virtuoso concert pianist requiring patience and dedication.

The most difficult part to learn is to trust and rely on Spirit (your guides on the other side) to deliver, because it isn't really the medium doing any of the work here, it is entirely Spirit utilizing the medium asan instrument (like a telephone). Just like Mozart relied on the muse to deliver his music, mediums rely on Spirit to deliver the evidence. Excellent *Evidential Mediumship* which consistently brings through names and other WOW details of evidence for complete strangers is a lifetime study, but anyone with dedication and persistence (even nerd scientists like me) can learn to do it well, because it is simply a process of surrender.

Accurate evidential mediumship *requires humility, gratefulness, suppression of the ego, and dedication to continual study.* It is not for the faint-hearted and once you realize its truth, it becomes compelling. When someone asks, "Why are you a Medium? my answer is, *"I can't help myself, this is part of why I live"*.

FINALLY, Mediumship when carefully examined scientifically proves that *Post-mortem ConsciousnessSurvival* is a scientific fact. What is required for a scientific fact are three things:

1. We have a logical possibility.

2. We have a great deal of evidence for it, and

3. There is no evidence against it!

Therefore, by our scientific requirement for **proof beyond a reasonable doubt**, it is indeed anestablished scientific fact. that consciousness survives and communicates with us.

Three videos that explain what we are doing at the Consciousness Research Lab (CRL) and at theLaboratory for Advances in Consciousness & Health (LACH) are listed below:

- Dr. Dean Radin, Discusses the work of the Consciousness Research Lab (at noetic.org)

- VIDEO CLIP (2 minutes) at http://vimeo.com/113981492

- Dr. Gary Schwartz, discusses the Mystery of Consciousness: Published on Mar 8, 2015, Dr. Gary Schwartz, professor of psychology, medicine, neurology, psychiatry and surgery at the University of Arizona and director of its Laboratory for Advances in Consciousness and Health. We asked Dr. Gary Schwartz for his thoughts on the mystery of consciousness. https://youtu.be/b1OeVvZCKVQ

- **Dr. Alan Hugenot, The Nature of consciousness,** has become one of the most popular videos on the you-tube and as of (12/10/2018) gets more than 400 hits a day. It explains where I am at. https://youtu.be/yByEQfaD314

2. HOW MEDIUMSHIP WORKS

A. TYPES OF MEDIUMSHIP

Not all readers will be familiar with mediumship. I certainly was never instructed in this taboo area of consciousness by my family.

Mediumship is defined as that portion of human psychic powers which involve sending and receiving communications with departed spirits in the afterlife (surviving consciousnesses), which is an intuitive ability which can be easily learned by most people. Mediumship involves the following intuitive abilities, which are defined below:

1. Clair-Sentience,

2. Clair-Voyance

    1. Subjective Clairvoyance

3. Clair-Audience

4. Impressional Mediumship,

    A. Inspirational and

    B. Impressional Writing.

    C. Automatic Writing

1. CLAIR-SENTIENCE - feeling the departed: This is the basis of all mediumship where the spirit makes you feel things. It can also be a very direct feeling. For example, as a medium I always ask certain questions of all spirits that I channel. in order to collect the evidencenecessary to identify them, and they deliver their messages through my feelings. I have posted the questions which any communicating Spirit must provide to get my cooperation.

First, I want to know their name. And, they give this to me through my feelings. While how I feel a name is difficult to explain, it is very real, I will have the distinct feeling of my uncle Floyd iftheir name is Floyd, I will feel basket balls if their name is Jack, I will feel an "M" or a "B" and literally sound out their names.

Getting a name right, if I were to guess, has odds of 200 to 1. But, because it is a surviving consciousness telling me their name comes through properly 85 to 100% of the time. The first name I get is usually them. It comes in one letter at a time often with me sounding it out. One example at a reading was that after feeling the L and the A, I sounded the name out to be **Avril**, and then I said *"or is it Daniel?"*. As it turns out is first name was Axel, and his middle name was Daniel. Through feelings I sounded our Avril which is nearly identical to Axel, but the Danieljust came through as a flash.

Second, I want to know what the departed's relationship to the sitter was. This comes with feelings of my own relatives. and if I feel my grandfather I say "This your grandfather ….. on your mother's side" … This answer has odds of 1 in 10 because there are only that many relations, Mother, father, brother, sister, grandma, grandpa, aunt, uncle, male cousin, female cousin etc. But, getting this correct without guessing, along with the name brings the odds to 2000 to 1

Third, I want to know how they died. Here, I may be short of breath and this tells me the Spirit died by drowning, emphysema, or lung cancer. Or, I will feel like my chest is being crushed and this means the spirit died of motorcycle wreck, car wreck or heart attack. Slightly differently my chest cavity will feel pain which can mean breast cancer or pleurisy. Sometimes I feel nothing which means they just died of old age. This has a 12 to 1 odds because there are a dozen normal ways you could have died. But when it is also correct it raises the odds to 24,000 to 1.

Fourth, I want to know what their occupation was, here I will feel them using their hands, smell baking, see them holding a pitch fork, etc. but there are about 10 occupations for each sex witha few more for men, but lets say odds of 10 to 1, and now if that fact also comes through accurately we are at 240,000 to 1 that this is the precise spirit we were seeking.

The list of questions numbers 25, but they usually only answer 4 or 5 and the sitter recognizes them. I have also studied on bringing through their distinct personality. Yet, all that is still done through clair-sentience.

2. CLAIRVOYANCE – Seeing the departed: This is a skill I am still working on, just allowing me to see them in my minds eye. It is not like video photography, rather it is more like dreaming. They are not fuzzy, they are more effervescent than that. But, I have learned that when I am becoming overwhelmed by the emotions of the feeling, which may ramp up quickly while in the clair-sentient mode, if i switch to clairvoyance and work at seeing them then the emotional feeling subsides.

My wife Gale finds clairvoyance to be the easiest form. She sits in a seance and sees the spiritsaround people. She also has very livid dreams, where I almost never remember a dream. Sothis seems to be an intuitive skill some have more of than others.

- Subjective clairvoyance

3. CLAIR-AUDIENCE – Hearing spirit: This is an intuitive skill which I have only experienced occasionally. However, Mozart says that he **"just heard the melodies"** and wrote them down. Obviously receiving them from the muse in complete form. So, again this is an intuitive skill which varies with each person, some have more of it than others. Obviously, Mozart had a very developed psychic ear.

4. IMPRESSIONAL MEDIUMSHIP – feeling the departed mentally: There are three forms ofthis intuitive skill

- Inspirational Speaking
- Inspirational / Impressional Writing
- Automatic Writing

A. Inspirational Speaking: This is when the spirit speaks through you by inspiring your mind. Itis similar to extemporaneous speaking, in that you have no prepared notes. But instead allow Spirit to give you the message. I have done this often and it is very freeing to just let spiritinspire my thoughts and voice. While doing this you are in a slightly altered state, but you arenot in trance, rather your analytical mind has been shut down and you are just transmitting what you receive.

B. Inspirational / Impressional Writing: This is the business of allowing spirit to fill your mind with thought which you write down, it is exactly like Inspirational Speaking, except that you write it instead of speaking it. Again, while you are in an altered state your are not in trance, rather your analytical mind has been shut down and you are just transmitting what you receive.

C. Automatic Writing: This is a trance like state where spirit takes over and does the writing. I have experienced this, but find it hard to edit later separating out the words which are written in script in one continues line. There is a message hidden in there but it is easier to use impressional writing.

3. BASICS OF MEDIUMSHIP - The Philosopher's Stone, How to Be a Medium.

A. OPEN TO IT: First things first. You cannot comprehend mediumship if you are at all skepticalof it. … It is like a non-swimmer who is afraid to go into the pool. … Believing is seeing. You will never be able to have it proven to you so that you can see it and then believe it. This is because the observer principle of *Quantum Electro-dynamics-QED* brings to the experimenter what he intended to find. "***What you want to see is what you get***".

This is simply am application of John von Neumann's "*Choice 1*". Consequently, if you want to find it is untrue,….. you will find evidence proving it to be untrue,…. The universe will simply deliver what you are looking for. … But, if you want to find it is true… … then you will find evidence proving it to be true.

If you think, ***"I'll believe it when I can see it,"*** that is your ego speaking out of fear. The ego is driven only by fear and tries to protect you from appearing foolish. But, because of the observer principle in QED, that what you see is what you get, and that what you expect is what you will always find, if you have any fears at all then mediumship will simply not work for you. If that is your attitude, go home and don't waste the mediums time.

Instead, before spirit can come to you, you have to open to spirit and be willing to be seen as a fool. You will only find the ***philosophers stone*** (the union of intellectuality and spirituality) if youwill first decide to believe it is actually possible to find it.

> ***"However bereft the human soul might be of illuminating grace….it bears in itselfthe categorical imperative, which makes it act and think as if it were eternal, immortal, and aspiring to infinite perfection"*** Immanuel Kant

You must therefore come to mediumship, without fear, feeling that you are divinely guided and always protected. You must come as *Don Quixote* a fool for love, a fool for God, and you must answer the question, ***"To be or not to be"*** before you can enter here.

It is the very trial of the satisfaction of our desires. You are faced with Goethe's Faustian question,

> ***"Can you renounce the wisdom of this world to give yourself the wisdom of divine love, which is folly in the eyes of the world?"***

If you can….. then this will be easy. if not then you will fail at this every time.

You must allow the search for spirit and mediumship to be real. Regardless of what first brought you to the quest for mediumship, whether you lost a family member, heard about someone's Near-Death experience, or merely had a deep desire to understand death andlook for evidence of an afterlife. When you heard about the idea that it might be possible to "see, hear, and sense" loved ones in spirit you need to open to it and allow it to make sense to you, orit simply cannot happen for you. It is only by allowing it to be a part of your pathway that you canopen this door.

Novices think that if they go to the "best medium" they will get through, but the energy of mediumship does not come from the medium. … The mediums task is to be open and available like a pay phone. They are just there present for you to use. … You, as the sitter placing the call have to provide the quarter for the pay phone to provide you with a dial tone."No quarter (no energy) no phone call (communication)".

But, if you are open to it, then the next step is to find an Evidential Medium, or do it yourself.

B. EMBRACE YOUR INTUITIVE SIXTH SENSE: Allow your intuitive sense to open. You will begin to expand your awareness, and in doing so you will most likely begin to attract the books, websites, and people you need to assist you on your journey.

This new "sixth sense" can come in many forms, but the three that tend to work most closelywith mediumship and spirit communication are clairvoyance ("clear seeing"), clairaudience("clear hearing"), and clairsentience ("clear feeling"), as mentioned above.

When you decide to take the step forward and declare to yourself, then your loved ones in spirit,and the universe as a whole; they will all assist you to open up your sixth sense and begin the process. So, embrace that sense and know it is being divinely presented to you. This sixthsense is something we are all born with. Some are aware of that sense as a young child, while others won't discover the sense until later in life.

Goethe said it this way, ***"When you definitely decide … the universe moves"***

C. FIND A MENTOR: This is not a road we can walk alone, you need a mentor. But, realize thatas you open to the universe your mentor will find you. … Indeed they are all around you. Having a mentor allows you to study under someone who can help you as you work through questions, challenges, and breakthroughs while you are building your connection to spirit. …

Right away I found fellow travelers as well as mentors.

D. BUILD YOUR SUPPORT: Join a developmental circle, most Spiritualist churches have groups that meet about once a week and work on mediumship. But, in this day and age there are all kinds of spirituality groups in operation. So, find a support group of like minded people.

E. RECOGNIZE THAT THIS IS A SACRED CALLING: What you are endeavoring to do is bringenlightenment to the world. This is not just a worthy calling, but is THE WORTHIEST of callings.Becoming the bridge that connects the world of the departed with the world of the physical is an awesome endeavor. ***Recognizing the sacredness of such communication is essential.*** Mediumship is not a career change, it is not a new way to make money and have your own business. It is a holy calling. In my experience the best mediums are successful in their careers and then discover, on the side, that they are also great mediums.

F. IT COMES FROM WITHIN: Everything you need for this work is to be found within, so begin to meditate regularly, set aside a time each day for this essential calming of the mind. I find this easiest at 3:00 AM after my mind is completely settled from 4 to 5 hours of sleep. I awake, go tomy library, light a candle and start to write in my journal as I receive info from Helen and the other side. You can do something very similar.

CHAPTER 5
HOW TO COMMUNICATE WITH SPIRITS:

1. GIVING READINGS TO THE PUBLIC IS AN EYE OPENER:

After I had been demonstrating mediumship on the platform at least once or twice a month as the medium at Spiritualist church services for over 5 years, each time giving 3 to 5 "readings" my total number of reading was approaching 350 to 450 "readings", but this had been in the relatively protected environment of a Spiritualist church. Although I had given an occasional individual private reading, I had not become a medium as a career change and had no ambition of "making a living" as a medium. At the same time during those 5 years I had been talking at conventions, and giving radio interviews on the *Science of Post-Mortem Consciousness Survival.*

And, one film quality interview which I gave in October 2015 (posted on youtube by the interviewer and film editor Anthony Chene) entitled *The Nature of Consciousness,* has gotten over 450,000 views worldwide. Just google Alan Hugenot Youtube, or this URL https://youtu.be/yByEQfaD314.

Consequently, all this generated hundreds of requests by email to provide private readings. So, due to this popular demand, I finally began in June of 2018 to providing private readings to the public by appointment. But, I chose to do this at the same professional fees that I charge for my design work as a Naval Architect, simply because that's what my time costs.

But, I quickly discovered how little most people understand about mediumship. Many novices seem to believe that:
- They pay for a reading,
- Tell the medium who they want to talk to.
- The medium then dials them up, and
- They then ask questions and get direct answers from the departed....

Well that just is not how it works. You may want to hear from your recently deceased spouse, and instead your Uncle George, the one who sexually abused you needs to talk instead. Well, Uncle George is the last departed soul you wish to hear from. Never mind that he is asking for your forgiveness, which he needs to acquire b before he can move on.

I also got a lot of abuse from the ignorant general public, which is why I also later stopped giving readings on line to the general public. I do sometimes give readings for the general public at psychic fairs.

But, I have included the following to educate the public about how to actually get a good reading.

2. ENHANCING YOUR MEDIUMSHIP READING:

This is excerpted from the instructions that I give to everyone who comes to me for an EvidentialMediumship reading.

HOW IT WORKS: Many things might prevent a successful communication. And there are several things you as a sitter can do to greatly improve the chances of a successful reading. During a reading the medium will be communicating with your departed loved ones. And although you probably have a certain loved one you want to contact, there will be several others who want to come through besides the oneyou are trying to get to.

Also, once the medium makes the connection across the divide, there'll be several personalities working together to make the communication take place. Further, each of them is trying to communicate using symbols and not words The several individuals are:

1. YOUR LOVED ONE: who is "talking" to the medium's "control" or "guide".

2. THE CONTROL: This person is a deceased Spirit who acts as the medium on the other side. Usually, the medium and the control are quire close, and have been working together for years. The "Control" is translating what your departed loved one is saying into symbolic impressions which will have specific meanings for the medium, and knowing which impressions within the medium's soul to use, the "Control" truly knows by heart, and this is why it works. In Mycase it is Helen.

3. THE MEDIUM: then translates those deeply felt impressions (which they "feel" and do not actually hear) into words, which they then will speak to you.

4. YOU then interpret those words they chose but will now apply your own meanings, andcolorings, based on your life experiences of those words.

Please realize that everyone of the four people in this chain has differing impressions based on the life they have lived and the emotional sentience involved. Finally, the message will always come through a bitgarbled at first.

Honestly, it is very much like playing the game ***"whisper down the lane"*** where four people sitting nextto each other at a party try to pass a whispered message to the next person, but when it gets to the fourthperson it is hardly recognizable as the same message. Consequently, if you are not open to re- interpretation of the meanings that your medium brings through then nothing will be clear.

SO, PLEASE BE AS OPEN MINDED AS POSSIBLE: Do try to see everything your medium brings through in a positive way. Instead of looking at what they may have mis-interpreted, look at what is rightin what they are getting and ignore what is wrong. If you can not be open minded, then you may miss out on a very special communication.

For example: Recently (2018), in an online reading, I brought a grand-mother through by giving her name (which was correct, and her exact relationship, which was also correct). And at first, the sitter agreed, ***"Yes, that is my grandma's name"***. Now, if you look at that single sentence of grandma's name,there are actually three pieces of evidence:

> **First,** Female (odds of 1 in 2),

> **Second,** Grandma (odds of say 1 in 10, when you consider mom, grandmother, aunt, sister,cousin, girl-friend, employer, etc.), and

> **Third,** her exact name (with odds of 1 in 200 considering all women's possible names).

Statistically, this already multiplies out to odds of 4,000 to one.....

So, this detailed evidence is already scientifically significant and the data is obvious that this could not simply be a lucky random guess by me (the medium) not at odds of 4000 to one. So, the only logical conclusion is that we have definitely made contact with her grandma.

But, then in this particular reading I next got the impression of **"Cook"**, and the way that specific impression comes to me is that I smell baking. ... Now, because I like to cook and absolutely love to bake I inadvertently added my own color to the feeling and so I said ,***"And, it appears that she <u>liked to cook</u>"***.

Now, the sitter, who was slightly distracted and not listening openly, emphatically said, ***"No, she did not.... you're wrong, grandma hated cooking,..... she spend the first 20 years of her life in service as the cook in a mansion, and she never liked it"*****.....**

Even though I had carefully prefaced this statement with ***"It appears"***, Yet the distracted sitter simply decided I was entirely (100%) wrong.

This caused her to also shut down her belief in the reading. Consequently, she now became increasingly dissatisfied when nothing else seemed to come through from Grandma....

Unfortunately, the sitter (who had probably also only lightly perused my clear instructions to be open minded). of course never realized that she herself had shut off the energy....

Not me or grandma, Basically, although she was still on-line, she had already "hung up the phone because she no longer trusted the phone company ... (me, the medium)".

Yet, the sad fact was that it was she herself that was destroying the communication. Strictly due to her personal distraction and lack of concentration; and her focusing on one word instead of the whole sentence. ("It appears that she liked").

All this took place simply because she did not see the reality of ***"Yes, grandma was a cook, in fact that was her occupation"***. Instead, she threw away the entire communication because I added my own impression and the single word ***"liked"***.

Further, grandma was merely answering the next question on my list of questions, which I ask Spirits to identify themselves with. ***"What was your occupation?"***. So, her grandma and I were actually spot on. **Grandma was a professional cook,** and although she may have hated her job situation of being "in service", she probably liked cooking better than being a ladies valet, or a scrub woman; or she probably would not have taken up being the cook.

In fact, this piece of valid evidential data, that she was a cook, raises the significance by another factor of 1 in 12 (because a woman of her grandma's age could have anyone of only about a dozen occupations before women's liberation; nurse, cook, telephone operator, clerk......), and adding odds of 1 in 12 to the prior three pieces of evidence we now have a statistical significance of **48,000 to one,.......** that is only a one in 48,000 chance that this is not her actual grandmother coming through........

But, instead of being open and concentrating on the reading, she decides my reading is 100% wrong, all based on the single word, **"liked".**

This unfortunate sitter, by not paying attention, and not putting positive spin on everything I said **uses an assumed contradiction** to negate all the prior evidence and then chooses to not believe that I have contacted her grandma. She ruins her own reading, even though we (Grandma and I) have provided statistical evidence of 48,000 to one. Needless to say the reading went down hill from there.

So, when you work with a medium, do not try to test them. if they only get half of the info right, they arestill batting 500 which is better than any professional baseball player that every lived. So, don't get confused by one wrong answer.

3. ***MEDIUMSHIP IS LIKE AN TOLD FASHIONED LONG DISTANCE PHONE CALL:*** 80 years ago you would wait until all the other people on the party line were done talking and it was finally your turn. … Then you would contact the long distance operator who would put your call through to the long distance operator in the city where your loved one lived, … and then that operator would make the analog (hard wired) connection at the switch board to ring up your loved one   and if their party line was free, or she could ask the other parties clogging the line, to shut up so your intended party could receive the long distance call. … Then, if they happened to be home they could answer the phone, or not…...

On weekends, when the rates were cheaper, sometimes all the long distance lines were too busy all day long and so you would have to wait, other times the other people on the party line would not get off the phone, and there was also sometimes static on the line.

But, if you were lucky and **everything worked** well and no one broke the connection you could often get through…... Indeed, in that era many people stayed home on Sunday afternoons and evenings just because a relative might try to get through on long distance.

So, please consider your medium is just a proficient telephone operator who has learned how to operate the switchboard correctly and is competent to place the call,……. but, it still might not get through So be open to revision in your interpretation of what comes through and please consider that:

FIRST - Your departed loved may not answer the phone. We can ring them up all day long, but maybethey are not yet ready to talk. Also, if this person seldom spoke to you in person or by phone when they were alive, here in the physical…. what would make them want to talk to you any more now?……

You may feel a strong need to talk, but they might not. So, plan to appreciate the communication thatdoes happen even if it is not what you originally set out to get, or even if who comes through is not who you planned to talk to.

SECOND - BELIEF IS VERY IMPORTANT: Mediumship will not work for you if you are skeptical about it of survival after death. Your negative energy will simply short circuit everything........ Skepticism, oran ***"I'll believe it when I see it",*** attitude will entirely dissipate the psychic energy and then no communication at all will happen..... So, if you are just getting a reading ***"to test the water"***, please save your money because your own skeptical attitude will prevent any communication at all from happening.

I know that sounds like a cop out to say that, *"mediumship only works for believers"*, but this is absolutely true. And, it is not some kind of placebo effect. Instead, it is simply the normal functioning of the observer principle of *Quantum Electro-dynamics-QED,* which says ***"You will find precisely what you are lookingfor"***. So, if you are skeptical and then you can leave the reading having "proven" that, ***"All mediums are frauds".*** ... It is a law of quantum physics, which you simply can't get around.

Also, if you believe but your spouse does not, then don't include your non-believing spouse at the reading. I had a reading the other day on SKYPE where the woman wanted to talk to her departed child, but the husband who thought all this was just so much rubbish was listening in the next room and he kept grunting and questioning everything I brought through. Simply, leave such people out of the equation they truly drain off the energy. She should have waited until he had gone fishing before contacting me.

THIRD - THE RECENTLY DEPARTED OFTEN DON'T YET KNOW HOW: People who who did not believe in an afterlife don't suddenly get wise just because they have now died......

When they find themselves still conscious they may easily think they could not possibly have died.......

"After all" they say, ***"Since I can still think, then I can not possibly be dead"*** .....To quote Descartes ***"I think therefore I am"*** .....

Things may be a bit strange where they now find themselves. For instance they no longer need to eat, and people no longer notice them no matter how loud they yell. But, according to their view point, ***"if they are still conscious they could not possibly be dead"***.

Also, even if they have figured out that they are dead, and do want to communicate back with you, they will still have to figure out how to do that from the strange new location they find themselves in. Also, if they never believed in the afterlife, they still may not believe that communication from the afterlife is possible, especially if they died believing that **"When you're dead you're dead"**, something will have to change their mind before they can even think about trying to communicate back.

Finally, even if they realize they are dead, and they do want to communicate they still may have no idea what they really need to do to accomplish that. On the other hand, they may learn this in a few more months and then they may communicate freely.

Consequently, we usually suggest that you give your departed loved one at least six months to figure all this out before you try to communicate with them. Unfortunately, most people left here in the physical really need to communicate in the first couple of weeks, but then six months later they have forgotten all about their need to talk to the departed.

FOURTH, YOU'RE NOT BUYING A DIRECT CALL TO A SPECIFIC INDIVIDUAL: Many people believe

that the medium simply dials up the deceased, and then they can have a conversation with them. But, what is really happening is that you are buying your medium's time similar to how you would buy your physician's time, or your lawyer's time. And you owe them for the time they spend with you whether or notthey solve the problem.

Also, If you do have a particular person you want to hear from, ... *Then Start talking to them right now*,

... telling them that you want to hear from them and invite them to the reading that you have scheduled, so they can get ready and be there, just as you would if you wanted them to accompany you to your Doctor's appointment.

When they were alive in the physical, you would not expect them to read your mind and know where you were going to be tomorrow. If they were still in the physical you would invite if you wanted them to come along when you visit your doctor..... Please believe me that nothing has changed, ... you still have to ask them to attend. If you do not invite them they really have no reason to be present .... Get a clue, here, *The truth is that they are still alive and have their own life to live.* So, you have to actually invite them.

And do remember to respect their time, *They may have left this dimension, but they are still alive andnot just waiting around for eternity to pass slowly by, as we might have learned from the church.* Instead, they likely have a life which is even more physical than ours and complete with scheduled activities, other friends etc. So, you need to impress upon them that you giving them a phone call is important.

FINALLY: If everyone attending the reading is a believer, then **There will definitely be communication from the other side**. and those of your departed relatives and/or friends who have been there long enough to figure it all out and want to communicate with you, will definitely come through. But, it is likely that the person you so desperately wanted to talk to will not come through, because they haven't figured itout yet.

Usually, the surviving consciousnesses who do communicate have been on the other side for some time. Yet, since they notice that a telephone line direct to you is currently available, they may line up and try to get through. So, your grand-parents and great grand-parents and your grand uncles and aunts will suddenly come through. So is also good to memorize the actual names of your ancestors so you know who they are when they come through by name. Also, your deceased grade school friends (many of whom you don't even know are dead) may suddenly come through. So, if the name of someone you haven't heard from in years comes through, and you aren't sure if they are dead or alive, do recognize them and welcome them.

Further, during the reading, for you to validate who the communicator actually is, you really need to know their first names. For example, just, what was your great grand-father's oldest brother's first name?......

He is your great grand uncle...... and did your great grand father have two or three brothers?.... If that fellow shows up and gives the Medium his first name, RICHARD, you need to be able to recognize

his name as being your great grand uncle RICHARD. Otherwise, you will think he is a stranger. For example, a medium will demonstrate before an audience of 10 people, and he will say *"I have a man here named George and he seems to be from the generation before this one, in other words at your parents level. Does anyone know a George?"* Now, out of ten people each with dozens of deceased relatives and hundreds of former acquaintances, there are probably 20 Georges, who are in their parents generation, yet amazingly no one can remember a George......

This is only because the audience have not done their own homework..... instead, they are expecting the medium and the deceased consciousness to do all the heavy lifting for them...... Likewise,there was one sitter for whom I brought through a David, and the sitter said *"I don't know a David"*, ...

yet she had been married to a David for over 15 years   It   was   after that reading, on the way home when her new husband reminded her that she had been married to a David   So, do realize that the person coming through could be someone you have simply put, "out of mind".

4. GET THE NAMES RIGHT:

Often, doing a mediumship reading, a spirit will show up and give their name, but the sitter does not recognize the name. Later, the sitter may find out who this person was, but by then the communication is over. So, before your mediumship reading it would be very helpful for you, if you look up (and write down) the first names of your four grand parents, eight great grand parents, and also the first names of your aunts uncles and cousins, and then bring that "family tree" with you to the readling.

And, make sure you have the names right, you may have called your grand mother "Granda" or "Gana" and always thought her given name was "Betsy", because some relatives called her that. But, when the medium says **"I have a female presence here named Elizabeth"** you might say **"I don't know an Elizabeth"** because the medium did not say "Gana" or "Betsy". So, it is good to get a family treefrom genealogy.com or other such site, and even bring it with you to the reading.

Finally, if one of those "forgotten" relatives does come through and even if you recognize their name, theymay tell the medium about how they died or their occupation, both details which you may not know at thattime, but write these details down when the medium gives them to you, and then you can check themlater with someone who does know, because when you can verify these additional details, which were unknown to you at the time of the reading, and certainly unknown to the medium it is evidence that because the medium received the correct facts, of which you were unaware, that the medium was not "psychically reading your mind", but was actually communicating with the mind of that deceased relative who gave that correct evidence to the medium.

Finally, if there is someone special you want to talk to during the reading, your job is to start inviting them to the reading before the appointment, just like you would talk to them, and tell them about the appointment, just like you would if they are still physically alive. ... Realize that they are alive still, with their own agenda for the day, and so be respectful and treat them that way.

WHAT MEDIUMSHIP COSTS: Lastly, 80 years ago when people made those *long distance phone calls* described above, average salaries were $35 to $50 a week yet the long distance call might cost $15 (20%of their weekly pay) and although they disliked the cost, people still made the long distance calls andloved being able to "get through".

Today, when nearly everyone graduates from the University and starting salaries for these people are a minimum of $120,000 per year ($10,000/ mo. or $2,325/week, $58.12/ hr). Yet, these wealthy folks audaciously will ask for free mediumship readings. When what I and other mediums charge is nowhere near 5% of their weekly pay. Yet, these free-loaders want an extremely difficult *"long distance phone call"*, across the divide into the afterlife, but amazingly think it should be for free. Give me a break.

CONCLUSION:

Now, after looking at all the objective and subjective evidence which supports *Post-Mortem Consciousness Survival,* the next question is **"*What is the afterlife like?*"** So, the following section describes and collates the best evidence for what the afterlife must be like.

CHAPTER 6
THE DEATH CHANGE, Transition to the NextDimension.

1. THE DEATH CHANGE:

As we begin our transition to the other side the importance of this side fades out, and we leave our physical body.

A. MY OWN NDE EXPERIENCE: My own experience of the death change during the NDE was that goingout-of-body was very simple. However, my experience of the return into the physical body is wrenching, and may always be a violent struggle. Mediums have told me that my difficulty in the returning is becauseI really do not want to come back into the physical.

My personal description of giving up the physical body as happened during my NDE, is that it is like taking off an overcoat and setting it aside. I like the phrases in the song "Going Home" as taken from the largo of Dvorak's New World Symphony.

"Quiet like, some still day.. I am going home

It's not far, just close by, Through an open door

There's no break, there's no end… Just living on"

My own experience of the death change (Described in Appendix 4) closely parallels the third description given below in item "D" by Edward C. Randall, which also closely collates with the Near-Death experienceas documented by the *International Association for Near Death Studies-IANDS*.

Here, in chronological order. are several descriptions of the death change

B. HORACE ABRAHAM ACKLEY, M.D. By Sophia Elizabeth Morgan, *From Matter to Spirit* **,** ©1863: One of the earliest descriptions of the death process communicated from the other side came from Dr. Ackley, who reported back through a medium his experience of dying:

"I experienced but very little suffering during the last few days of my life, though at first there werestruggles, and my features were distorted; but I learned, after my spirit had burst its barriers and was freed from its connection with the external body, that these were produced by it in an attemptto sever its connection, which in all cases is more or less difficult; the vital points of contact being suddenly broken by disease, the union in other portions of the system is necessarily severed with violence, but, as far as I have learned, without consciousness of pain.

Like many others, I found that I was unable to leave the form at once. I could feel myselfgradually raised from my body, and in a dreamy, half conscious state. It seemed as though I was not a united being — that I was separated into parts, and yet despite this there seemed to by an indissoluble connecting link. My spirit was freed a short time after the organs of my physical body had entirely ceased to preform their functions. My spiritual form was then united into one, and I was raised a short distance above the body, standing over it by what power I was unable to tell. I could see those who were in the room around me, and knew by what was going on that a considerable time may have elapsed since dissolution had taken place. and I presume I could have been for some time unconscious; and this I find is a common experience, not however unusual."

So, here in the first known "modern" description we have a "connection being severed" but no mention of such connection being a cord.

C. ANDREW JACKSON DAVIS: *Death and the Afterlife* , ©1865:

Two years later, Davis reported seeing many spirits leaving he body, and being connected by *"A very finecord"*. But, in the same narrative Davis also witnessed a soldier blow apart, ***"I saw that all the particles streamed up and met together in the air"***.

So, while Davis sometimes saw this cord, yet other times it was apparently not even necessary.

D. EDWARD C. RANDALL'S DESCRIPTION FROM 1906, taken from *The French Revelation* by N.Riley Heagerty ©1995:

This is probably the most reliable description, which was received by Edward C. Randall, through the mediumship of Mrs. Emily French. One Spirit told Randall that:

> *"Death change is simply the liberation of the spirit form from the physical body, composing the outer flesh garment, perfectly natural and painless. Every change in nature is beautiful and dissolution is not exception to that rule. One simply ceases to be an inhabitant of the world in which we now live. The second world or plane is just as natural to us as the first, but, of course, we live under different conditions. We pass our daily life as before. Our spirit is just as perfect a human form as it ever was. For your clear understanding of the* modus operandi *of the death change to this plane we may say, One parts with the physical body only, We lose none of our intelligence, neither is any thing added to our understanding."*

"The insane pass from earth-life insane still. and countless numbers of our people are required to care for them and give them proper treatment so that their mentality may be restored to the normal. Murderers at war with humanity, hanged or electrocuted on the earth-plane, are liberated in this community, we are obliged to do what the world of men failed to do — control and educate them. Then again, we have the ignorant and vicious. The atom of good that has found expressionin them must be developed and directed.

*"**Few people come into this life with any conception of what or where it is, or the controlling laws. The ignorance of the masses is pitiful.** They enter our portals as helpless asthe babe enters yours. So, you see dissolution making no mental change, and life being material and continuous, there is just as great a need for schools, colleges, and universities as exists with you. If fact, it may be said that anything you have in your earth life is but a poor imitation of what exists here and is largely the result of spirit influence and power.*

The law of attraction is the dominate force here. *We have a great number of thoughtful men seeking to discover and develop the hidden forces of nature; we have great lecture halls where those who are learned discourse upon the hidden forces; we have teachers who develop the spirituality, and discourse upon that great force called Good and its function in the universe. It is abusy world where everyone is doing his or her part. **We do not have strife for money or need for money. So you see the occupation of a great many people is gone***.

The above is the description that most resembles what I personally experienced during my NDE.

E. FREDRICK H.W. MYERS: Here the renowned SPR scientist is speaking through the mediumship of Geraldine Cummins, seems to repeat the idea of a "cord" first mentioned by Andrew Jackson Davis in 1865. Myers referred to the spirit body as the "double" explaining it to be an exact duplicate of thephysical body, and clearly stating that ***death results from a change in vibration"***.

However, this would seem to contradict the idea reported earlier through the same medium that *"Death occurs when these two principal communicating lines with the brain and solar plexus are severed."*

Now I have to ask "Did death occur when the vibration changed or when the alleged two cords were severed?

Observing such a contradiction in terms within a single communication, tells me that **the medium was coloring some of it with her own interpretation when the communicator was stating it differently, which results in the contradiction**. Here is what Cummins reported as being received from Myers:

> *"the two are bound together by many little threads, by two silver cords. One of which makes contact with the solar plexus and the other with the brain. They all may lengthen or extend during sleep or during half-sleep for they have considerable elasticity. When a man slowly dies these threads and two cords are gradually broken. Death occurs when these two principal communicating lines with the brain and solar plexus are severed"*

Yet, Myers went on to explain in the same communication that life occasionally lingers in certain cells of the body after the soul has departed, and then is reported as having said that that during this time the "double" is still attached to the physical shell by some threads which have not been broken. However, he also pointed out that the soul does not suffer during this time. So, here from Myers we have those cords again.

"As a rule" Myers stated, *"the soul achieves complete freedom within an hour or two of the of physical death."* He added that *"there is usually no pain associated with the separation."* So, if the soul has departed, according to this doctrine of the silver cord, then the cord is severed. But, if these remaining parts later join the departed soul through the still attached cord then the doctrine contradicts itself. Which is why I see a good deal of coloring it to be the way the medium thinks it "should be".

Further, according to Myers, *"death results from a change in vibration. the physical body vibrates at a much slower rate than the "double". There is a temporary dislocation as the soul passes from the confinesof the physical body to the spirit body."*

But, after Myers (speaking through the interpretation of Geraldine Cummins) apparently introduces two cords, that rumor is now in vogue. and we see it being repeated again in 1917.

F. WESLEY TUDOR POLE'S DESCRIPTION (BRITISH MEDIUM) : *Private Dowding* , ©1917"

Pole reports on what he as a medium saw during the death of "Major P", when he saw a form begin to appear above the body:

> *"This form is attached to the physical body on the bed by two transparent*

elastic cords. One of them appears to be attached to the solar plexus and the other to the brain. As I watch this form it grows more distinct in outline, until I can see that it is an exact counterpart, so far as the form is concerned, of the body on the bed. I can see what looks like spiral currents passing up through these two cords, and as the physical body grows more lifeless, the form hovering above seems tobecome more vital.

About 40 minutes later, Pole noticed that the "double" had become more distinct and that he could seethe currents passing through the cords gathering greater momentum:

"The life force is steadily ebbing out of the body, and is apparently passing into the form above."

Some 15 minutes later, Pole observed two figures stoop down over the bead and break the cords atpoints close to the physical body:

"Immediately I see that the form or double rises about two feet from its original position, but remains horizontal, and at this same moment Major P.'s heart stopped beating."

Obviously, he got the memo about the two cords, but now has added spirit overseers to sever the cords. So the rumor is enlarged yet again.

G. FRANCIS BANKS: On the other hand, Francis Banks mentions no cords in the book ***Testimony ofLight* by Helen Greaves, ©1967**

BANKS p.28: ***"After the change was over and I was free of my earthly "covering" I "woke up" here in the hospital of the Rest Home".*** what Francis describes is nearly identical to what I experienced.

BANKS p.29: ***"As soon as I was able to bring myself to a conscious state of mind, after my withdrawal from my worn-out body, I knew that I was the same essence".***

BANKS p.29: ***"I have discovered that I can use telepathy both ways, to receive and to relay.Indeed, I am already able to contact your mind, and what is more important, to hold that contactso as to poueas out to you".***

BANKS p.31: ***"So this is death…life separated by density, that is all. I knew that I could 'tune in' and even 'see' the earth plane. Now I dwelt in a calm of thought: and such thought Power, when rightly implemented, can penetrate the dense plane which is the world of human habitation. I did not feel that I had really gone away to a far country…I could still keep in touch".***

BANKS p. 37: *"I am exactly the same person now. I will have to go over and over again in my mind the possibilities I had when on earth, the failures and mistakes I made, in the light of this new approach. I will baulk at admitting much that was perhaps reprehensible, and which could halve been managed without my human bungling".*

BANKS p. 66: *"I have met my family, and visited my father, mother, sister and brother"*

BANKS p. 71: *"You must by now be realizing the tremendous importance and reality associated with Light. If you recall, we worked on earth (as well as we could in the 'heavy earth association) trying to attain Light. But, how difficult there to penetrate the inert forces which seemed to holdus. I wrote in my book Frontiers of Revelation (c) 1962, of the experience I had of 'etheric light';*

"Such experiences (NDE-like) must be thought more positively, and with greater use of theintuitive powers, by those in the world who would wish to lift the slow vibration of the planet."

BANKS p. 72: *"When I caught but a glimpse of Light on earth, and it uplifted and changed me, andchanged also the direction of my life, that impermanent glimpse was as nothing to the immersion of Light that is possible here.*

"Psychiatrists would call these 'subjective experiences'. Yet, what do any of us really know of the subjective extensions of the mind?

"Here we are mind (stepped down to our individual potency, I grant), but still mind, untrammeled by the destructive and apparent reality of matter... Therefore, by thought and will, we can travelfar out beyond what constitutes our immediate circumstances, if you wish".

H. LILLIAN BAILY, *a Tapestry of Life,* **by Marjorie Arrons ,** ©1979:

Bill Wooten, A World War I victim, communicated back through Lillian Baily that:

> The life cord (singular) is silver and thick, glowing and glistening. He said that it emerges from thepineal gland and extends to the solar plexus. Wooten added that spirits are able to tell the health of a person by the cord. When they see the cord getting down to a hair's breadth, they know that the cord is about to snap. When it does snap, it is as if a rope were breaking, and death takes place.

Wooten apparently had not gotten the memo about two cords and that they are snapped by two angels. So, in his narrative we are back to just one cord. On the other hand, he definitely did get the memo about the spirits on the other side monitoring the death and waiting for those cords to break, and he added tothe rumor his own "factoid" that the spirits can tell the health of the dying by the condition of the cords.

CURRENT SCIENTIFIC SUPPORT FOR THE "SILVER CORD":

1. **DR. SAM PARNIA:** One NDE'r told him that she found herself standing beside herself looking at a cord that connected her to her body and how thin and wispy it was.

2. **Dr. PETER FENWICK & ELIZABETH FENWICK:** *The Art of Dying,* **(c)2008** One NDE'r told them: ***"Like a kite on an endless string",*** this) cord seemed to be attached to the back and that she could feel it pulling her back to her body. Another NDE'r told the Fenwicks that although he could not see hisbody, he could see that he was attached by a ***"light grey rope".***

3. **MY PERSONAL EXPERIENCE:** I saw no cords, silver, pulsating or otherwise, while going to the otherside and none while returning. Of course, this makes sense because from **QED and Non-locality** we know scientifically that physical space and dimensions are merely illusions, constructed by our minds to provide a frame of reference. So, since there is no actual space then there is no place for these cords to exist, they are merely mental illusions like the physical body itself.

4. **AT THE SAME TIME:** Try to remember that NDErs are attempting to talk about ineffable concepts. So, they use 'similar" concepts to describe the in-describable. When interpreting an NDE narrative make allowance for the fact that our earthly languages are based on THINGS, so an emotion holding us back might be described as a cord.

5. **THE PHYSICS OF IT:** To remain in accord with the physics of *QED* and *Non-Locality*, what actually happens is that we merely change vibration and appear in a new dimension (as Fred Myer originally said, before all the coloring began). Indeed, even our illusion of what constitutes reality moves intothat new plane of reference.

    Try to also remember that all references to physical resurrection are related to our *intoxication with matter.* Since everything we perceive as real seems to be solid and physical we want the next dimension to be the same, so we delight in the resurrection of the physical body. But, the scientific factis that all matter is an illusion produced for us from the infinite potential o the conscious universe, all done to suit our "Choice 1" intentions.

On the other hand it is easy to see how speculations, misinterpretations and dogmas enter our religious beliefs.

2. **THE LIFE REVIEW:**

A. The ancient Egyptian belief in the "***Weighing of the Heart***" is explained in Appendix 2, including how that ancient legend occurs immediately after death. This matches the NDE life review, which *TheInternational Association for Near Death Studies-IANDS* has verified by our best NDE science.

Unfortunately, according to Francis Banks and others, that quicky re-examination apparently does not complete the process. Instead, after we pass on permanently into eternity we will review our entire life very carefully.

B. FRANCIS BANKS - ON REMORSE: p. 34 & 35 in *Testimony of Light*, by Helen Greaves ©1967 *"Somewhere in the deeps of my mind two 'blueprints' are brought forward into my consciousness. These are so clear that I can (literally) take them out, materialize them and study them.*

One is the PERFECT IDEA with which my spirit went bravely into incarnation. the other is the RESULTANT of only a partially understood plan.....First of all the mind looks at the whole comparison, and sets the blueprints side by side.

*This is the first shock; a true humbling of yourself to find that **you did so little when you would have done so much**, that you went wrong so often when you were sure you were in the right.*

"During this experience the whole cycle of your life-term unfolds before you in a kaleidoscopic series of pictures. During this crisis one seems to be entirely alone. Yours is the judgement, You stand at your own bar of judgement. You make your own decisions, You take your own blame…You are accused, the judge and the jury. This is where quite a few souls in the rest home have become immobilized. Their pictures were too searing in their exposes.

"The second stage in this recapitulation starts when the soul feels strong enough and calmed sufficiently to take the earth life round by round (so to speak). .....Now you seem no longer alone.

'Someone is beside you. whether it is your own Higher Spirit or a Great Helper I have to discover. Only now, as you ponder, work out, go over, tabulate, and

judge what you did and WHY AND WHAT WERE THE RESULTS (good or bad) you are gloriously aware of this great Being beside you giving strength, peace, tranquility and helping with constructive criticism.

BANKS P. 37. *"This is a slow process, I progress slowly,…*

BANKS P.45. Francis is assisting with the review or Dr. X's life: *"Suddenly, without preamble, this blue vista broke up, and became a cinema or television screen, Pictures began to emerge on it, They were notsuperimposed as in a cinema, but seemed to 'grow into it' from the very ether itself. These pictures appeared to form themselves.*

"They showed moments of stress, moments of triumph, moments of failure in the earth life of Doctor X. We saw patients; we watched him with his diagnoses; we followed him to the theatre (Operating room) and witnessed his operations, and as we watched, we became conscious (as he did) of the great Light that enfolded him as he worked.

"The picture on the 'screen' went on and on. We were taken into the homes, lives, families of those on whom the Doctor had performed his successful operations. We saw the benefit to humanity, the healings, the resumption of happy, useful lives which were the results of this man's skill. Even when he wasworking under the influence of drugs (as he said) we were allowed to view the results of what he had accomplished.

"As the film of his life unwound for us, the Doctor saw (though he could scarcely credit it) that he had indeed done his part. He had followed his Patten, worked out his Blue-Print, seen though he had badly smudged it in the performance.

"At the end he saw! He understood.

"His fault has been a weakness in the soul's contact with the personality which he had allowed to widen until it threatened to break completely. But he had been released before that had happened. His failure had been his refusal to delve into that Inner one whom he knew; to contact Him deliberately and reverently at times other than when the 'Celestial Surgeon's' skill was needed. The Light had been within him and about him and he had comprehended it not.

C. FRANCIS BANKS on RETRIBUTION / PURGATORY p.27: *"Here there is no compulsoryconfinement, and no punishment, except what you meet out to yourself.*

BANKS p.33: *"Here we live so much more in the realm of the mind. As we ponder over an experience or a Purpose, the mind stretches out to see all sides of the problem.*

BANKS p.37: *"Here no one is kept against their will or desire. Mostly the patients are happy enough and wish to stay in this temporary security. They cannot move on until they have (literally) seen the Light, or at least as much of the Light as they can assimilate at their present stages.*

BANKS p.41: *"You see how this purgatorial experience works? We don't alter fundamentally, But bit by bit, we move away from earth ideas and limitations, and advance more into Light and Wisdom.*

BANKS p. 80: *"It seems to me now that we only understand properly and without emotional prejudices when we are separated from life on earth. How useless is remorse here ... Remorsefor those things we did not do as well as for those we did. Our actions mostly resulting from the fact that our minds, and therefore our reactions to circumstances, were clouded by partial judgment, and by preconceived (and totally wrong) conclusions. We here do regret this lack very acutely, all the more so because scales have fallen from our eyes and we behold Truth (or perhaps I should say a "wider state of Truth"' than could penetrate and neutralize the negative emotions of the body-mind).*

"I said that remorse here is useless... but that statement might have been too sweeping. To know all is to forgive all, so the more constructive thought one brings to bare on this regrets the better. ..

BANKS p.81: *"Some of the souls who come to our side and who have perpetrated much evil, take a great deal of advising and helping on this point. Remorse overwhelms them and often they choose to live in the floor of regret. This is rightly termed 'gloom' (and I am not referring to the Place of Shadows) because, even here, by their sadness and remorse they are shutting themselves away from the very Light which should illumine their minds, dissolve their guilts and bring a constructive ray to bear o their problems.....*

CHAPTER 7
THAT "UNDISCOVERED COUNTRY" - A NEW TERRAIN

"Who would fardels (a bundle of emotions) bear, to grunt and sweat under a weary life, But, that the dread of something after death,... ***THAT UNDISCOVERED COUNTRY*** *from whose bourn no traveler returns,... puzzles the will...*

And makes us rather bear those ills we have, than fly to others that we know not of?.... Thus conscience doth make cowards of us all." William Shakespeare, Hamlet Act 3 Scene 1, (c)1599 –**1601**

1. STRUCTURE OF THE AFTERLIFE - THE ETHERIC ENVIRONMENT

During my *Near-Death experience* I moved through an alternate fourth dimension, traveling to the edge of the etheric. Arriving at a borderland which if crossed would be the end of this physical reality,

Today, astro-physicists call this border *"the Event Horizon"* and what lies beyond it a *"Dark Hole".* This is the place where light disappears entirely.

In the half century since that day, much has been learned about the Near-Death experience as frontier scientists have studied it extensively. And, I personally have worked closely with some of those same scientists. Yet, while they now know much about the terrain between our dissolution from the physical cadaver and this boundary at the event horizon edge of the fourth dimension; not much has been learned objectively about what lies just beyond.

In this chapter we will examine the subjective evidence about those alternate dimensions which lie beyond the event horizon, as discovered in the research of frontier scientists over the last century, describing what it will be like when you go there yourself into the afterlife.

Accordingly, the following road map. which is based on Edward Randall's synopsis, as received through direct voice mediumship with Emily French; and as taken from taken from *The French Revelation* by N. Riley Heagerty ©1995: has been modified by other collating descriptions. The synopsis shows that there are **seven sphere**s of existential reality existing in the alternative dimensions of the Universe where our surviving consciousnesses congregate in the afterlife.

Not surprisingly, this agrees remarkably well with physics understanding of *Dark Energy* & *Dark Matter*, and *String Theory*, which postulates **seven additional undiscerned alternative dimensions**; and *M- theory* which postulates an eighth additional dimension, which correlates with Ain Soph in the Cabalistic Tree of Life.

This *non-local* "structure" is more about levels of mental attitude (consciousness) than it is about specific places. Think of these alternative "dimensions" as higher and lower frequencies.

All of this is also similarly represented by Francis Banks, Arthur Findlay and others. Further, thesespheres are compared to Swedenborg's earlier vision which he couched in the more Christian terminology of his era. So, there is an overall consistency here and the spheres can be designated as follows:

LOWER SPHERES

Sphere (Randall & Hossack)	Alternate Dimensions (string theory)	Description	Swedenborg's vision	TIBETAN	Catholic Heaven
A. FIRST SPHERE	3RD DIMENSION + time	"PHYSICAL LIFE"			
B.	Lower 4TH DIMENSION	"EARTHBOUND"	Swedenborg's 1st state	FIRST BARDO	Limbo
C.	Upper 4TH DIMENSION	"RESTITUTION"	Swedenborg's 1st state	SECOND BARDO	Purgatory
D. SECOND SPHERE	5TH DIMENSION	"RESTORATION"	Swedenborg's 2nd state	THIRD BARDO	
E. THIRD SPHERE	6TH DIMENSION	"INSTRUCTION"	Swedenborg's 3rd state		HEAVEN
F. FOURTH SPHERE	7TH DIMENSION	"TRIAL & TEMPTATION	Swedenborg's 3rd state		

HIGHER SPHERES

Sphere (Randall & Hossack)	Alternate Dimensions (string theory)	Description	Swedenborg's vision
G. FIFTH SPHERE -	8TH DIMENSION	"TRUTH	Swedenborg's Heaven
H. SIXTH SPHERE -	9TH DIMENSION	"HARMONY"	Swedenborg's Heaven
I. SEVENTH SPHERE -	10TH DIMENSION	"EXALTATION".	Swedenborg's Heaven
J. AIN SOPH -	11TH DIMENSION	"SUPERNAL"	Swedenborg's Heaven

It is also understandable that the further we get from our physical perspective of three dimensions plus time, the more imperceptible is the reality of the other side. Again, please remember that none of this is cast in stone, but it is what has been reported back about an area we can not discern with our fivesenses. But, this subjective evidence is the best our science can yet produce.

All of this has also be analyzed in relation to what has been reported in the ***Tibetan Book of the Dead*** and also what might be loosely called, "***The Egyptian Book of the Dead***", as congealed from the coffin texts at the necropolis at Saqqara, the Hebrew Cabala & the Tree of Life, as well as the Bhagavad Gita

A. SUBDIVIDED SPHERES:

Each sphere (or alternative dimension) contains many planes of existence and is divided into six societiesor circles, in which kindred and congenial spirits are united and subsist together, under the ***Law of Affiliation*** or *Law of Attraction.*

Each of these circles also has teachers who come from the circles above and even from higher spheres. And, the moral and intellectual faculties of the spirits residing there are expanded to higher concepts and more exalted views of nature. And, as their understanding grows spirits can rise to whatever the mind of man is capable of conceiving. The noble and sublime sciences of Astronomy, Chemistry, and Mathematics afford inexhaustible subjects for study and reflection. And, within these "circles" there are thousands of planes of existence, all rounded into complete worlds, and all the habitations of those who cherish the special idea which rules that particular plane.

Considering this it is easy to see that all the Baptists are all in one place, with Methodists all in another each worshiping their image of God in their own way. All the Muslims are praising Allah in their peculiar ways, and all the psychopaths are in another place praising themselves, all the thieves in yet another place, etc. etc.

These planes are not permanent, but are the temporary homes of those who pass through them. Theyare the barns into which are gathered the sheaves of earth, there to rest and gain experience until they become distributed and amalgamated into life eternal. There are also planes of love, where tendernatures calling to one another until they are drawn by higher, broader aspirations to broader planes of thought. Apparently, because like attracts in these dimensions, loving souls are no longer affected by psychopaths, and there are no longer any infidels to kill.

There are planes for every shade of mental light, thought and knowledge; planes of special grades of intellect and wisdom, In all and each there is a special need or happiness; but also, in all and each there are prevalent impulses to stretch out further, to press on, to grow, so that every soul, can partake of the special characteristics of every plane in turn, each person to glean and gather in at least the good of it all and thus become a perfect spirit.

Never-the-Less, don't imagine that everyone here is interested in progression. Just as in the physical life, there are millions of spirits who are not yet sufficiently advanced to take an interest in such pursuits as progression. There are myriads of duller, grosser beings living in their own planes, gathering together withlike minded individuals, and all unconscious of the fact that their existence is permeated by the frequencies of these other more radiant worlds. Not seeing these other dimensions thronged with glorious life, which is to fine for the gross to view from their limited perspective.

Each living creature is surrounded and enclosed by the chosen atmosphere (Karma) to which it has belonged, whether higher or lower, and which restrains their vision to the special plane in which they dwell. Similarly to how you cannot see us in your sphere of physical life, likewise those who do not look above their ego's pre-occupations can not see.

Yet, in the lower spheres, when those who are held there realize that the only way to improve their condition is by helping others, and finally have a change of heart and a genuine desire to help, then the way will be shown to them.

FRANCIS BANKS P. 48 & 49, from *Testimony of Light,* **by Helen Greaves** ©1967

I went with Doctor X to visit some of his contemporaries and his friends in another part of this new life. I suppose you would call this the higher Planes. I cannot say for sure……. But, we had both had a taste of the beauty of the Higher Spheres and of communion with progressed souls."

FRANCIS BANKS p. 60

"The Planes of the Spirits stretch onward into infinity."

FRANCIS BANKS p.81. I have visited the lower regions though, I assure you, with Conductors who were able to guide and protect us, Believe me it is a terrible region, or regions, of semi-gloom, of unwholesome 'sticky' emotions, of utter distortion of all that is beautiful. One's feelings are wrung by the pitiful sights; compassion flows out for those poor half-alive creatures in their self-darkness".

FRANCIS BANKS p 82. I thought a lot about those words… "They that sit in darkness and the shadow of death" and a new meaning and connotation was added to our old scriptural one. That place was *shadow* indeed. The *shadow of deat*h, but not so definitely the death of the body as the death of the *mind,* forthere the mind is *inert* in the density caused by the wrong used of God given faculty, man's mind and free will. This density causes the soul to be starved to such a deficiency as to render it 'cut-off' and its Light shut away. Surely that is death… or rather the *shadow of death.*

The *shadow of death* is a gruesome *fact,* but thank God, not one that will ever be experienced by those who try to live the good life and to open their minds to Truth.

B. CURRENT SCIENTIFIC SUPPORT - ALTERNATIVE DIMENSIONS OF MODERN PHYSICS: When the Hubble Space Telescope became operational in 1998, Astronomers began to look into deep space only to find that the universe was expanding faster and faster, instead of slowing down due to gravity as previously assumed. The only viable explanation for this force of expansion, which also fits in with our known mathematics is an undiscerned force called "dark energy", and "dark matter", which makes up 96%of the Universe., and the light energy that we can discern makes up only 4%.

Basically, Astronomers have pointed out to the materialists that their best Newtonian science discernsonly 4% of what is out there. And that their perceptual belief system entirely misses 96% of the existing Universe. At the same time Quantum Theorists have begun to investigate "String Theory", which, so that the mathematics will work out, postulates 10 dimensions. The three dimensions plus time that we know here in the physical, and an additional 7 dimensions which remain undiscerned. If you place what iscalled "M" Theory along side this you get an 8th undiscerned dimension.

So, Randall's "Seven Spheres" very nicely matches the *Quantum Electro-dynamics* "String Theory"including "M" Theory,

C. RELIGIOUS SUPPORT: This system of 8 levels also agrees with the *Hebrew Cabala,* (if you include Ain Soph or Ein Sop as the limitless light at the top) Further, it also agrees with the pagan (pre-christian) religion's descriptions of the afterlife, as well as the Gnostic Christian's descriptions of the afterlife. So, it all begins to add up quite concisely. Finally, here is a confirmation from the New International Version (NIV) of the "approved" Christian Bible:

> ***"I will go on to visions and revelations, I know a man in Christ who fourteen years ago wascaught up to THE THIRD HEAVEN. Whether he was in the body or out of the body, I do not know (but) God knows"*** this is Saint Paul speaking in 2nd Corinthians chapter 12 verses 1 & 2 NIV)

Apparently, the man St. Paul is talking about had a Near-Death experience and went to what Randall's communicators called the Third Sphere.

2. AND WHAT ABOUT DIFFERING RELIGIONS?

Apparently, at first, after they arrive on the other side, people continue to practice their own religions, but as they advance to higher planes these petty differences disappear, as they slowly discover that God (theforce behind the conscious universe) loves everyone. And that not just those in their little religious clique who dress a certain way, or cut their hair and shave their beards a certain way, or women who cover theirhair with a wig, or wear a veil or a burka or men wearing a hat from the 1880's, etc. etc. etc.

Realizing that no people is "chosen" neither the Jews (Sons of Issac) nor the Islamists (sons of Ishmael) ,not the Christians, nor the Americans, nor the Communist Chinese. Finally, everyone learns that all such *hocus-pocus non-sense* is simply man made speculations which have nothing to do with the Conscious Universe or God.

A. Rev. ALBERT DRAYTON THOMAS, *Life Beyond Death with Evidence* **©1928**: A Wesleyan Minister and investigator for the *Society of Psychical Research-SPR*, sat with Gladys Osborne Leonard over 500 times. His discarnate father told him:

> *"When one is fitted for a low plane, no amount of desire to be on a higher or more beautiful one would suffice to take one there. The habit of life on earth decides, and not any chance desire. If a man has qualified for a lower sphere, he will find himself there and he cannot get away from it. That is just and right, and it saves a vast amount of supervision. Accordingly as a soul moulds itself while in the body, so it decides the place to which it must go on leaving the body. Those who simply live in the physical senses find themselves exceedingly limited on leaving earth (where they no longer have physical senses) We wish such people understood the facts, so that they might realize how fatally unwise and short-sighted is their manner of life."*

> *"The lower the sphere the more correspondence there is with places on earth"*

> *"looking very far ahead indeed, I know there is a great design which awaits us someday, somewhere, somehow. We shall continue to be ourselves, but in a state higher than anything realized upon these spheres. I know that there is a world above and beyond our present one, but I do not seek to know too much until it is given to me.*

His father was on the Third Sphere and had not been to higher spheres, but teachers from those higher spheres had informed him of these laws. Then Etta, Thomas' sister came through with the thought that people on the earth plane and the lower spheres are unable to see or grasp the entire divine plan:

> *"Of the whole plan were given to you at once, you would probably be dazzled, confused, weighted down by it. On those high spheres it is difficult for them to explain to me how they know things, because they can comprehend the whole and although they are no longer in close touch with detail, yet detail is attended by them; for they do perfectly what they undertake".*

B. Rev. ALVIN MATTSON'S DESCRIPTION: *Witness From Beyond*
©*1975* by Ruth Mattson Taylor: A Lutheran Minister who passed in 1970, communicated with his daughter through the British Medium Margaret Flavell Tweddell, saying:

"From this point we can progress to higher planes — to higher levels of consciousness… By higher planes I do not mean spatially higher, but rather those planes which have a finer vibration".

Mattson, also said that many of the religious denominations continue to practice the rites of thererespective churches on the lower and intermediate planes, where he was currently at. But, he had been permitted to visit higher planes:

"Where there is a unity of God-praise, not a segregation of God-praise"

C. ANDREW JACKSON DAVIS: *Death and the Afterlife* ©1865

"Jews believe in the doctrine of their fathers — Abraham, Isaac, and Jacob; the Roman Catholics hold the same views they did before death; and there are other sects (here) who think andbelieve in the same things and forms of faith they learned on earth… They are so far below the higher planes that this is required in order to make them feel at home. However, eventually all evolve toward a single understanding of spirit."

D. Dr. DAVID C. HOSSACK: taken from *The French Revelation* by N. Riley Heagerty ©1995: Dr. Hossack answered Randall's question **"What of the religious movement among your people?"** as follows:

"In the lowest spheres, that is, in the earthbound spheres sectarian strife and religious movements are just as strenuous among the people as they were before these persons left her physical body.

"That state of transition is but little removed from the physical, for, while the majority there know they have left the body, others have such an imperfect appreciation of the change, or have led such immoral lives that they are not conscious of the fact.

"Here the dogmas of orthodoxy are dominant, and the old religious teachings are promulgated, and the priesthood still hold power.

Yet, another spirit told Randall:

"There is no progress possible in the afterlife for one occupying the position of spiritual leader when here (on earth), until he had searched out in this plane all those who had followed his teaching, and brought them to

the truth. Moreover, he must stand and wait until the coming of those still in the earth life, in order that his error should be corrected at the earliest possible moment."

"To promulgate unknown or impractical teachings while on this earth-plane is a serious matter, and results in punishment in the afterlife.

ARTHUR FINDLAY- *On the Edge of the Etheric* ©1924:

"A clergyman who had died, told me that he could make no progress until the last of his congregation had arrived from this world. I asked him why, and he said that the reason was because he had preached to them orthodox Christianity, namely, the forgiveness of sins through the belief in Christ's death on the cross, and the punishment of all who had not this belief. He was waiting to tell each one of his congregation, as they came over, that he was wrong, and that he had given then an entirely wrong impression of the afterlife.

"I was once told that all young children who had passed into the etheric world as infants, without any knowledge of this earth's religious dogmas and creeds, grew up quite ignorant of these, as these earth-made beliefs meant nothing to the inhabitants of that world. Those passing over, holding such beliefs, are taught to see their error, and those who have not preached them very quickly forget them in their new surroundings. Those, however, responsible for preaching and teaching error may have to endure mental remorse until they have forgotten their mistake."

This would appear to be a case of normal remorse and reparation, and not "punishment" other than thatwhich we create for ourselves, and all of which will be described later.

CHAPTER 8
SEVEN OR EIGHT ALTERNATIVE DIMENSIONS

THE FIRST or LOWER SPHERE:

This includes the earth plane of our physical universe of three dimensions, but extends beyond to include those who are "earth bound". Earth bound consciousnesses are those who don't believe they are dead. This is where Poltergeists hang our. After they finally realize they have passed over, they will begin to do reparation work. But, it is not the most pleasant place to find oneself after dissolution.

MICHAEL TYMN'S DESCRIPTION: *The Afterlife Revealed, What happens after we die,* ©*2011* So it appears the lowest sphere is comprised of the earthbound souls, most of whom don't seem to fully comprehend the fact that they have "died". Souls at this level apparently did very little during theirlifetimes to develop any spiritual consciousness and contented themselves with living selfish and materialistic lifestyles, perhaps even depraved ones. This lowest or first level is what religions call "Hell" but it is not an eternal state.

THE FOURTH DIMENSION (First Sphere)

This earthbound area is what is experienced in the preliminary stages of the Near-Death experience,when people are out of body and viewing the doctors working on their cadaver. Some NDE's go beyond this area but tend to recall passing through an area of darkness or passing through a tunnel to get to the light. This shadowy dark area lies just beyond the preliminary Near-Death experience of the 4th dimension.

1. EDMUND C. RANDALL'S DESCRIPTION: taken from *The French Revelation* by N. Riley Heagerty ©1995:

One Spirit told Randall that:

"The First or rudimental sphere is nearest the earth plane. It is just one step higher in vibration and it really blends in with your earth sphere"

Another spirit said to him:

"The first step in progression after death is so earth-like that it is at first difficult to comprehend"

"In the Lowest Sphere one sees much suffering among those still "earthbound", they too are busy working out past faults and they are

often heavy hearted. The First Sphere is where restitution must be made, and where there final wrenching away from earth conditions takes place.

Many mediums and other consciousness survival researchers simply call this level "Earthbound". But, the second communicator went on to tell Randall"

"We have been so long taught that the death change is so marvelous, having been given visions of sitting on clouds, that a newly arrived spirit is reluctant to accept the simple situation. It has been compared to the going from one room into another. While the surroundings are changed they are similar; like, yet unlike. But, the thought and individuality are in no-wise altered. these areidentical, the mode of expression and the touch only are different. This is not what is ordinarily expected, therefore it is oftentimes reluctantly accepted."

"The inability to touch the bodies of those still in earth life, or to speak so they can hear you, together with the meeting with those who have gone on before you, slowly bring those who have just passed over to appreciate the natural change that has come to them. Then comes the thought of what and where they now are. This vision is enlarged, and while they see all that was visible to their material eyes, a mental curtain is parted, and there comes a conception of sights and sounds not possessed before. They then find, not a walled city with guarded gates and streets of gold, not a judgement throne before which they must appear like criminals at the bar of justice, but a simple, natural world, this same world spiritualized."

To comprehend what is here in the earth bound conditions just beyond death, but which is most often bypassed by those having a positive Near-Death experience, is fully shown in one Spirit encounter Randall had, while working with Mrs. French, as given in the following verbatim dialog:

"By what right do you presume to compel my presence in this house?" *The room wasin absolute darkness; the voice of one celled by the world, "dead"" trembling with anger broke upon the stillness of the night.*

"Do you understand the situation in which you find yourself?" *I asked.*

"I do not, and will not allow any man to dictate to me", *he replied.*

"You are not afraid?" *I said.*

"Afraid!, I am not afraid of God or man, and I will not remain here."

"It might be to our advantage if you would", I answered, *"I did not force you to come, You are a stranger to me as I am to you"*.

"Who did force me to come?", he asked.

"I do not know, tell me about it?"

"As it comes to me now", he answered, "an irresistible force seemed to urge me froma dream-like condition. Suddenly I was awake, in your presence, and immediately concluded that in some manner you controlled my conduct. That I can not permit".

"You are mistaken there, but does it occur to you that some great good may come of this meeting?" I inquired.

"I cannot in any way understand your suggestion" the stranger said, *"or see how any good can come out of an enforced conference. If you did not bring me, who did? I had no desire to come, nor do I wish to remain. This house and its surroundings are unfamiliar to me. With your permission, I will retire."*

"Before you go", I said, *"I should like to have you know something of the work we are doing which may account for your coming"*.

"Well sir, finding myself in this unfamiliar situation I will not be lacking in courtesy", hesaid.

"For many years", I replied, *"I have been engaged in psychical research, with this psychic who sits opposite me, trying to obtain a practical solution of that great physical change called death."*

"What has that got to do with me? I am not dead nor am I interested in the subject," he answered.

"Wait a moment, please. You will be interested when I tell you that I have discovered something of the daily life and environment of the individual after he has ceased to be an inhabitant of the earth-plane."

"You are entirely mistaken in your statements; There is no survival — no continuity of life. Death is the end."

"Are you sure?" "Absolutely", he replied.

"Suppose," I answered, *"I could prove to you here and now, that death, so called , isbut a physical change, the separation of the life-force from the flesh garment, that substance with which it is clothed during its journey on this plane — suppose I could demonstrate here and now that the individual has a spirit body*

composed of matter with form, features, and expression during his entire earth-life, and at dissolution simply becomes an inhabitant of the next plane of consciousness with the same spirit body, is in short, the same identical man?"

"There is no such thing as life after death," he said.

"I am going to try to explain what life is before I give you the absolute proof of what I state. Now follow me. At the point of conception, an Atom of the Universal Force called Good is clothed with substance vibrating more slowly than the life-force clothed. The individual is as perfect at that moment as he giant oak in the heart of the acorn. We cannotsee the individual or the oak tree before or after birth and growth. Life-force vibrates so fast that it is not visible to the physical eye, but ultimately we see the outer covering, that substance which makes both possible. This outer garment of the individual is composed largely of water. The physical body of ours changes once in seven years at least, but with such change we retain individuality, form, and feature. How is it done?" I asked.

"I don't know and I don't care", he answered.

"Follow me a little farther, please. This entity, this life-force,, this individuality, this soul, this 'us' if you like, is composed of matter, differing only from the flesh substance in its vibratory condition. This accounts for its permanency of form, but no physical eye ever saw or ever will see this self, this spirit form, this soul, so called, unless possessed of the psychic sight with which speaking generally very few are endowed. Without it one individual can never see the spirit form of another while an inhabitant of the earth. We are conscious only of the physical expression and sound. Now in dissolution from accident or physical weakness, the body covering that is visible to use is no longer fit for habitation; then separation, dissolution — death so-called — occurs; the individual through a natural process releases itself from the flesh garment, and stands forth the same man or woman as before, though invisible to the inhabitants of earth. They see but the old flesh body that housed the spirit. They could not, as I have said, see the true self before, nor can they see it after dissolution, because of the intensity, because of the rapidity of the vibration of the etheric body, for our eyes are limited as to motion, as well as to distance."

"That is all vey well, but what has that got to do with me? I am not dead"*, he answered.*

"If you will be patient I will lead up to the personal application. When one has gone through this death change, one of two conditions may follow; we may never for a moment lose consciousness — it is then just good night to the old and good morning to the new environment. This usually follows a respectable life. The man is the same still, nothing subtracted from or added to his personality, and in the mirror of Nature he sees himself with the same outlines the same expression, the same thoughts, the same attachments, still a material body dissociated from the flesh covering, the same spirit form that hasbeen his during his journey in the world. But he then appreciated that his body is lighter and more transparent than the flesh substance he has been accustomed to look upon, andhe does not resist muscular effort as he did in the old covering; then but for assurance of friends and relatives who assist in the change as at earth-birth, and explain to the quickening consciousness, many would be afraid. There is this great difference in the two births. When this atom of life-force first becomes individual, an inhabitant of the earth plane, it possesses instinct but no intelligence; it continues to develop, with no knowledgeof its previous existence. It could have none, for it came from the mass of universal life forces. The next great change is similar except that the individual retains all previous development; He knows little more of the laws governing, and the means available to aid his progression than an infant.

"On the other hand, those who have led unclean earth lives, who have been selfish, immoral, and have committed crimes against man and Nature, may not soon awaken; if they do, they find themselves in mental darkness, in a prison of their own building, and there they remain until a desire comes from within for better things. Then the way will be shown by spirit people engaged in such charitable work. In the beginning each awakening spirit is told that each wrong act done in earth life must be lived over, that as he works he will encounter like conditions under which the wrong was done, and in the new life hemust correct the error in the old, in order to advance. I recall that an inhabitant of the next plane once said; "The justice that meets a naked soul on the threshold of the afterlife is terrible in its completeness".

"I cannot accept a word you say about a life after death. There is no other life — there can be none — man dies like a dog", said the visitor.

"That is true in a sense," I said, "for the life force and individuality both go on. You cannot destroy an atom of matter, you will admit; so if life-force is matter, that can not be destroyed."

"This is very strong talk, but why speak on such a subject to me? I am not dead; If I were and there life beyond the grave, should not be here talking to you".

"I have talked, just as I am talking to you, with many who have made that change", I said.

"Do you mean to tell me you have talked to dead people?"

"I did not say that; I said that I had talked to those who have made the change called death. There is in reality no death, there are no dead."

"Talk sense", he retorted, *"we have all seen dead people, have seen their bodiesburied, and you tell me there are no dead"*.

Again I said, *"You fail to understand what I have been telling you. We bury the physical bodies but not the spirit bodies; one is just as material as the other."*

"I don't comprehend you, and I don't care to continue the discussion. I think I will say good night."

"Just a moment, and I will demonstrate the fact. Did I tell you a moment ago that I talked with many so-called dead?"

"Yes", he answered. *"But, I did not take what you said seriously' I made up my mind onthat subject long ago"*.

"Now to begin the proof — do you know where you are at this moment? Tell me if you know."

"I don't seem to know. This is not my home; the room is strange to me; you arestrange too. It is all unreal. Can you explain the situation in which I find myself?"

"Listen to me, this frail little woman, over 80 years old, who sits opposite me, is the most gifted psychic in the world. More than twenty years ago it was discovered that under favorable psychic conditions, such as prevail tonight, we could have speech with spirit people."

"It can't be possible", *he said.*

"The suggestion", I replied, "is so far beyond the experience of man, that I am not surprised at your inability to comprehend the fact. Wait! Having such means of communication, we have not only learned much of the future state, but acting in conjunction with a group of people in the next life, we have been able to bring many to a state of consciousness, after the death change, in quasi-material, quasi-spiritual conditions, such as prevail here to-night; and when we are doing work of this character, many out of body are brought for help by their friends, as you have been, that they may comprehend the situation."

"But, I am not one of these; the suggestion is absurd, I tell you. I am as much alive asyou, and my body is quite as substantial as yours" *he said.*

"Hold up your hand as I do mine, and see if there is any difference between the two". "Yes" *he answered,* ***"Yours is opaque, but mine is transparent. I can see right through***

my hand. Is this hypnotic suggestion?"

"No", *I said,* ***"You are facing new conditions tonight. Do you know that we sit in intensedarkness and can not see you, although we hear your voice distinctly?"***

"I know" *he answered* ***"that it is not dark for I can see you, and if I can see you, you cansee me. But, never mind that; what is the matter with my body?. I think I have been very ill,and one always looks as I do after long sickness"*** *he replied.*

"Speaking of illness what do you recall about your last illness?"

"My memory seems hazy, but it is coming back to me. I recall lying in bed, thephysician waiting, my wife and children sobbing. The doctor said, "He is passing now", and that gave me a start, there were many who would like to see me dead — but I fooled them — for I did not die. If I had died, How could I be here?"

"What do you know about death?" I said.

"I don't know anything about it, and I don't want to".

"But the that time comes to you, you will be obliged to know, whether your desire it ornot", *I replied.*

"Well I am willing to wait, and I don't want to talk about it, I never did."Suppose I tell you that you have already made that change".

"It would be foolish to tell me such a thing, when I am here talking to you."

"Suppose I now prove it to you. Those in spirit life co-operate with me in this work and are often able to bring to the stranger those whom he has known in earth -life, and face to face and voice to voice the proposition proves itself."

"I tell you", he said ,"There are no dead people, and if there were, I don't want to see them".

"You are not afraid?"

"No", he answered. "But, I don't want to see them. I have enough trouble with the living without bothering with the dead."

"Is there no one in the next life with whom you would like to talk if you could?. Remember that your sickness may have ended in dissolution; your body is different, and you know you find yourself in a strange city."

"Things have changed, but I don't want to see or talk to dead people".

"You find life so material, so like the earth life, that I believe no method but actual experience will convince you that you have left the mortal state, and that lesson must be learned. You have been so intent on our conversation, I think that you have not looked around — look, what do you see?

"My God!, People, people, people! All stranger and all looking at me, all with bodieslike my own; what strange hallucination is this? Where am I? What am I?

"You are no longer an inhabitant of this world, but are actually living in the afterlife.Are there none you know among those you see, who, to your knowledge, are counted among the dead, so called?" *I asked.*

"Not one, but wait, there comes — John — my old partner. Why does he, of all men, come? He is dead. I helped bury him. I was his executor. Take him and that woman andthat boy away, I don't want to see them, I tell you. They are dead, all dead. They are coming to arrest me. How can they when they are all dead? Tell me, tell me, tell me quick"

*"**What wrong did you do?**" I asked.*

*"**Wrong? Who said I did them wrong? I was faithful to the trust.**"*

*In answer another spirit spoke. "**No, you were not faithful. You stole the money I entrusted to you for my wife and child, and and left them to suffer. There never was, and never can be a secret in the world. When you kept from my loved ones that which I left for their support and let them die in want, I saw, and all your friends in spirit life saw your act and the working of your mind.**"*

"No secret in the world?" My crime known! The dead alive! Have I too left my physical body to find life when I thought to find oblivion? Am I to meet all those I have wronged? I cannot face the future! Darkness is gathering!, I am falling! God help me!"

The voice faltered, struggled for further speech, and was lost. The gross material that clothed his organs of respiration, disintegrated, and he spoke no more.

We had participated in one of the most remarkable experiences that it has been the privilege of man to have. We had talked with one who had left the physical body, and witnessed hisawakening.

2. ALICE BAILEY'S DESCRIPTION, Death the Great Adventure ©1985:

"In the case of the spiritual undeveloped person, the etheric body can linger for a long time in the neighborhood of its out disintegrating shell because the pull of the should is not potent and the material aspect is"… "Where the person is advanced, and therefore detached in his thinking from the physical plane, the dissolution of the vital body can be exceedingly rapid.

3. EDGAR CASEY'S DESCRIPTION, *No Death: God's Other Door* ©1998:

"Many an individual has remained in that called death for what ye call years without realizing it wasdead!"

Casey further explains that the entity becomes conscious gradually and that this is contingent upon "how great are the appetites and desires of a physical body"

*4. **WILLIAM STANTON MOSES DESCRIPTIONS:** Imperator told him about the earthbound conditions: "They are states not places", as Moses understood them. "The difference between spheres," he said, "is based upon the* *moral, intellectual, and spiritual state of the inhabitants. The progress of spirits is made through seven states, during which the spirit is laboring either to purge away the contracted impurities of Earth, or to gain further knowledge to prepare oneself for a life of contemplation.*

"The first three spheres are near about your Earth and are filled thus: **The First** *with those who, from many causes, are attached to the Earth. Such are they who have made little progress on the Earth sphere; not the wholly bad, but the vacillating, aimless souls who have frittered away their opportunities and made no use of them. Those. again, whom the affections and affinity for pursuits of their friends restrain them from soaring, and who prefer to remain in the Earth sphere, though they might progress. In addition, there are the imperfectly trained souls who's education is still young, and who are in course of elementary training; those who have been incarcerated in imperfect bodies, and have to learn still what the should have learned on earth. Those, too, who have been prematurely withdrawn from Earth, and from no fault of their own, have still to learn before they can progress.*

5. The TIBETAN BOOK OF THE DEAD'S DESCRIPTION: *The Tibetan Book of Living and Dying* (c)1993: which fully describes these same forlorn beings standing inert in endless fields, saying that the vast majority of people do not immediately recognize the "Ground Luminosity" (The Being of Light) and are therefore plunged into a state of unconsciousness.

Traditional Buddhism states that the consciousness continues without the body and goes through a series of "bardos", where most of them go on grasping at a false sense of self, with its ghostly grasping at physical solidity and this continuation of that illusion which has been the root of all suffering in life, exposes them in death to more suffering, especially in the "bardo of becoming".

6. FREDERICK H.W. MYERS DESCRIPTION:

On February 19, 1901, A month after he died on January 17, 1901, Myers came through medium Rosalie Thompson to Oliver Lodge. It was clear that Myers was struggling to communicate. He told Lodge that he was confused when he first arrived on the other side, before he realized he was dead.

> *"I thought I had lost my way in a strange town, and I groped my way along the passage. And, even when I saw people that I knew were dead, I thought they were only visions."*

7. CLAUDE'S BOOK, *by L. Kelway-Bamber, Psychic Book Club, London.*

Claude was a British pilot shot down in World War One, who communicated with his motherthrough Gladys Osbourne Leonard:

"It may have been a fortnight or more later that I became conscious again"…

He went on to explain that he received an orientation and then was put to work greeting new arrivals.

"We bring them away so that they may return to consciousness far from their mutilated physical bodies, and on, Mum, I feel quite tired sometimes of explaining to men that they are dead. They wake up feeling so much the same; some go about for days, and even months, believing they are dreaming."

CURRENT SCIENTIFIC SUPPORT FOR THESE INITIAL CONDITIONS: Much of this same inability to touch or communicate with those still living in the physical, has very often been experienced during Near- Death experience out-of-body episodes. For example, the NDEr watches the doctors from the top of the room, or tries to console loved ones in the next room. So, it is obvious that the preliminary NDE occurs in this same earthbound sphere, but in the 4th dimension, just beyond our sight.

Research on thousands of narrative accounts of NDE'rs finds that most pass through a tunnel (wormhole) to get to the light. What is in the darkness outside that tunnel?

The testimony of several Near-Death experiencers, whom I have personally interviewed, who passedover vast fields of inert spirits standing alone thinking selfish thoughts. One NDEr when inquiring with her guides about these seemingly lost souls was told, *"Don't touch them…When they finally decide thatothers are important and angel will come and minister until them."*

IGNORANT IMMIGRANTS:

Here in physical life, all developed nations have huge problems with immigrants who manage to get across their borders, but then refuse to learn the language or assimilate into the culture of their new host country. … It is similar in the afterlife only a bit more catastrophic because they have insufficient evolvedsouls who can assist these "ignorant immigrants".

1. SILVER BIRCH'S DESCRIPTION:

"We receive, day after day, the misfits, the derelicts, the outcasts, the flotsam and jetsam, **the millions who come unprepared, unready, unequipped and who have to learn all over again.***Instead of passing to our world a stream of evolved souls ready to take up the tasks that was meant for them, there come millions who have to be treated and nursed and tended because theyare like bruised little children.*

2. EDMUND C. RANDALL'S DESCRIPTION:t taken from *The French Revelation* by N. Riley Heagerty ©1995: Another Spirit told Randall about the continual arrival of people unaware that they were dead. ***One of the biggest problems in the spirit world is that few of those arriving there evergave the subject of the afterlife a single thought......*** *And, so they come, one by one, but withal becoming a great crowd every hour, and* **only now and then is there a solitary spirit thatcan take up and do good work immediately upon arrival.** *The others all have to be taught the simplest things about their new "country".*

> *"Indeed many thousands of your people cannot even read, and they reach us with so limited a mental development as to need all our energies in their advancement out of ignorance, wrong education and false religious teachings...... Few on your earth,* regardless of intellect and education, *have any idea of the changes that take place along the lifeline. As they come, we gather and instruct them as you do in your schools, and especially as you do in your night schools, where the ignorant seek enlightenment. And,* **very many of those called "learned", in the physical world, will realize that at the end of their earth life, as they arrive here, theywill be among those that need teachers, and will find it necessary to attend night school here in the spirit world."**

Further, a woman who had lived an unselfish life on earth and had passed through the change called death told Randall that:

> *"You wish to know where I went on leaving the earth. Well, there seemed to be a period of unconsciousness; then I awoke and found myself in an entirely different place from any I had known on earth. I was somewhat confused at first, most people are, and find it difficult to realize where they are and what has happened to them. I was not afraid, however, because I believed I would be taken care of, and would go on living somewhere. My ideas about the afterlife however, were very vague, as are those of the majority of people.*

Her description of the arrival conditions parallels the descriptions of the "initial conditions" experienced by NDErs. as documented by the *International Association for Near-Death Studies - IANDS.*

NOTE: *Also,* in my own NDE, I, "*experienced a period of unconsciousness; then I awoke to find myself in an entirely different place from any I had known on earth. But, although I had never heard of the spheres at that time, looking back I obviously was not in that earthbound level*"

This same woman went on to tell Randall and her attending relatives that:

"Psychic work will change all this confusion, however and people will know better what to expect; instead of fearing and dreading the dissolution of the body, as so many millions do now, it will appear to them as it really is, Just a sleep and an awakening"

"You are wondering, and often have wondered, why I was taken when I seemed to be, and was, so much needed on earth. You have blamed God, and thought it cruel and hard and not by any means as an act of love. This is the result of your limited vision."

"I will give you a description of the place in which I found myself when I awoke after what you call "death". It took me some time to realize the beauty of my surroundings. But this was because my eyes were blinded by the sorrow which my going had caused on earth. The grief of my people leftbehind kept me so sad at first that I was not able to see or think of anything but their earthly sorrow.

That is why grief for departed friends and relatives is so wrong. and is so harmful to those onearth and to those who come over...... The longer the grief continues and the more hopeless it is, the more those mourned for are kept to earth. .....

Instead, of being able to go straight on when they come over, seeing and realizing the beauty andwonders of their surroundings and helping others to see them also, they are instead kept in astate of helpless grief, which renders them incapable of either helping themselves or others. Fortunately, the grief of my people on earth was not of this desperately hopeless variety, and I was enabled in time to rise above it and get on with my work of helping others."

"This is a life of service, and self must be eliminated. *That is why folk who have livedunselfish lives on earth get on so well here. They do not need the preliminary training which moreselfish spirits need. Unfortunately, it is a very long time before some spirits who came over are of any use at all in helping others. This is caused partly by their own selfishness and partly by the selfish grief of their friends and relatives on earth. This is why so many of the messages sentback to earth through* *mediums are a plea to those relatives to have a more helpful outlook.*"

"On the other hand, it is almost impossible for us to help some spirits, as they have no desire tobe different or better than they have always been.... Prayer by those still on the earth is the only thing which can help them. It will give them the desire for better things."

"Until there is that desire in their hearts, they will remain much as the were when in the flesh.Their spirits still inhabiting the earth and they are the evil or sometimes mischievous spirits I have told you of before. Prayer is not only a protection against them, but is also their only hope of salvation. Indifference is the greatest sin there is. As long as folk desire to be better, there issome foundation to build on, but if that desire is lacking it is very difficult to do anything withthem."

"The great pity is that it is so long before some spirits even begin.... to progress. Some who have not progressed, when communicating with their friends on earth, give them quite wrong and dissimilar impressions of conditions over here.

But, all is not charity work over there. The spirits also told Randall that:

"At the same time, those in the finer realms of being do not have such limited perspectives and can view, at will, the grosser planes (including the physical life), just as I found I could do. I am putting this knowledge into practice in coming now to you. In fact, I found the secret of will, which is power.

The mind being freed from the physical constraints of a gross material body can perceive through intuition (ESP) the truths on which science is based and we have many other sources ofintellectual, moral and heartfelt enjoyments. And, anyone who wants to can progress.

Those who have lead clean, fine lives, and have enriched the world, come here and without a break take up their work and go on.

What position will the average individual occupy when he enters the new life? What position has he/she qualified themselves to fill intelligently?

You arrive here stripped of all earthly possessions, money, goods and chattels gone, they have nothing left but your spirit, and that clothed only with kindly acts that have enriched your soul. If you have made the world happier and better then you proceed radiant and glorious.

3. FRANCIS BANKS' DESCRIPTION: Now let's compare that to what Francis Banks sent back in December 1965. Francis Banks, who understood that there would be an afterlife, and had lived a very exemplary life did not have a lot of remorse and reparations work to do.

However, she still spend some time in the earthbound conditions, and makes reference to the samedesire for the earth life and being drawn back to the earth because of peoples grief over her passing,

Yet, she does not see it as an obstacle like the first woman did. This difference in their reports on the same grief concept, illustrates how "personality" is involved in every interpretation. In other words **surviving consciousness retains its character.**

"After the Change was over and I was free of my earthly covering, I woke up here in this 'hospital'

of the Rest Home. My room had no walls and the sunlight seems to flow over one all the time. I opened my eyes… or came back to consciousness….. I knew that I was the same in essence." I was the same but not the same…….

"With a flash of realization I decided that I must be stone deaf, for I could no longer hear any ofthe usual sounds of everyday life, the chatter and movement of human beings around; the whistleof trains, the twittering of birds…. There were no noises in this new consciousness. One of my first recollections was "I am still conscious…the change has taken place…But, I can not hear, neither can I see!"

"And for a space of time I seemed to lose my identity. I recall endeavoring anxious to pierce through this new state to recall memory…..Who am I?…..What did I do?…"

"It was strange; almost eerie experience, for the name I had borne for over seventy years eluded me… At length I recall telling myself to give it up and go to sleep….When I next came back to consciousness I seemed to be puling myself out of a thin sea of silver….Those are the only wordsI can use to describe the experience. "

"As soon as I can re-orient myself sufficiently, I shall be tasting or tutoring again. It is the service I can give… I'm already learning so much…. I have discovered that I can use telepathy both ways, to receive and to relay There are not the difficulties here that we experienced on earth. This holdsout all sorts of exciting possibilities.

Indeed, I am already able to contact your mind, and what is more important, to hold that contact so as to pour ideas out to you.

"Because this plane is only a few rungs or so higher than the earth plane, there are the same conditions, hospitals, as with our civilizations, and prisons, only here they are self-made.

"I speak of the patients here. "I said we had all grades and classes in this Home, Illiterate, uneducated, educated and cultured, rather as I had to teach when I worked (in the physical life)as a Tutor-Organizer in the Maidstone Prison Experiment. Only those were prisoners of the State;segregated from their fellows by rule and power. Here, no one is kept against his/her will ordesire. Mostly the patients are happy enough and wish to stay in this temporary security. They cannot move on until they have (literally) seen the Light , or at least as much of the Light as they can assimilate at their present stages...."

"I still have the same experience, the same problems, the same hopes, with even greater and wider aspirations for work, only now I view them from an entirely different angle and with far greater dawning of comprehension.

In another communication Francis told Helen Greaves this:

"As soon as I was able to bring myself to a conscious state of mind, after my withdrawal from my worn-out body,

"And, the first face I saw was the smiling face of my dear Mother in religion — Mother Florence, I was so overwhelmed that I couldn't speak...... From then on I remember that I was in and out of consciousness....But, now I found that I was lying in an open porch with a vista of blue and silver before me.... This was beautiful beyond words and calming to my spirit. Trouble, anxiety and all sense of loss abated; a great feeling of peace enwrapped me."

This is it, I kept reassuring myself in wonder, I have made the change!...I realized then that I could both see and hear as before only now in a more intense way. I thought immediately "I wonder how I can get through"...I must tell Helen about this."

"Later as I grew more accustomed to this new consciousness, I was able to 'commune" with both Mother Florence and Father Joseph, How delighted I was to meet them! and to know that Father Joseph was indeed the same splendid, wise could I had known in my

Community days… He was agains bye to help me much. He gave me confidence."

"I felt as if I was 'convalescing" as indeed I suppose I was from the effects of my last painful illness…"

"It was borne in on my throughs that an 'aura' of sadness surrounded me…."They will be burning my body" I said to myself."

"Immediately, an intense desire filled me to be again with all those friends I had loved and those who had loved me, at this solemn ceremony."

"In an inexplicable way, and due no doubt to my intense desire, I was able to e present with you all in mind and consciousness, Whilst lying here in this slivery light, I wondered if this was what astral traveling must have been like….. But, it was a wonderful experience…."

"Then just as inexplicably as I had become part of these scenes, it all faded. I was lying there at peace."

"So this is death!" I recall saying to one of the Sisters who was beside me…Life separated by density…. that is all"

"Elation filled me, I knew that I could tune in and even see the earth plane, if desire was strong enough to loosen the barrier between your world and my new one. The possibility rested with me….This I realized was my first lesson…… Now I dwelt in a ream of Thought; and such thought Power, when rightly implemented, can penetrate the dense plane which is the world of human habitation.I did not feel that I had really gone away into a far country… I could still keep in touch….

"With this blessed feeling of consolation I must have drifted again, or slipped into a state of passivity. My next experience came with a strong thought….Exeter.

"Again I was with you in spirit, in the vast Cathedral where a small gathering to remember me wasalmost swallowed up in the big empty building. This time I was less emotional. I was able to participate in an objective way. My mind could apprehend the order of service… I felt humbled as never before by the kindliness of the would gathered in that chapel, by the excellently thought out oration of Colonel Lester, by the constructive 'aura' of the prayer forms as well as by the expressed faith of that Memorial Service."

"This is a change you will all make (some very soon), I recall thinking, ant then Truth will become apparent. How I longed to materialize before you to show that there is no death; but that was beyond my power to do…

"By the time the London Memorial Service was held I had "Progressed' sufficiently in this method of extension of consciousness to be able to make my presence known to those who could open their minds to this new dimension of thought. I felt that certain present 'saw' me or were 'aware' ofmy presence with the Sisters. To me this was uplifting and comforting. I relaxed into peace.. Life goes on for me now on a roller and more abundant scale of living.

4. PERSONAL EXPERIENTIAL SUPPORT FOR THESE INITIAL CONDITIONS: Although my Helen hadbegun communicating with me in early 2013, as I began to work as an evidential medium. She is a relative and all that seemed normal, family communicating with family.

But, in December 2014, I had a second earth changing experience with a discarnate spirit who was not family. and which proved to me unequivocally that consciousness survives the physical death, and thatwe aren't just imagining the communications we receive from the other side. This personal experience also documents much of what the two prior communicators told Randall, and also what Francis Banks stated about the "ignorant immigrants". It was an experience with simply no-other-explanation (NOE).Here is the narrative of that earth changing event.

BARBARA LEVINE'S MESSAGE: In the first week in December 2014, I was attending my first session oftwo weeks of courses on *Evidential Mediumship* at ***Arthur Findlay College of Psychic Science,*** in Stansted-Monfichet, Essex England. Having arrived on Sunday afternoon, it was Wednesday night of the first week (December 3), and I chose to attend the Spiritualist church service in the college chapel. There were over 120 people attending from the school and the surrounding communities, and I was sitting near the back. On the platform demonstrating mediumship was a Spiritualist medium (SNU Minister Simone Key). Spiritualist services always include a medium who brings through messages received from discarnate souls in the afterlife thus "demonstrating" the reality of consciousness survival.

Simone Key, the demonstrating medium, was also at that time chief instructor at the college, but not beingone of the instructors on the course I was taking she and I had not previously met. She proceeded to deliver two very evidential readings for two persons in the audience, each of whom could claim all the evidence given by the particular spirit communicator coming through. And, although those receiving thosemessages could verify the evidential facts delivered within those communications, I could not.

But, then she began to deliver a communication from the third and final spirit for the evening, by saying,

> ***"I have a woman here in spirit and she is showing me herself as having been in a wheel chair,...... she died in her late 50's or 60's...... of a disease much worse than Multiple Sclerosis,...... and she has a specific message for someone in this room....***
>
> ***"She was an educated woman whom you helped through her illness at a time when therest of her friends abandoned her. ....***
>
> ***"You weren't family just a friend...... Can anyone take those details."***

Sitting near the back of the auditorium, and being a stranger visiting from America, I had never attended aBritish demonstration of mediumship, so I was not used to this method of identifying the spirit and then finding who they belonged to. In America the medium usually picks a member of the audience and then looks for their departed loved ones.

But beyond that I was shocked by the fact that I could indeed accept all those details with regard to a recently deceased friend...... But, before I decided to raise my hand as one who could take all thosefacts, two women in the audience near the front raised their hands. ... ... These were regular attendees who simply hoped to "qualify" for the message (As a more experienced medium I now call these selfishly motivated sitters "body snatchers", because they are more interested in telling their friends *"I got a message"* than they are in the truths of Spirit communication). But, not wanting to be a "body snatcher" myself I demurred.

However, the medium now had to decide who the message was actually for, and apparently the was usedto this crowd. So she began to question each of the women, and quickly it was revealed that each was only able to accept "part of the details"......

The medium asked each of them, ***"How old was your friend when they died, and what disease did she have?...."*** One lady said, ***"80 years old and she had Parkinson's"***, the other said ***"90 years old and also with Parkinson's".***

The medium then firmly said,

"No... it can not be for either of you..... this discarnate communicator is very definite that she died in her late 50's or 60's and had a disease worse than Multiple Sclerosis.... Parkinson's simply does not qualify, and also both of these women were too old"....."

"I will ask the spirit communicator for some additional details".

The medium was silent for a few moments and then said,

"This woman is now telling me that you had to physically modify her house to allow for her disease........ and also that she was an educated woman but as her disease slowly progressed all her intellectual friends abandoned her, because her condition was toomuch for them to take;.....

"but you,..... just a casual friendly neighbor, still came and took her to events or the museum every week, and even continued to do that after the wheel chair fell one time........

And, as an educated woman she so appreciated your intellectual discussions".

Now, I was fully emotionally overcome, I teared up as I realized that I could accept all the additional

details as well, and knew undeniably that it was a communication for me from Barbara Levine; a Jewish friend that I would never have expected to hear from, yet she was definitely seeking me through this medium...... choked up and unable to speak... I shakily raised my hand.

Barbara had been a fellow San Franciscan. In the years before her death I had even brought my family and celebrated Jewish Chanukah's First Candle and also had eaten *seder* meals on the first night of passover with her family. Barbara had a Master's Degree in Education, and had passed on three years earlier in September 2011 due to ALS, (Lou Gehrig's disease). I had known her for about 5 years before the onset of the disease which slowly destroyed her physically over three and a half years. and I had witnessed the remodel of her house to suit her advancing ALS. And my wife Gale had taken her somewhere in the van at least every other week, while I was at work. So, Barbara was obviously also sending a message to Gale, and not just me.

But, now the medium, in order to make sure I was the right receiver, questioned me, *"How old was she when she died and what was her disease?"*,

with a wavering voice and choking back my tears, I said, *"I believe she was in or late 50's or early 60's, and she had ALS,.... Lou Gehrig's disease"*, (Checking later I know she was actually 68).

"I am not familiar with that disease, is it worse than MS?", asked the medium...... Now severalpeople the audience quickly responded *"ALS is what we call Motor Neuron Syndrome"* (the British name for it) and *"Yes, its much worse than MS"*.....

But, the medium now interjected,

> *"Never mind, the spirit communicator herself is now excitedly telling me that 'YES, it is aman, and that this man is in fact you".*

Having now successfully placed the message with me, the medium said,

> *"The communicator wants to thank you specifically for telling her that she wouldn't bedead when she passed on......*

> *"Because that knowledge saved her so much time in the new life.......*

> *"She said that she is already assisting new arrivals in their adjustment to the same facts, and to help them awake to their new lives there."... "*

> *"She also says, and with much emotion, that WHEN SHE COULD NO LONGER EVENHAND YOU A COOKIE, STILL YOU CAME IN ORDER TO TELL HER THE MESSAGE THAT SHE WOULD STILL BE ALIVE...... She says THAT she loves you, and to thank you againfor having the courage to give her that message"*

The evidence within the message was phenomenal,.....

How could the medium have possibly imagined the cookies which had sat on the kitchen counter betweenme and Barbra (completely immobilized and braced in her wheelchair). That was three years earlier in March of 2011, on the evening of Barbara's birthday party which was when I had told her that I knew she would still be alive after her impending "so-called" death.

There is simply no way the Medium could know these details and that Barbara could not hand me acookie at the same time that I told her this important message. For me personally this is undeniable proof that Barbara is still alive and telling these details to the medium.

Barbara's spirit's reaction in real time as the medium identified me, and Barbara said ***"Yes, it is a man and that is the man".*** is experiential scientific proof replicating other experiences I have had as a medium delivering messages to other people.

Further, the message itself overwhelmed me entirely because every single fact was perfectly accurate and could not have been known or guessed by the medium or anyone there. And, the statistical odds of the medium guessing all that is beyond astronomical.

This powerful message left hardly a dry eye in the house, and everyone in the the audience had no doubt that this message was real and had coming directly from a still living spirit whom I knew and cared for, and further that all the evidential details had been absolutely correct, and that the still living consciousness of the communicator (Barbara) was alive and also watching all of us in real time.

The verifiable truth of the evidence received is what matters in any scientifically observed data, and although this is a personal anecdote, yet it is my own empirical data and I treat it scientifically.

1. **First,** the medium did not know me, nor that I was even in the room or for that matter even in Europe. We were complete strangers and she did not use the direct method popular in the USA of picking me out as the sitter, instead she used the indirect method (which I have learned to prefer), of letting the spirit's evidence isolate who the receiver must be. This "indirect" method allows Spirit to pick the "best" message for the assembled audience. Consequently, it is difficult for anyone to argue that she was "psychically reading" my mind through ESP, since she had not previously identified me and so could not have "dialed me up" psychically.

2. **Second,** the discarnate communicator was not someone the medium could have known anything about, and further, I never expected to hear from Barbara. She was not my relative and just a friend that I had known casually, and she and I were not exceptionally close during our physical lives. But, was merely someone I had kindly helped to face death.

3. **Third,** the spirit communicator's message was very personal to me, with multiple facts in evidence that only I would know; like the house had to be modified to suit her illness, and the cookies which sitting on the counter between us when, during a private moment in a house full of birthday party guests, I had courageously told her during her

struggle to face her demise, that **"she would not be dead when she died"**.

4. **Fourth,** the content of that statement ***"You said that I would not be dead when I died"***. The fact is that most people (even spiritualists) have great difficulty sharing such intimate details of belief with people facing death. I am one of very few I have met who are confident enough in the reality of the afterlife (due to my NDE and my experiences as a medium), to openly share this with people facing death. Yet, the medium confidently states that, ***"She is thanking you for telling her she would not be dead when she died"***, and to me it is obvious that the medium was also fully aware that I would accept this detail as being true.

That is a deeply heartfelt story, which puts tears in my eyes every time I proof read it, but what pertains toour discussion is the fact that, Barbara ***"is already assisting new arrivals in their adjustment to the same facts, and to help them awake to their new lives there"***.

Barbara's story personally confirms for me what Randall's first communicator, and many of the others above had said, and which Francis Banks' communication had corroborated;

> ***"Only now and then is there a solitary spirit that can take up and do good work immediately upon arrival. The others all have to be taught the simplest things about their new "country".***

5. **ALLAN KARDEC'S DESCRIPTION,** *Heaven & Hell ©1878*: Apparently when Allan Kardec tried to invoke an old friend Mr. Van Durst, he was told by the medium's spirit control that Van Durst was still in a state of confusion and was unable to communicate. When Kardec eventually made contact, Van Durst said that his state of confusion WOULD HAVE BEEN SHORTER AND LESS PAINFULL if he had been more concerned with the spiritual when he was alive.

"You strive to regain the consciousness or your ME, and you cannot grasp it"... "You no longer exist, and yet you feel that, never-the-less, you do exist, but in what an abyss of confusion and trouble! ..... And, presently, after a lapse of time that you are unable to measure, a time of latent distress — for you have no longer the strength to feel it understandingly — after this lapse of timewhich seems to you interminable, to be slowly reborn into existence, to wake up in a new world."

"But, if before quitting the earth, I had known what you know, how much more easy andagreeable would have been my initiation into this other life".

This backs up what Barbara Levine told me personally, and also Randall's report of what the confused individual felt in the first dialog above, as well as what many others have reported.

And it fully agrees with what Dr. Fredrick H.W. Myers did finding and helping Raymond Lodge communicate back to Dr. Oliver Lodge from the other side in just 11 days. But, 6 years earlier Dr. Lodge had issued an his definitive book *The Survival of Man,* ©1909:

6.   SCIENTIFIC SUPPORT:

Dr. Oliver Lodge stated a "Tentative Conclusion" on page 343 of his 1909 book (Survival of Man), which he had written as President of the Society for Psychical Research after extensive study for 25 years(1883 until 1908) with numerous mediums and especially the cross-correspondences.

Lodge validates what Francis Banks just said (at No. 3 above) *"I still have the same experiences, the same problems, the same hopes, with even greater and wider aspirations for work, "* and also what was said earlier, *"On the other hand, it is almost impossible for us to help some spirits, as they have no desire to be different or better than they have always been…"* Francis Banks.

Dr. Oliver Lodge:

"The evidence for the survival of man, that is for the persistence of human intelligence and individual personality beyond bodily death has always been cumulative; and now, through recent developments of the ancient phenomena of automatic writing, it is beginning to be crucial."

"We find deceased friends — some of them well know to us, and active members of the Societyof Psychical Research while alive — Especially Gurney, Hodgson and Myers — constantly purporting to communicate, with the express purpose of patiently proving their identity and giving us cross correspondences between different mediums. We also find them answering specific questions in a manner characteristic of their known personalities and giving evidence of knowledge appropriate to them.

Not easily or early do we make this admission. In spite of long conversations with what purported to be the surviving intelligence of these friends and investigators, we were by no means convinced of their identity by mere general conversation — even when of a friendly and intimate character, such as in normal cases would be considered amply and overwhelmingly sufficient for the identification of friends speaking through a telephone or typewriter. We required definite and crucial proof — a proof difficult even to imagine as well as difficult to supply.

Yet, the ostensible communicators realize the need of such proof just as fully as we do, and have done their best to satisfy the rational demand. Some of us think they have succeeded, others are still doubtful. I am one of those who, though they would like to see more continued proofs, are of the opinion that a good case has been faded out, and that as the best working hypothesis at the present time it is legitimate to grant that lucid moments of intercourse with deceased persons mayin the best cases supervene; — amid a mass of supplementary material, quite natural under the circumstances, but mostly of a presumably subliminal and less evidential kind.

Carefully constructed evidence, I say. The constructive infinity exists quite as much on the other side of the partition as on our side; there has been distinct co-operation between those on the material and those on the immaterial side; and we are at liberty, not indeed to announce any definite conclusion, but to adopt as a working hypothesis the ancient doctrine of a possible intercourse of intelligence between the material and some other, perhaps ethereal order ofexistence.

"The first thing we learn, perhaps the only thing we clearly learn in the first instance is continuity (survival of consciousness).

"Essential belongings, such as memory, culture, education, habits, character, and affection, — all these, and to a certain extent tastes and interests — for better or worse, are retained. Terrestrial accretions, such as worldly possessions, bodily pain and disabilities, these for the most part naturally drop away.

"Meanwhile, it would appear that knowledge is not suddenly advanced — it would be unnatural if it were — we are not suddenly flooded with new information — nor do we at all change our identity; *but powers and faculties are enlarged, and the scope of our outlook on the universe may be sidelined and depend, if effort has rendered the acquisition of such extra insight legitimate and possible."*

"On the other hand, there are doubtless some whom the removal of temporary accretion and accidents of existence will leave in a feeble and impoverished condition; for the things are gone inwhich they trusted, and they are left poor indeed. Such doctrines have been taught on thestrength of vision and revelations, quite short of any recognized Divine revelation, for more than acentury. The visions of Swedenborg, divested of their exuberant trappings, are not wholly unreal, and are by no means wholly untrue. There is a general consistency in the doctrines that havethus been taught through the various sensitives, and all I do is to add my testimony to the rational character of the general survey of the universe indicated by Fredrick Myers in his great and eloquent work."

At this point we have anecdotal evidence from several discarnate communicators, My own unequivocal personal empirical evidence, and careful scientific evidence proving that:

1. Our consciousness can survive outside the physical body during an NDE, and

2. The consciousness can also survive the permanent death of the physical body, and

3. Can (given the right circumstances) communicate with us.

4. Due to our culture's materialist perspective (that the physical is all there is), most people arrive inthe afterlife totally unaware of what is coming.

5. This is why Spirit is so concerned and trying to communicate with us now that **THIS PHYSICALLIFE IS NOT THE END.**

RESTITUTION (Upper 4th Dimension)

We can now move on to the "Restitution Phase", which is the upper level of the next stage or fourth dimension. This is the plane of existence where the "life review", which was first found scientifically in a shortened version occurring during the Near-Death experience, now becomes a full time activity, andmust be dealt with before a soul can progress further.

Here is what one spirit told Randall:

"We also have no sectarian or ecclesiastical feuds, no metaphysical dogmas; our religiousteachers instead belong to that class of persons who were noted during their probation on earth for their philanthropy and deeds of morel bravery; who, regardless of the scoffs and sneers of time-serving multitude, dared to promulgate and defend the doctrines of civil

and religious liberty."

These teachers urge upon us the necessity of cooperation in the reformation and advancement of our more degraded brethren, by all of us instructing them in the divine principles of love, wisdom and benevolence. They instruct them in the soul inspiring and elevating doctrines of universal and eternal progression, and in the sublime truth that evil is not an indestructible and positive principle, but a negative condition, a mere temporary circumstance of existence; and furthermore, that suffering for sin is not a revengeful and malevolent infliction of god, but is a necessary and invariable consequence of violating the law.

They teach also that, according to the divine moral economy, there is no such thing as pardon for sins committed — no immediate mercy — no possible escape fro the natural results of crime, no matter where or by whom committed, no healing of a deceased moral constitution by any outward appliances or ceremonial absurdities; and finally, that the ***ONLY WAY TO ESCAPE SIN AND ITS CONSEQUENCES, IS BY PROGRESSING ABOVE AND BEYOND IT".***

REPARATION & RESTITUTION RATHER THAN RETRIBUTION:

A spirit told Randall:

"Remember", said one who had been in spirit life nearly four hundred years "The world in which you live is in a very low order of development. in many of the other planets this philosophy of life is universally taught, but you have comparatively only a few minds high enough out of the slough of materialism to comprehend it."…

"In the lower sphere one sees much suffering among those still earth bound, they too are busy working out past faults and they are often heavy hearted. Generally speaking, the first sphere (4th dimension) is the one where restitution must be made, and where the final wrenching away from earth conditions takes place."

Francis Banks said to Helen Greaves that:

"Somewhere in the deeps of my mind two "blueprints" are brought forward into my consciousness. These are so clear that I can (literally) take them out, materialize them and study them. One is the PERFECT IDEA with which my spirit went bravely into incarnation. The second is the resultant of only a partially understood plan…. In fact my life as it was actually lived. It was a shock to me, and a very salutary experience, to find that these two plans differed exceedingly. And, yet one learns so

much by facing the results....."

"*First of all the mind looks at the whole comparison, and sets the blueprints side by side. This is the first shock; a true humbling of yourself to find that you did so little when you would have done so much. That you went wrong so often when you were sure you were right.*"

"*During the experience the whole cycle of your life-term unfolds before you in a kaleidoscopic series of pictures. During the crisis one seems to be entirely alone. Yours is the judgement, You stand at your own bar of judgement. You make your own decisions. You take your own blame..... You are the accused, the judge and the jury. This is here quite a few should in this Rest Home have become immobilized. Their pictures were too searing n their exposure. So, we try to help them along, but only when they have made the 'inner desire' to right their wrongs. Until that moment I do not know what happens to them, but I should think that they are 'prisoners of theself'*"

"*Immediately, as they are ready to face themselves again they are guided to these beautiful and peaceful homes. Here,the Sisters devote their love and thought, their skill and experience, to aiding the stumblers*"

"*The second stage (of the First Sphere) of this recapitulation starts the the soul feels strong enough and calmed sufficiently to take the earth life, round by round (so to speak).. Then the blueprints are brought into the mind again; only this time the start is made from the moment of departure from the body. the mind works slowly, oh so slowly backwards through one's experiences, but now you seem no longer alone you are aware of this great Being beside you helping you giving you strength, peace, tranquility, and helping with constructive criticism.*

"*Lots of those here have got STUCK on their first picture. So we sisters try to link up with these great ones and bring help and strength to the stumblers' level....There is one man in the wards. He had been brutal and bitter to his wife and family. Now he is stuck. He has spent a long period of your earth time(thought there is no time as such over here) since his changeover to this life, in being tied to the places and people where his cruelty and his bitterness had been exercised.Now he is here and is trying to go on, But the film reel of his life appalled him; and he hasbecome completely immobile.*

THE FIFTH DIMENSION (Second Sphere)

The second sphere is the one of being instructed, a period of study, during which the spirit gains knowledge of self and natural law. Some would call this '**Purgatory**".

MICHAEL TYMN'S DESCRIPTION: The Afterlife Revealed, What happens after we die, © 2011:

The second sphere is populated by souls who developed a modicum of spiritual consciousness during their lifetimes but still, for the most part, led selfish and materialistic lives. Also souls from the first sphere may have gained a little consciousness and advanced to this level after some time, however time is measured in that state. Although, partially conscious, souls at this level are in something of a stupor, aware that they have died, but still very confused or bewildered, yet more easily educated by missionary spirits from higher spheres.

Tymn's description agrees with the *Tibetan Book of the Dead.* and with descriptions I have heard from NDEr.s

1. EDMUND C. RANDALL'S DESCRIPTION:

One Spirit told Randall that:

"The second is one of instruction a period of study, during which the spirit gains knowledge of selfand the natural law"

"Those in the second sphere do little, except to fit themselves for a broader and better work. Before reaching this sphere they have freed their spirit from the burden of wrong done in thebody, repaid every debt due mankind, dispelled the darkness of the First Sphere."

"They work with open eyes and clear spiritual vision, and are at peace with all. This must precedethe sphere of Study and Development. I have classes on Purity, Beauty, and Patience, and there are classes on every conceivable subject, Music, Chemistry, everything. They are different from those in earth-life, and one has to adopt different ideas. One of our engineers magnetizes your room each time you hear our voices. It is easier for those who have advanced to higher life to reach us than for us to reach you; there are not so many barriers."

'Yes we always have places that resemble homes. Thought is not indefinite, and that makes our homes, and while we keep that thought our homes are permanent. You asked where is that home located. I would say to you that all that is space is peopled with spirits.

2. **PROFESSOR HARE'S DESCRIPTION:** Professor Hare's father told him:

> *"There are seven spheres, the* **First Sphere** *is the terrestrial sphere which we occupy in their Earth reality. The* **Second Sphere** *is where the depraved spirits find themselves until they can begin the process of purification that allows them to ascend to higher spheres. The spirit goes toa sphere for which it is morally and intellectually adapted; thus the first sphere above theterrestrial one (the Second Sphere) is the abode of degraded spirits, meaning not only evil spirits but "mis-directed" ones as well.*

> *"He pointed out that* **there are millions of such spirits in the second sphere***, what the religionscall Hell, Hades, or Purgatory, who are groping and unable to free themselves from the fetters of earthly conditions. This sphere is said to be the abode of as many spirits as all the five spheres above it. However, contrary to the teachings of many religions, the spirits on this sphere are not permanently confined there. Sooner or later, spirits from the higher levels are able to reach them and help them see the light.*

"As there are no words in the human language in which spiritual ideas may be embodied so as to convey their literal and exact signification, we are obliged ofttimes to have recourse to the use of analogous and metaphorical modes of expression. In our communion with you we have to complywith the peculiar structure and rules of your language; but the genius of our language is such that we can impart more ideas to each other in a single word, then you can possibly convey in a hundred.

"Each sphere is divided into six circles, or societies, in which congenial spirits are united and subsist together according to the law of affinity. While these spirits generally agree in moral and intellectual matters, there are individual differences and some disagreements.

"Spirits united by ties of sanguinity and marriage, may or may not be linked together in the spheres and in the same society. It depends on the affinity between them, including the level of advancement. However, a spirit in a higher sphere can pass to a lower sphere to visit with loved ones but a spirit can never ascend to the higher level spheres until fully prepared for such a transition.

A spirit named Maria, daughter of Professor Hare's friend said:

"As her vision became clearer, she perceived a group from which her brother William emerged to greet her. He accompanied her to the Third Sphere, but they had to pass through the Second Sphere. She described it as gloomy and uncomfortable, appearing like a vast desert without a green spot to relieve the eyes. She observed its denizens straggling here and there with no fixed objective in view. All seeking to minister to their perverted tastes, Some are holding forth in loud tones, and painting in false and gaudy colors the joy of their home.

"Others who commanded high station on Earth, hang their heads in confusion, and would fain hide themselves from view, but they are taunted with red jests, and told that their 'pride of position will avail them nothing here'. One heart-sickening feature of this place is the absence of children. No purity can exist where such evils abound. The loud laugh which bespeaks a vacant mind is heard pealing forth in derision, as the teachers from the higher spheres approach the motley group. Some in whom the work of regeneration has commenced, are seen ascending the spiral stairway of progress which leads to the Third Sphere.

THE SIXTH DIMENSION (Third Sphere)

MICHAEL TYMN'S DESCRIPTION: Paraphrased from *The Afterlife Revealed, What happens after we die, (c)2011* Referred to as "Summerland" by Spiritualists, the third sphere is said to be the one where the average decent person — one who has led a relatively good life even though still grounded in materialism and lacking in significant spiritual consciousness — finds him or herself after separating from the physical body. He or she will be reunited with loved ones who have also made it here (based on their own karma) and will experience conditions very similar to those left on the earth plane. It has been referred to as a "dream life", but *less of a dream life than was experienced on the earth plane*. Many will continue to practice their old religions at this level, but missionary spirits from even higher spheres will slowly wean them away from their limited beliefs and engender a more unified belief system.

1. EDMUND C. RANDALL'S DESCRIPTION:

One Spirit told Randall that:

"The third is one of teaching those in the lower spheres, as I have said."

*"**The law of attraction is the dominate force here**. We have a great number of thoughtful men seeking to discover and develop the hidden forces of Nature; we have great lecture halls where those who are learned discourse upon the hidden forces. We have teachers who develop the spirituality, and discourse upon the great force called Good and its function in the universe. It is a busy world where everyone is doing his or her part. **We do not have strife for money, or need for money; so you see the occupation of the great majority of your** (earth) **people is gone.** It is only by helping others in this life — and this is equally true of earth life — that one betters his conditions and enriches himself. This is the law. The only happiness that the inhabitants of earth really get is through being charitable, doing good, and making the world happier. The only wealth that any man carries beyond the grave is what he gives away before he reaches the grave."*

"There is" Dr. Hossack told Randall," No aristocracy in this land of ours, but mind and merit. The law of Nature which is the Supreme Force, called Universal Law, has to be obeyed, in order that each sphere may be reached. Every individual remains upon the plane for which he is fitted, until he subjects his will to the Universal Law. As he progresses, he learns new laws, but they are fundamentally the same, only they grow more intense and vital, until he becomes a part of thatlaw himself."

2. **PROFESSOR HARE'S DESCRIPTION:** Professor Hare's friend's daughter Maria told him:

*"On approaching the **Third Sphere** William and Maria were met by a company of angels from theSeventh Sphere, among whom she recognized two brothers who had died in infancy and had since grown to the stature of men.... The inhabitants of this Third Sphere are anxious for instruction. The teachers from the higher spheres are listened to with profound respect and attention.*

"But they were just passing through en route to Maria's new home in the Fourth Sphere. She observed a band of children carrying wreaths of flowers and singing after welcoming a child who had just arrived from the earth plane. And while she had never been to the Fifth, Sixth or SeventhSphere she had been told about them.

THE SEVENTH DIMENSION (Fourth Sphere)

MICHAEL TYMN'S DESCRIPTION: The Afterlife Revealed, What happens after we die, ©2011

The fourth sphere seems to be the abode for those with more than average spiritual consciousness whenalive in there flesh. They were less grounded in materialism and more interested in service to fellow humans than serving oneself. Also, souls from the third sphere may have advanced to this level. While fourth sphere is mostly beyond human comprehension, conditions in the fifth, sixth, and seventh spheres are reportedly far beyond human comprehension and vocabulary. Indications are that most Spirit Communicators reside on the third and fourth levels.

1. EDMUND C. RANDALL'S DESCRIPTION:

One Spirit told Randall that:

"The Fourth Sphere is one of trial and temptation"

"In the Fourth Sphere, that of Trial where I am we are fitted for a higher order of life. Here, any weakness a spirit may still hold becomes a doubly alluring and seemingly irresistible. We finally overcome this by throwing it out of our spirit. Sometimes it is a long, hard task. We are made todo anything that we do not like to do, or, rather, we must learn to like to do it. Often when we help others, the task is irksome and we long to keep ourselves free for spiritual development, forgetting that each deed for others helps our own growth.

In the Sphere of Truth (Fifth Sphere) the spirits learn all about the other planets and become wise and uplifted, so that they can enter into perfect harmony with the universe. Of course, this needs special preparations and a high degree of development. There they are not taught by contact withteachers from the higher spheres — in fact, in that sphere we see no teachers, everything comes through suggestion. Our minds are receptive enough to be taught and guided in that way. Each sphere makes suggestions just a a little clearer and easier to grasp than the one before, and so we are fitted for the last, where we are able to throw out individuality into the nominating forces of the universe

Above this first level growing more intense and increasing in action are six more spheres, which are distinguished from this first sphere as the "Spiritual Spheres" Each sphere is separated from the other and regulated by fixed laws. These spheres are not hapless chimeras or mental projections, but are absolute entities, just as tangible as the planets of the solar system or the earth upon which you reside. They have latitude and longitude, and an atmosphere of peculiarly vitalized air. The undulating currents, soft and balmy, are invigorating and pleasurable.

Professor' Hare's Sister Martha communicated:

"The language of the mortals is inadequate to convey even a tenth part of the joy that she experienced when liberated from the physical body. She recalled being dazzled by brilliant light emanated by the beings who surrounded her, as she passed from death to life, and welcomed her. Her father was the first to greet her. "Father watched my emotion with deep interest, and wasdelighted with the stating and happy effect produced on my mind. We passed quickly through the different stages of our progress, till we arrived at the Fifth Sphere, which is my present home.

"I am often with my friends on Earth, and would gladly influence them, and prove my identity to them, if they would render themselves receptive to my power. When we desire to be with our friends on earth, we have only to will it, and out desire is instantly gratified. We can visit the spheres below, but not those above us until we are prepared for admission into them by a gradualprocess of development."

She also reiterated what the others had said that the Second Sphere is the abode of those spirits whose desires are low and sensuous. They maintain interest in the things that attracted them on Earth until their moral faculties become strengthened.

But, for the last 170 years Spiritualists have been publicizing the simple statement that "***There is not death, there are no dead***", which our best science is now completely verifying. Those Spiritualists continue to provide mediums weekly at every church service, who by bringing through evidence theycould not have known demonstrate this fact of consciousness survival.

Indeed, I do this myself as a scientist. After years of study and honing my skills I can bring through the name, relationship, how they died, and what their occupation was, for the departed loved ones of complete strangers. And it is easy to do, even though the odds of guessing all that would be billions to one.......".***It is easy because I am not the one doing it***." ... I am just the telephone. I have no ego here......The departed are the ones delivering the information to and through me, I am just an open channel. The communicating discarnate souls of loved ones just use me. Yet, all of this is still vehementlydisputed, and militantly resisted by ignorant materialist minded skeptics. Who can only feel safe if this isall impossible. Frankly, I think they are afraid of hell-fire and so have to remove any hint of a Universal Consciousness (God) and Consciousness Survival, simply because they believe they have hell to pay.

THE EIGHTH DIMENSIONS (Fifth Sphere)

The fifth is one of truth , where error and falsehood are unknown.

MICHAEL TYMN'S DESCRIPTION: The Afterlife Revealed, What happens after we die, ©2011

While fourth sphere is mostly beyond human comprehension, conditions in the fifth, sixth, and seventh spheres are reportedly far beyond human comprehension and vocabulary. Indications are that most Spirit Communicators reside on the third and fourth levels.

1. EDMUND C. RANDALL'S DESCRIPTION:

One Spirit told Randall that:

"The fifth is one of truth , where error and falsehood are unknown."

THE NINTH & TENTH DIMENSIONS (Sixth & Seventh Spheres)

In the Sixth all is harmony. In the Seventh the spirits reach the plane exaltation and become one with the great spirit that rules the universe."

MICHAEL TYMN'S DESCRIPTION: The Afterlife Revealed, What happens after we die, ©2011

… conditions in the … Sixth (9th dimension), and Seventh spheres (10th dimension) are reportedly far beyond human comprehension and vocabulary. Indications are that most Spirit Communicators reside on the third and fourth levels. My communicators and guides tell me that they can not see much father than we can into these higher level spheres.

D. ELEVENTH DIMENSION (Ain Soph, or Pure Consciousness)

No one who has gone here has come back to tell about it. Apparently, here we enter the Universal Consciousness to become one with Universe (God) and there is no longer any separation.

APPENDIX 1
THE PROBLEM WITH "SCIENCE"

The following quotations are by the late Dr. Carl Sagan (1934-1996), the Cornell University Astronomer who created the television series *"Cosmos"* and who is also one of the most famous atheist scientists of the 20th century. He is also one of my personal hero's.

"For me, it is far better to grasp the Universe as it really is than to persist in delusion, however satisfying and reassuring." Dr. Carl Sagan (1934-1996)

"It is the responsibility of scientists never to suppress knowledge, no matter how awkward that knowledge is, no matter how it may bother those in power. We arenot smart enough to decide which pieces of knowledge are permissible and which are not." Dr. Carl Sagan (1934-1996)

"I would like to suggest that superstition is very simple: it is merely belief without any evidence." Dr. Carl Sagan, Gifford Lecture No. 1, 1985[1]

UNDERSTANDING MATERIALIST SUPERSTITIONS PERVADING WESTERN CULTURE:

Materialism, is simply the belief that everything is made of matter. And, that this matter (stuff) is the basis of the universe. Unfortunately, this archaic belief which was the foundational tenant of Materialism is no longer supported by our best science. For example: The force of gravity is not made of matter, it may be caused by matter's attraction for other matter, but the force itself is not matter. Electric forces are not matter, they cause matter to do things, but the forces themselves are not made of matter.

ThE classical Newtonian perspective of physics, culminated in the 1890's with a mechanistic view of a "clock-work" universe, everything working according to the *First Principles of Physics*. A view that remains very comfortable to the world's scientific community who persist in wanting to believe thatscience knows everything there is to know.

This "*We almost know everything*" perspective was stated by Lord Kelvin (British physicist William Thompson, and 1st Barron Kelvin) in April of 1900, at a lecture given to the Royal Society of London. At the time the the most eminent scientific society in the world.

Lord Kelvin stated that Physics was "nearly complete", and that the careful application of mathematics to science had been so successful that the mysteries of the universe were all known and reduced to equations. **Except for two "small clouds" on the far horizon of physics, which needed to be cleared up.**

The first cloud was that we needed to explain the "*luminous ether*" (what it is that fills up empty space), and **the second cloud** was the "*ultraviolet catastrophe*", also known as the Rayleigh-Jeans Law that a "blackbody" would radiate unlimited amounts of ultraviolet radiation, but did not exactly follow the known laws or Physics.

These "small clouds" both concerned anomalous physical properties of light, which were simply not fully explained by best physical theories of the day, yet they appeared to be only minor issues which research would shortly clear up.

Instead, researching the "*ultraviolet catastrophe*", led to Max Planck a German physicist and ChiefScientist at the University of Berlin, just eight months after Lord Kelvin's speech, identified the Quantum. which quickly evolved into Quantum Physics. This proved not to be some small cloud, but was instead a force 5 hurricane which destroyed the entire structure of classical materialist physics.

And, the luminous ether disappeared as a problem because for years it was thought to have been disproven by the Michelson-Morely experiment in 1881. And, so not much research was done here, even though Michelson-Morely discovered in 1887 that their "experiment" had been greatly flawed. But, unfortunately failed experiments are seldom later retracted. And, as a consequence many people still today continue to believe Michelson-Morely had proven the ether could not exist.

On the other hand, knowing physicists consider the Michelson-Morely experiment to be ***the most famous failed experiment in history"***.

But the faulty science of Michelson-Morely had stalemated the question of what un-discerned force allowed for the transmission of light waves for over a century. Then in 1998 with the launch of the Hubble Telescope, Astronomers and Astro-Physicists discovered the undiscerned forces of *Dark Energy* and *Dark Matter,* and *Dark Energy*, although still undiscerned, is a valid candidate to be the force which allows the transmission of light as the "Luminiferous Ether"

LOSS OF THAT COMFORTABLE PERSPECTIVE: However, Max Planck, proposed a radical solution forthe "*Ultraviolet Catastrophe*", which Planck now called the "Quantum", with the help of several other Nobel Laureate physicists, within the next three decades that radical solution had become what isproperly named ***Quantum Electro-dynamics-QED.***

Today, QED is the most proven scientific theory of all time. Without QED being true, we would have no cell phones, no fMRI, no computers no digital photography, In fact no electronics at all because without QED being true we would have no transistors.

This single theory alone has entirely disproven Materialism, and shown it to be the archaic religious belief that it actually always has been.

Max Planck had gone on to say:

"All matter originates and exists only by virtue of a force which brings the particle of an atom to vibration and holds this most minute solar system of the atom together. We must assume behind this force the existence of a conscious and intelligent mind. This mind is the matrix of all matter." Max Planck (1858-1947) speaking in 1900., Nobel prize 1918

And his compatriot in the creation of QED, Erin Schrödinger also stated that:

"What we observe as material bodies and forces are nothing but shapes and variations in the structure of space" Erwin Schrödinger, Nobel Prize 1933

Then along came Albert Einstein, in 1905 with his solution for Brownian Motion. which added impetus to Planck's theory of atoms emitting quanta of energy.

Einstein also later introduced his two theories General and Special Relativity, which when combined with Maxwells equations of Electro-Magnetic force allow the creation of **QED**, when observed separately provide another perspective for explaining the cosmos. But, Max Planck quickly found a place at the University of Berlin for Einstein.

However, with the second cloud having been resolved by *QED*, that left that first cloud, about what made up the "luminous ether" still unresolved. Space still appeared to be empty space and yet space could transmit light without any apparent medium through which the light could be transmitted. This issues was further confused by the flawed experiment made by Michelson-Morely which had seemed to prove there was no luminiferous ether. So, that would take a little longer, and would not be resolved until the end of the 20th century 98 years after Lord Kelvin's speech.

It was with the launching of the Hubble Telescope in 1998, that this was finally to be solved. When we could finally see into very deep space and it was discovered that the expansion of the Universe was speeding up, and was not slowing down as Newton's theory of gravity would suppose. Gravity was not slowing the universe down, something else was overcoming that gravity and speeding up the expansion.

> Note: The materialists still have no intelligible explanation for what causes gravity. They say "large objects attract each other", but their explanation stops there. That statement may be a fact, but it is not an answer to the question of what is gravity?

After much conjecture, the physics community has begun to agree with the astronomers that this undiscerned force is what we now call *Dark Energy*, and *Dark Matter*. And, their best calculation is that although as yet totally undiscerned these two do in fact make up 96% of the universe. So, then it would appear that Materialist Physics looking only inside the limited perspective of the Standard Model is really only about 4% complete and 96% incomplete. Just a little more egg on Lord Kelvin's arrogant face. But, that is yet another story.

On the other hand, the Materialism belief system (BS) has within the 120 years since Lord Kelvin's prediction of physics being complete, been completely overturned and disproven, just as have all other religious belief systems (BS), or superstitions, which are based on faith (beliefs), rather than facts.

Logically this should be obvious. No matter how much you WANT something you choose to believe to be true, your willing it to be so can't make it so.

And, regardless of the objections of most Materialist believers, "Materialism" is absolutely a superstition. As Dr. Carl Sagan said ***"superstition" is belief not baed on any facts.*** So, Materialism is no more than a chosen religion.

Instead, Materialism is based on those six ***First Principles*** all being true. If any one were not true then Materialism has no foundation. Just as Dr. James E. Alcock, Ph.D, (BS-Physics, Graduated with honors in Physics from McGill University, But he is not a physicist and is instead, a Professor of Psychology and not a scientist at all. Yet he is however one of the chief Pseudo Science skeptics.

Dr. Alcock said that if the claims of parapsychology (and QED) were true, that they would,

> ***"stand in defiance of the modern scientific worldview"...And "if the claims of parapsychology prove to be true, then physics, biology and neuroscience are horribly wrong in some fundamental respects."***

But, isn't that the same problem with all religions?...

And by the way, Dr. Alcock, the classic newtonian "materialism", has no longer been the "modern scientificworld view" for over 100 years. ... So, you had better get busy revising those fundamental respects which are wrong. ... ... The least you can do is to stop using your cell phone and your computer since you don't believe in QED !!!

It is easy to see that back in the 1650's all these *First Principles* were simply presumed to be "selfevident" when Issac Newton and Rene Descartes were forming the basis of classical physics, and when the Royal Society was formed in 1660, they simply had no way to test these *First Principles* to determineif they were actually true. So at the time "Self Evident" would have to suffice.

For example, ***"As anyone can see, it is self evident that space is empty. You don't see any matter there so how could anything be there..... Duh?... It is obvious that there is no Dark Energy, or we would be able to see it?....***

Likewise, **"Reality is obviously there.....Isn't it..... You are sitting on your chair, not a bunch of atoms made of nothing but electron clouds.... To think reality is an illusion is just stupid"......** And, **"Time passes, so you know that.... Time is real and can't be a mere illusion... we've wasted enough time on this"**...

But, unfortunately, most honest physicists agree that both time and space are illusions, as illustrated by Einstein's theories of Relativity.

Unfortunately, although it is completely untrue, in Western culture Materialism is still taught at our universities as being the equivalent of science. And this untruth is perpetuated by the very same professors who would protest vehemently if any other "religion" were being taught in their ivory towers. These professors all believe that the *First Principles of Physics* are already scientifically proven facts, when they have never been more than mere presumptions..... simply widely accepted religious "beliefs" with no proof.

So, for the skeptics I have below disproved the *First Principles* of Materialist Physics, one by one using *QED* and *Non-locality*. These unproven but "assumed to be true concepts are these; **reality, locality, causality, continuity, determinism** *and* **certainty**. as defined below:

REALITY: This is the unproven presumption that asserts the physical world to be objectively real. This means that the observed world exists independent of our creative thought. In other words, this is a belief that we don't just conger up the physical world in our thinking, but instead the physical world actually exists whether we are there to observe it or not. Yet, this concept is based on the next four concepts (locality, causality, continuity and determinism) all being true, which they are now know not to be.

LOCALITY: This is the unproven presumption that asserts that things can actually be separated by space and dimension. This carries with it the idea that objects can only be influenced by direct contact. Unmediated "actionat a distance" is simply prohibited. Remember, this was a mechanistic concept invented before the discovery of radio waves and other forms of higher- frequency radiation, which all seem to operate *without* benefit ofphysical contact.

Further, we now have John Bell's **Theory of Non-Locality,** which has been proven nearly a dozen times between 1972 and 2009, which entirely refutes any concept of locality. John Bell's theory is possibly the most important discovery of the 20th Century, more important than Einstein's Theory of Relativity. It proves conclusively that space and distance are truly illusions. And, as a consequence, **it also proves that the concept of "locality" on which materialism is based is entirely false.**

CAUSALITY: This unproven presumption which asserts that the arrow of time points only in one direction and that it cannot be reversed; and assumes that cause and effect sequences are absolutely fixed. However, logical this may seem to our perception, QED has shown that time can be measured in both directions, and further, that certain actions can be measured which show retro-causality. That is, observations made later can change what has been held in a quantum state from the past. Here we are back to the thought experiment ofSchrodinger's Cat, and in some instances, decisions made later can act with retro-causality. Several scientists have recently been able to show retro-causality in scientific experiments. So, this also disproves the idea that time only moves in one direction.

CONTINUITY: This unproven presumption asserts that there are no discontinuous jumps in nature, and that thefabric of space and time is "smooth". This means that there are no holes in the fabric of space and time. But, at the micro-scale QED, nature is neither smooth nor continuous, and mostly exists only in a quantum state until it is observed by a living consciousness. In other words, it is one big vacuum until we observe it.

DETERMINISM: This unproven presumption asserts that things progress in an orderly predictable way. Takento its extremes this belief says that: if we were able to know all the starting conditions, and to anticipate all the causal linkages that would unfold, then we could, in principle, predict the future completely. Unfortunately, this belief is based, too, on the validity of causality, reality and certainty.

CERTAINTY: This is the unproven presumption that something can be proven to a mathematical certainty. In other words "knowing for sure". However, GÖdel's incompleteness theorems proved in **1931** that essential aspects of *certainty* could not be attained, and he found that.

> ***"in any sufficiently powerful mathematical system, such as arithmetic, a statement that can be shown to be true, but that does not follow from the rule of the system will always exist."***

Thus, it became clear that the notion of a mathematical certainty cannot be reduced to a purely formal system. Gödel showed that such a system was not powerful enough for proving its own consistency, let alone that a simpler system could do the job. Also, Heisenberg had already restated this in **1927** as the "uncertainty principle".

Although it maybe comfortable to believe as your religion that these basic "*First Principle*" presumptions are inviolable, all of them lack any basis in modern science because each of them has been proven to be false by Quantum electro-dynamics and Non-locality.

On the other hand, Materialism is a great approximation of reality and it works very well in daily life. I haveused the classical Newtonian "Standard Model" throughout my career because it is still a wonderful approximation of the Universe, and so is very useful in the practical applied science of engineering.

But, the ***First Principles*** just are not "truths" or "facts" they are merely approximations.

Most religions do realize that their belief system (their BS) is based on belief. They clearly state we have faith in our religion. While they believe it is true, they also realize it is only a belief.

Unfortunately, Materialist scientists, taught by their professors that Materialism is scientific fact, pride themselves on the idea that their personal BS (belief system) is the only truth. Further complicating the issue is the fact that many scientists are atheists who honestly believe they have no "religion". However, just like Islamic terrorists these "non-religion" scientists try to stifle any resistance to their "truth", (Kill the infidel seems to be their motto).

Further, science does not equate to Materialism. Science itself is not a body of beliefs, instead, science is actually a way of doing things in order to find out the truth. Since is an investigative process.

THE PSYCHOLOGICAL PROBLEM WITH MATERIALIST BELIEVERS:

Carl Gustav Jung, one of the founders of modern psychiatry, while a young medical school student was fascinated when he read about psychic phenomena as observed by such noted scientists as **William Crookes** (inventor of the vacuum tube) and **Johann Zellner** (astrophysicist at University of Leipzig) Yet, when he spoke of them to his friends and classmates, they all reacted with derision and disbelief, or with an anxious defensiveness.:

"I wondered at the sureness with which they could assert that things like ghosts and table-turning were impossible and therefore fraudulent, and on the other hand (I wondered) at the evidently anxious nature of their defensiveness." Carl Gustav Jung

Later, in his practice as a psychiatrist Jung found that the majority of his patients were those who had lost their faith:

"They seek position, marriage, reputation, outward success or money, and remain unhappy and neurotic even when they have attained what they were seeking. Such people are usually confined within too narrow a spiritual horizon. Their life has not sufficient content, sufficient meaning."

Carl Gustav Jung

Finally, he referred to the reality of most people as:

"a submission to the vow to believe only in what is probable, average, commonplace, barren of meaning, to renounce everything strange and significant, and reduce anything extraordinary to the banal." Carl Gustav Jung

DISCLAIMER FOR ANYONE FEELING A BIT SKEPTICAL: So, for any readers that are newcomers to Psychic Science (the careful and systematic study of psychic phenomena), I do understand your concerns, because I had some of the same concerns after having myself been schooled in the main stream materialist perspective. Your first reaction may be that we now seem to be stepping off the edge of rationality and delving into some kind of *"hocus pocus"*.

In fact, it may appear to some that if we believe in psychic phenomena at all then we have chosen to believe a complete superstition.

But, we are just talking about scientific data, actual objective clinical results which dedicated medical professionals have been reporting for years. Further, we can witness Evidential Mediumship to acquire subjective evidence for ourselves.

It becomes clear to anyone after honestly and carefully examining the data that psychic phenomena are just as natural as electricity, magnetism or gravity (again, all three are concepts which modern science simply can not explain because in each instance we know the symptoms, but no the actual cause).

So, just because we also can not also explain psychic phenomena within our current limited perspectiveof materialism, that does not mean that it not true, just like our inability to explain electricity, magnetism and gravity does not make them untrue.

Again I come back to Dr. Carl Sagan's favorite phrase ***"We just don't know"***.

APPENDIX 2
THE PROBLEM WITH RELIGIONS & THEWEIGHING OF THE HEART

The problem with all religions, is that they want science to prove that the way their specific religion chooses to believe is correct, and every other religion is wrong.

But, the science or *Post Mortem Consciousness Survival* is instead revealing that all religions are correct, in there belief that there is an afterlife. But, at the same time our best science is also telling us that this afterlife it is not at all like any of their priests and imams have been speculating it to be for the last several thousand years.

Consequently, *Quantum Electro-Dynamics, Entanglement* and *Non-locality* are showing us an ontology which supersedes all the world's religions. Basically, all religions are a little bit off they all have egg on their face.

The new ontology ("religion") which science is rapidly revealing is that:

1. The conscious universe (God) is real, but

2. There is no retribution other than our own remorse, and

3. As Saint Paul said, ***Heaven (eternal life) is a free gift which is not earned or deserved.*** We all will experience Post-Mortem Conscious Survival.

The one religion which is most compatible with these new scientific truths is Spiritualism, which not only believes that none of us die, but that everyone will experience Post-Mortem Consciousness Survival. And, further that we can communicate with those in the next dimension.

SPIRITUALISM & QUANTUM ELECTRO-DYNAMICS: A COMING PARADIGM SHIFT: In the early

1850's, James Clerk-Maxwell developed the classical theory of electro-magnetism. This breakthrough formed the basis of wireless (radio) communications technology, and when combined with relativity gives us ***Quantum Electro-Dynamics-QED.*** In fact, Albert Einstein believed that Maxwell's equations are basicto everything.

Later, in the latter half of the 20th Century, Dr. Richard Feynman felt that this one breakthrough, as quantified in Maxwell's equations ***"is the most important change in all of the history of science".***

Synergistically, this scientific advance of defining electro-magnetic vibrations happened in parallel with therise of Spiritualism (i.e., the belief in the possibility of communicating with departed souls continuing to exist at higher vibrations). Consequently, there are deep connections between these two separatephilosophies.

Modern Spiritualism, as it is called by its proponents, began in 1848, at Hydesville, New York, when the Fox family was contacted by the disincarnate spirit of a salesman, Charles B. Rosna, who had, five years earlier, having been murdered in the house they were now renting, and buried in the basement. Digging inthe basement, hair and teeth were found, but the rest of the body had been apparently been moved. However, 40+ years later Rosna's bones and his salesmen's pack were found behind a false basement wall in the foundation structure, which the murderer had constructed.

The Fox sisters soon began holding séances receiving messages from many deceased persons. Thetruth of this concept spread rapidly, and within three decades prominent scientists like **William James** of Harvard and **Sir Oliver Lodge** of England were carefully testing spiritualist mediums. Both of these men worked extensively with both Lenora Piper in Boston and Gladys Osborne Leonard in London betweenthe 1880's and 1920 (James died in 1910, and Lodge in 1947). Yet, the rigorous scientific reports of these prominent scientists on the subject are fascinating to read even 100 years later.

Both Lodge and James were convinced that the individual human consciousness (soul) does survive death and continues in some mode of existence capable of interacting with the living through mediumship.

AN AKASHIC RECORD: One explanation popular 100 years ago was that the souls of the departed are somehow permanently imprinted in an "ethereal medium" that surrounds and permeates all ordinary matter, which conveniently explains psychometry (where a person brings an object to the medium which belonged to the departed person and the medium "reads" the person's story off the object).

Today, physicists call this imprinting "decoherence". But, the energy field where all this takes place is *Dark Matter* and *Dark Energy*. The late Edgar Mitchell, Lunar Astronaut, has recently described the "recording" as the *quantum hologram* which physically registers, by electro-magnetic decoherence, everything that has ever happened. This recording process and reading the information is very similar to the information gathered by fMRI scans.

At about the same time that Modern Spiritualism was born (1848), **James Clerk Maxwell** began to conceive of electric and magnetic effects in a completely different way. Building on the earlier suggestions of Faraday, Maxwell, who is undoubtedly as great a physicist as Newton and Einstein because he combined electricity, magnetism and light into one medium, also conceived of an all-embracing aether (dark matter) as being the mechanism and embodiment of the forces of electro-magnetism.

Maxwell showed that this ethereal medium was capable of conveying energy in the form of electro- magnetic waves propagating at the speed of light. Indeed he surmised that light itself is an electromagnetic wave. Maxwell's final synthesis of these ideas was published in 1873, and in the 1880s Hertz, who succeeded in producing and detecting them directly by means of oscillating electrical circuits, showed the reality of electromagnetic waves. In an article on "Ether" for the Encyclopedia Britannica Maxwell wrote:

> "Ether or Aether: A material substance of a more subtle kind than visible bodies, supposed to exist in those parts of space which are apparently empty... Whatever difficulties we may have in forming a consistent idea of the constitution of the aether, there can be no doubt that the interplanetary and interstellar spaces are not empty, but are occupied by a material substance or body, which is certainly the largest, and probably the most uniform body of which we have any knowledge. Whether, this vast homogeneous expanse of isotropic matter is fitted not only to be a medium of physical interaction between distant bodies, and to fulfill other physical functions of which, perhaps, we have as yet no conception, but also ... to constitute the material organism of beings exercising functions of life and mind as high or higher than ours are at present - is a question far transcending the limits of physical speculation".

Today, from the perspective of QED, it is obvious that Maxwell is attempting to describe *Dark Energy* and

Dark Matter as explaining our *non-local* conscious universe.

But, some of Maxwell's close friends and followers were less cautious in their ethereal speculations. For example, in 1873, Peter Guthrie Tait, along with Balfour Stewart, wrote a book entitled *"The Unseen Universe"*, expounding on the probable spiritual functions of the luminiferous ether.

> "We attempt to show that we are absolutely driven by scientific principles to acknowledge the existence of an Unseen Universe, and by scientific analogy to conclude that it is full of life and intelligence - that it is in fact a spiritual universe and not a dead one."

The book (which enjoyed huge popularity in its time) argued that

> ***"the forms of matter and mind survive eternally as configurations of spirit in the ether".***

Sir Oliver Lodge had written in another of his books *The Ether of Space* that:

> ***"The universe we are living in is an extraordinary one; and our investigation of it has only just begun. We know that matter has a psychical significance, since it can constitute brain, which links together the physical and the psychical worlds. If anyone thinks that the ether, with all its massiveness and energy, has probably no psychical significance, I find myself unable to agree with him."***

Quantum electro-dynamics-QED lends itself to various forms of neo-spiritualism based on the phenomena of quantum entanglement (*non-locality*). Consequently, with the realization accepted by most *Quantum electro-dynamic* theoretical physicists that the Universe is formed of conscious thought, rigorousscience is finally filling in all the blanks which previously seemed to defeat the original Spiritualist theories of the late 19th Century.

Today the mounting evidence is actually proving that Spiritualism is indeed true, and the dream of the materialists that there is no soul (a religion in itself) is being completely undermined.

Now, it appears that in the 21st Century, rapidly continuing over the next 30 years, there will be a reawakening of Spiritualism in the US and Canada (as well as Great Britain, Australia, and New Zealand),which will dwarf the tremendous growth this philosophy experienced in 1848-1888, and again in 1914-1927.

Rigorous triple-blind science is currently verifying the phenomena of Spiritualism (Evidential Mediumship) and these discoveries are spreading across the Internet so rapidly that this is forcing a paradigm shift on the scientific community. By mid-century, any 21st Century scientist who still chooses to cleave desperately to the formerly comfortable Newtonian materialist theories of the 19th Century with noConscious Universe (God) will be seen as the old "quacks" that they truly are.

"la Pesée du Coeur"

THE WEIGHING OF THE HEART - A candid look at where "Christianity" began

Have you ever wondered why it is that, **_ONLY POPULATIONS DESCENDED FROM THE ROMAN EMPIRE BELIEVE IN A SINGLE LIFETIME_**, … … while the rest of the world, indeed the majority opinion is that we live multiple lifetimes?

> "That's the paradox,…, "In the west people say, 'Why are you spending money to study reincarnation when we know it is impossible'. In the East they say, 'Why are you spending money to study reincarnation when we know it is a fact?"

Dr. Ian Stevenson, University of Virginia researcher on children who remember past lives.

> **_"…there are three claims in the ESP field which, in my opinion, deserve serious study… One of these is that young children sometimes report the details of a previous life, which upon checking turn out to be accurate …………and which they could not have known about in any other way than reincarnation…"_**

the late Dr. Carl Sagan

"The transmigrations (reincarnation) of souls was taught for a long time among the early Christians as an esoteric and traditional doctrine which was to be divulged to only a small number of the elect." Jerome (340-420AD) in a letter to Dimeterias

THE ANCIENT EGYPTIAN WEIGHING OF THE HEART:

On my desk sits this print of the ancient Egyptian papyrus, The original is held at the Louvre in Paris andis entitled *"la Pesée du Coeur"*.

The papyrus Illustrates, the ancient Egyptian myth of *"The Weighing of the Heart"*, the philosophy of which has been documented in surviving written artifacts from as far back as 4500 years ago (2500 BCE)[70]. In fact, remnants of this same ancient myth in the *Bahgavad Gita*, dated by scholars around 3000BCE (and archeo-astrologically dated to as early as 5561 BCE),

So, the archetypal myth portrayed in the papyrus precedes Christianity, Islam, Judaism and Buddhism by a good thousand years if not several thousand. Yet, parts of it appear to be incorporated into each.

To any honest scholar, carefully not allowing his perception to be clouded by any preconceived "belief system" (BS) ..... these facts indicate that this myth is a basic part of mankind's inner psyche asunderstood by Carl Jung and Joseph Campbell.

THE WEIGHING OF THE HEART: This papyrus shows the goddess Maat, representing the Divine Attributes of Truth, Honesty, Justice and Fairness observing a balance-scale that is weighing the heart ofa disincarnate individual just recently deceased. On the other side of the balance, being weighed against the heart, is Maat's feather of righteousness. Maat holds in her left hand the key of life (ankh), ready to award it to this deceased person if she finds the weight of their heart to be "light as a feather"

(i.e. She is asking him whether his experiences in the physical life have given him enough trials, tribulations and lessons to achieve the growth necessary for his spirit to finally be at peace sothat his heart is therefore light).

Standing on a pedestal on the side of the deceased, and shown as a monkey, is Horus, the Son of the God Osiris. Horus is himself a god who was born of a virgin (immaculate conception). His mother, Isis, was impregnated by the spirit (Holy Ghost) of the deceased god Osiris. Horus is actually waiting to tilt the scale in favor of the deceased. This *Son of God* is ready to literally "make up for the sins of thedeceased".

TWO POSSIBLE OUTCOMES:

If the deceased's heart is not weighted down with the burden of sin, then Maat will give him the key of life and the deceased will travel on into the heavens to the star Sirius (Isis) and Orion (Osiris) to rejoin the gods from which he came, and live with them in the heavens eternally, having after many lifetimes escaped the wheel of repeated lives and finally achieved Buddha-hood.

On the other hand, if his heart is still weighted down with the burdens of this life, then his experiences in the physical life have not brought him enough pain to garner the gnosis necessary to no longer careabout the things of this physical existence in time and space. And, therefore, because his heart is still heavy, he will have to travel back through the underworld led by the guide dog Anuket to be "Born Again" and reincarnate as a human for another physical lifetime of seeking wisdom from the trials of physical life.

The only part of the Egyptian myth which is missing from today's Christian version of the salvation story is the opportunity for rebirth into another physical life (reincarnation). Otherwise, the 21th Century Christian salvation story is identical to the ancient Egyptian afterlife myth, but with the single addition of "retribution" that is hellfire and damnation, in the Christian version the "underworld" has been transformed into a place of eternal retribution.

BUT, THE AFTERLIFE SALVATION MYTHS OF ALL RELIGIONS BEGAN HERE: Not surprisingly, this ancient myth also contains all the significant beliefs of most modern religions(Christian, Moslem, Jewish, Hindu & Buddhist).

"… man is destined to die once, and after that to face judgment."

Hebrews 9:27 (NIV)

Yet, beyond the various religion's beliefs the Egyptian myth is obviously also describing **the *life review* asreported by the 21ˢᵗ century NDE.** That now scientifically proven "life review" examines how the recentlydeceased feels about all the events that transpired in their immediately prior life. Obviously the surviving parts of the legend which still appear in the salvation myths of each of the world's religions must have came from prior knowledge of the NDE.

THE LIFE REVIEW: Although, it is not recalled by all NDE survivors, this life review occurs in t0henarrative accounts of hundreds of NDE's. Consistently it provides the participant with a review of all the significant events of their lifetime. Typically, it takes place shortly after the consciousness has left the physical body. After conclusion of this life review, the NDE continues with an important question which takes this form,

"Was it enough?" or "Have you learned enough that you are ready to move on?"

If the answer is "No", and the deceased individual still has unfinished business in the prior life, then the decision is made to return to that prior life, and reincarnate *in the same body*. Apparently, if the answer to this question is "YES", then the person moves on into the afterlife, because no one who answered "YES" has returned to the prior life to report an NDE.

EARLY CHRISTIANS BELIEVED IN THE NDE AND REINCARNATION: Ancient historic accounts of thislife review occurring in the NDE, have been discovered throughout the written literature. Indeed, several accounts of the NDE and life review were recorded by highly revered early Christian fathers, prior to the sixth century. which clearly agree with the modern NDE of the 21st Century, all telling the same story of what lies just beyond death. It has also become evident that earlier so called "pagan" civilizations knew of NDE's.

But, most shocking of all to the Christian faiths, and as I will shortly show, even the early Christians in the first three centuries after Christ, believed in reincarnation. Long before the Roman emperors, beginning with Constantine in 312 AD, imposed illiteracy and "group think" onto Western Christianity, including burning the Library at Alexandria the first time at the close of the 4th century (in 390AD).

This revision of Christianity finally culminated with emperor Justinian (not the Pope) outlawing belief in NDE's and transmigration (reincarnation) after 553AD.

COMPARISON OF RELIGIOUS SALVATION MYTH BELIEFS:

ORIGINAL EGYPTIAN   CURRENT AFTERLIFE BELIEFS OF MAJOR RELIGIONS

AFTERLIFE BELIEF ELEMENT	CHRISTIAN	MUSLIM	HINDU	BUDDHIST
1. Belief in Afterlife/Eternal life	YES	YES	YES	YES
2. Belief in Universal Salvation	NO	NO	YES	YES
3. Belief in Final Judgment	YES	YES	YES	NO
4. Belief in Crown of Life (Ankh)	YES	YES	YES	YES

And going to live with God

AFTERLIFE BELIEF ELEMENT	CHRISTIAN	MUSLIM	HINDU	BUDDHIST
5. Belief in Savior (Christ/Horus)	YES	NO	NO	NO
6. Belief in REINCARNATION [a,b]	NO	NO	YES	YES
7. Belief in Hell/Hades/underworld	YES	YES	NO	NO

ADD-ON BELIEFS

8.	Belief in Eternal Damnation	YES	YES	NO	NO

a Modern Christians misinterpret reincarnation to be "Born Again" which means having the Spirit "re-born" in the same physical body during a single physical life lived in the" one lifetime hypothesis".

b Two small Muslim sects do believe in reincarnation.

THE CHRISTIAN RELIGION IS THE PAGAN RELIGION: Although, after late fourth century the Roman church has officially condemned the 'Pagan" religions which preceded Christ. St. Augustine (November 13, 354 AD – August 28, 430 AD) The revered "Doctor of the Church, and Roman Catholic Bishop at Hippo in Carthage (Tunisia): wrote in 427 AD just three years before his death, that **this so-called "new" Christian religion was merely a rebranding of the pre-existing "pagan" religion:**

"That which is called the "Christian" religion existed among the ancients, and never did not exist, from the beginning of the human race until Christ came in the flesh, at whichtime the true religion WHICH ALREADY EXISTED began to be called Christianity"

St. Augustine, *Retractions*,

The above quote is taken from P.54 ***The Fathers of the Church, Saint Augustine, The Retractions***. *Brogan ©1968, Catholic University of America Press.* My personal copy caries the *Nihil Obstat* of John C. Selner, S.S., S.T.D. the Censor Librorum, and also the *Imprimatur*, of Patrick Cardinal A. O'Boyle, D.D. Archbishop of Washington D.C.

These are both official declarations by the Catholic Church that a book or pamphlet is FREE OFDOCTRINAL OR MORAL ERROR.

Augustine's "**Retractions**" were written as a clarification in 428 AD (c.e.), after publication of his seminal work the City of God in 427 AD (c.e.)

CHRISTIAN "LAST JUDGMENT": For example, the Christians believe that after death there is a final judgment where Christ, who like Horus in the papyrus, is believed to be the Son of God and born of a virgin, makes up for one's sins. At the Christian *Last Judgment*, if you are found righteous you are given the, "crown of life" (the ankh), and you then go to be with God (Isis & Osiris) in the heavens (the stars Sirius & Orion). But, if your sins are too great (i.e. your heart is too heavy) and you don't seek help from Christ (or Horus) to tip the balance in your favor (propitiation) then you are condemned to go down intothe underworld (Hades or hell). But, the Christian story forgets to allow additional lifetimes, which is the single missing element which appeared in the original myth.

20th Century Biblical scholarship on early Christianity has shown that reincarnation was the accepted doctrine in early Christianity. It is now well-documented that reincarnation was taught by the early Christian fathers, including Origen of Alexandria (185-254 AD) who is considered one of the greatest of the early Christian theologians.

NOTE: This means that the theology of the early Christian church of the 1st Century, which included reincarnation in their original Christian Salvation Myth, was IDENTICAL to the ancient Egyptian Salvation Myth from 2450 years earlier.

THE SINGLE LIFE THEORY: Unfortunately, politics has always been the force behind any form of "organized" religion.

125 years after St. Augustine, the Christian salvation myth was drastically reduced by the Roman emperor Justinian in order to allow only a single physical life. In 553AD, Emperor Justinian called the Fifth Ecumenical Council (2nd Council at Constantinople), the sitting Pope Viligis refused to even attend this council. At the ecumenical council itself, Justinian pushed for this rejection of reincarnation. Yet, the alleged adoption of these "Anathemas against Origen", which shunned all those who believed in reincarnation, were never actually recorded in the official minutes of this Ecumenical Council. So, from that record it appears that the attending bishops also did not want to grant the Emperor's desires.

Biblical scholars are not agreed on how these anathemas ever became connected with the 5th Council.

Understanding the underlying regional differences in Christianity raging between Byzantium (Constantinople), Rome and Africa (Carthage-Alexandria) a full 550 years after Christ, is important in comprehending how the Emperor played the factions against each other. And, helps to realize that the doctrinal Christianity which has been handed down to us by history, is indeed the watered down version which the Roman emperors needed to control the populace.

Justinian did not murder "heretics" because he was a zealous Christian, it was instead because he was consolidating his power over his subjects. Justinian simply claimed that these anathemas were in fact adopted at the council and then set about enforcing this change in doctrine and belief throughout the Roman Empire. Anyone who disagreed was simply killed. Justinian insured that those who continued the original beliefs, but whom he called, "Backsliders into paganism" were to be put to death.

WHAT DIFFERENCE DOES REINCARNATION MAKE? Jesus had clearly spoken in the canon gospels about multiple lifetimes But, now to suit the emperor, the church had to reinterpret Jesus remarks. Instead of being "born again" into multiple lifetimes to live in the "Life of the World to Come" (as it says in the Nicene Creed) where you could work out your karma and get it right with God. All in agreement with the ancient myth, a Christian believer now had to be spiritually "born again" in the same physical body during that single lifetime.

That original ancient religion which St. Augustine identified as the *true faith* had always allowed for second chances in additional lifetimes without threat of hellfire.

But, now to Justinian's single lifetime theory if you simply add "Original Sin" and there is no way to now escape hellfire unless you "kiss up" to the Roman Emperor's church. Emperor Justinian had no desire for true religion, only power and control.

Unfortunately, Islam which came along in 667 AD, is simply a more watered down version of this works righteous christianity of Justinian's

BRINGING BACK THE MISSING PIECES TO CHRISTIANITY AND ISLAM: Today, bringing back into

the Christian salvation myth and the Muslim salvation myth the knowledge which the Near-Death experience provides about transmigration of the consciousness (out of body reincarnation) and also the awareness that the life review includes no retribution, would make Christianity and Islam nearly identical with the Ancient Egyptian religion,

This acceptance of the restoration of reincarnation with no damnation, would allow Christians more life times to improve their spirituality, and the realization of future lifetimes in which Muslims could continue to improve their karma by following the five pillars of the faith and would overcome any need to 'HELP GOD" through jihad......

SAINT PAUL'S PERSONAL NEAR DEATH EXPERIENCE

St. Paul's description of his own Near-Death experience appears in 2nd Corinthians 12, where Saint Paul describes his own NDE, which occurred during the decade after Jesus death (about 35 AD), Although St. Paul tells the story in the third person, he is here speaking about his own conversion experience on the road to Damascus when he saw the light. He clearly is speaking about an *out-of-body* experience.

But, the church likes to use the second hand account related by Luke in the book of Acts, Luke was not present during this event, but was only a later follower of St. Paul. The being of light that St. Paul is supposedly speaking to on the road to Damascus is identified by Luke as Jesus, but, in St. Paul's own telling of the story in 2nd Corinthians he himself does not identify Jesus.

> *"I must go on boasting. Although there is nothing to be gained, I will go on to visions and revelations from the Lord. I know a man in Christ, who fourteen years ago was caught upto the third heaven. Whether it was in the body or out of the body, I do not know – God knows. And I know that this man, whether in the body or apart from the body I do notknow, but God knows, was caught up to paradise. He heard inexpressible things, things that man is not permitted to tell. I will boast about a man like that, but I will not boast about myself, except about my weaknesses. Even if I should choose to boast, I would not be a fool, because I would be speaking the truth. But I refrain, so no one will think more of me than is warranted by what I do or say."* St Paul's second letter to Corinthians 12:1-5 (NIV)

Saint Paul describes that he went out-of-body and "heard inexpressible things" just as happens in the modern NDE narratives where the experiencer travels out-of-body to commune with *the light,* and finds it to be ineffable.

For me, this was concrete evidence that I was not alone. Now, I knew that this revered apostle Saint Paul, a great Christian had also "been there" with *the light,* just as I had. This changed my opinion of him and I then began to study the *real* Saint Paul. No longer would I study him from the *proper* perspective of the Roman church and its prodigal child the Protestant church, but instead from the perspective of a fellow Near-Death survivor.

But, the NDE appears even further back in the Bible's Old Testament

Approx. 1000 BC – JOB'S NDE:

This narrative is related by the writer of the book of job, which most scholars believe was writtensometime after the reign of Solomon and prior to the first exile of the Hebrews (Babylonian Captivity), this means it could have been written as early as 931 BC and as late as 597 BC.

But, the events in Job's lifetime took place sometime between 2000 and 1000 BC, and most likely nearer to 1000 BC, having been transmitted *orally* prior to being written (which of course allows for great distortions to have inadvertently crept in).

The following verses from the NIV version of Job are a favorite of mine and also many other Christians. Often they are enthusiastically quoted on Easter Sunday. And, they come from the Hebrew of the Old Testament.

> "I know that my Redeemer lives, and that in the end he will stand upon the earth. And after my skin has been destroyed, yet, in my

flesh I will see God. I myself will see him with my own eyes – I and not another – How my heart yearns within me."

Job 19:25-27 (NIV – text as printed)

But, several ancient Hebrew texts for these same verses provide alternative translations. Naturally, the NIV translators have chosen those translations that fit their current chosen dogma of, a single lifetime and "resurrection of the physical body".

Yet, when I examined the alternative texts, which the NIV mentions in the foot notes, I found that **those alternative versions actually agree in all details with what NDE has been reporting for thousandsof years**.

When I worked out the alternative translation I found that it contains no resurrection of the physical body but only resurrection of the spirit. Here is how the alternative Hebrew text reads:

> "I know that my Redeemer lives, and that in the end he will stand upon my grave. After I awake, though this body has been destroyed, then (while) yet apart from my flesh (i.e. out- of-body), I will see God. I myself will see him with my own eyes – I and not another – How my heart yearns within me."

Job 19:25-27 (NIV - Alternative Hebrew texts, as listed in NIV foot notes

This earlier text shows clearly that Job is describing what he learned during an NDE. Certainly, all theconditions for an NDE were present for him, as described earlier in the book of Job.

- He is very sick,
- His entire body is covered with boils and
- He has wasted away to skin and bones.

The details of his disease are sketchy but it is obviously a walking death condition and he has come very close to death (i.e. Near-Death proximity). But, seeing that Job relates the same gnosis which Near-Deathsurvivors return with today verifies that Job had an actual NDE with several "standard" items of the NDE gnosis were shared by Job:

1. He knows that after death he will be *out-of-body*….. "apart from my flesh".

2. He knows his body will be destroyed, but he will still live on without it

3. He describes the experiences much as it has been described in the NDE reports "apart from my flesh I will see God, I myself will see

God with my own eyes".

4. He knows he will see *the light* (see God).

5. He knows that he has eternal life and cannot wait to get back there.

Further, Job's remark in Job 14:14; ***"If a man die, shall he live again? All the days of my appointed time will I wait, till my change comes."***, reminds me of my own NDE impression that, ***"Yet, a little while, and you can return to the Light"***.

SCRIPTURAL SUPPORT FOR REINCARNATION:

There are many Bible verses which are suggestive of reincarnation. One episode in particular from thehealing miracles of Christ seems to point to reincarnation:

FIRST: we have John 9:1

"And as he was passing by, he saw a man blind from birth. And his disciples asked him, 'Rabbi, who has sinned, this man or his parents, that he should be born blind?" Jesus answered, *'Neither has this man sinned, nor his parents, but the works of God were to be made manifest in him.'"* (John 9:1)

The disciples ask the Lord if the man himself could have committed the sin that led to his blindness. Given the fact that the man has been blind from birth, we are confronted with a provocative question. When could he have made such transgressions as to make him blind at birth? The only conceivable answer is in some prenatal state. The question as posed by the disciples explicitly presupposes prenatal existence. It will also be noted that Christ says nothing to dispel or correct the presupposition. Here is incontrovertible support for a doctrine of human pre-existence.

SECOND: Matthew 11:13-14

This is the episode where Jesus identifies John the Baptist as Elijah.

> ***"For all the prophets and the law have prophesied until John. And if you are willing to receive it,*** *he is Elijah who was to come.***"** ***(Matthew 11:13-14)***

THIRD: Matthew 17:10-13

> ***"And the disciples asked him, saying, 'Why then do the scribes say that Elijah must come first?' But he answered them and said,*** *'Elijah indeed is to come and will restore all things. But I say to you that Elijah has come already, and they did not know him, but*

did to him whatever they wished. So also shall the Son of Man suffer at their hand.' **Then the disciples understood that he had spoken of John the Baptist.** " (Matthew 17:10-13)

Here again is a clear statement of preexistence.

Consequently, Despite the edict of the Emperor Justinian agains Origen, there is firm and explicittestimony for pre-existence in both the Old and the New Testament of the Bible. Indeed, the ban against Origen notwithstanding, contemporary Christian scholarship acknowledges pre-existence as one of the elements of Judeo-Christian theology.

As for the John the Baptist-Elijah episode, there can be little question as to its purpose. By identifying theJohn Baptist as Elijah, Jesus is identifying himself as the Messiah. Throughout the gospel narrative there are explicit references to the signs that will precede the Messiah.

"Behold I will send you Elijah the prophet, before the coming of the great and dreadful day of the Lord." (Malachi 4:5)

This is one of the many messianic promises of the Old Testament. One of the signs that the true Messiahhas come, according to this passage from Malachi, is that he be preceded by a forerunner, by Elijah. Although the Bible also contains other re-incarnation passages, these Elijah-John passages constitute clear proof of reincarnation:

1. The Old Testament prophesied that Elijah himself (not someone "like" him or someone "similar" to him, but Elijah *himself*) would return before the advent of the Messiah.

2. Jesus declared that John the Baptist was Elijah who had returned, stating bluntly "Elijah has come".

Now, based on these passages alone, either (A) or (B) following must be true:

A. **John the Baptist *was* Elijah himself**, meaning that Elijah *had* reincarnated. If true, thenreincarnation must belong in Christian theology, and the entire doctrinal Engerpretation of "Life After Death" and the "Last Day Resurrection", must be radically revised, or...

B. **John the Baptist *was not* Elijah himself,** meaning that Elijah himself had *not* returned. But, If this is so, then either:

1. The Old Testament prophecy about Elijah returning before the Messiah failed to come to pass (meaning that **Biblical prophecy is fallible**), or

2. Jesus was not the Messiah.

Basically, **What do you want to believe?** One of the following A, B, or C, must logically be true:

A. Reincarnation is true, or

B. Jesus was not the Messiah, or

C. The prophecies of the Bible are unreliable.

As surely as two and two make four, one of the above must be true. At any rate, the passage in which Jesus says in no uncertain terms that John *was* Elijah is "overt" and direct:

CONSIDERING REINCARNATION One of the most controversial religious discussions in the West is about reincarnation. Both Western science and Western religions (All those originating in the Roman Empire), are vehemently opposed to the idea of multiple lifetimes. Yet, the majority view in the world is that we live multiple lifetimes.

As stated in **The Weighing of the Heart**, The West's single lifetime view was imposed by Emperor Justinian after 553 AD. But, it was not the original position of the Early Christians nor the pagan Greek religions prior to that. So, if you haven't read that already, please do so you can understand the rest of this Appendix 2.

Here is the feed back we have from two discarnate souls who reported back from the other side.

FREDRICK H.W. MEYERS: One of the best considerations of reincarnation was given by psychicexplorer Fredrick H.W. Myers speaking from the afterlife, through the mediumship of Geraldine Cummins:

"When I was on earth, I belonged to a group-soul, but its branches and the spirit — which might be compared to the roots — were in the invisible. Now, if you would understand psychic evolution, this group-soul must be studied and understood. For instance, it explains many of the difficulties that people will assure you can be removed only by the doctrine of reincarnation. You may think my statement is frivolous, but the fact that we do appear on earth to be paying for the sins of another

life, is in a certain sense, true. It is our life and yet not our life. In other words, a soul belonging to the group of which I am a part, lived that previous life which built up for me the framework of my earthly life, lived it before I had passed through the gates of birth."

Myers further explained that the group soul might contain twenty souls, a hundred, or a thousand. "The number varies. It is different of each man. But what the Buddhist would call the karma I hadbrought with me from a previous life is, very frequently, not that of my life, but the life of a soul thatpreceded me by many years on earth and left for me the pattern which made my life. I too, wove apattern for another of my group during my earthly career".

Myers added that the Buddhist's idea of rebirth, of man's continual return to earth, is but a half truth. *"And often a half truth is more inaccurate than an entire misstatement. I shall not live again onearth, but a new soul, one who will join our group, will shortly enter into the pattern or karma, I havewoven for him on earth.*

FRANCIS BANKS, p. 83-84 of Testimony of Light said:

"No doubt when I am more proficient in the study of individual lives and their results, together with the life courses of nations and their results, food or apparently not good, which have been set in motion through the Law of Cause and Effect, I shall be better able to appreciate how the Divine Pattern of individual growth and group growth is linking up from life to life and from age to age. It is only logical to assume that we take up, as it were, where we left off in a previous trial of strength and weakness. This presupposes a chain of lives, of experiences, or reincarnation in its little understood form.

"But, I am more than convinced, as I observe stories of effort and success and failure, that thesouls needs to 'project' some part of Itself back into the denser environment of earth in repeated attempts to master the trials and stresses of those vibrations. But, which part of Itself, and whetherit is always the same part, is still a mystery, and must remain so until we have advanced much in wisdom and insight."

"After talking with savants I have been privileged to meet here, there seems to be no reason for me to change my earthly acceptance of the fact of repeated lives, and therefore of a possibility of pre- viewing the presentable future, even when in a material body. When a soul (or that portion of a soulwhich seeks enlargement of experience) reincarnates, it is at a certain stage in its Divine Blueprint. It will seek a trial of strength in some experiences, a leading rule in human affairs in others, an emotional compensation in personal relationships and so forth."

APPENDIX 3
HELEN & MY PERSONAL JOURNEY TOMEDIUMSHIP:

After the NDE changed everything in my psychic nature, I had to overcome all the erroneous religious nurture learned as a child, and all the erroneous science learned as a physics student. Raised in a fundamentalist Baptist family, it was never a goal in my wildest dreams to become apsychic medium. Indeed, my mother taught us that talking to the dead was *"of the devil"*.

Consequently, my conversion to this occult persuasion was not easy. Indeed, *"Spirit had to kill me to get my attention"*. and then after becoming an intuitive and beginning work as an Evidential Medium, Spirit later gave me a series of seizures to *"re-arrange my psyche"*.

But as my spirituality increased so did the synergisms, miracles and unexplainablecoincidences. Everything I relate throughout this book actually happened.

After having my NDE in **1970** (see Appendix 4) **I had acquired the first two clues:**

1. **That the consciousness could survive while out-ot-body. and therefore,**

2. **That *Post-Mortem Consciousness Survival* must be real.**

I had personally journeyed to somewhere outside my body, and outside this physical world. Therefore all the religious views about consciousness survival and an afterlife which I had been taught as a child no longer made sense, and neither did the materialist physics I had been taught.

Also, from that NDE I had gained an ability to empathize with everyone around me…. Yet, to survive in the working world, build a career, raise a family, etc. I had to figure out how to shut down that empathy. You simply don't do to well in a design office when you can psychically readeveryone else's mind. So, I held all that back.

But, once the Universe starts you down a path of enlightenment, you won't be allowed to turn back. It was long after I completed college while raising a family and still building a career in 1988 that I received **the third and fourth clues:**

1. **There are *Post-Mortem Surviving Consciousnesses* who want to communicate with us from the other side. And**

2. **That they will communicate through dreams and intuition.**

Whether we payattention is our problem.

This happened when I personally encountered a surviving consciousness haunting the scene of his murder 96 years later. The evidence in its order of presentation made these facts undeniable. The following story, *"Charlie's Ghost"* is an excerpt from in my first book *The Death Experience ©2012.*

CHARLIE'S GHOST – Sometimes life leads us into events which provide a gnosis whichwe then can no longer deny, because there is simply no other explanation. Such a personal encounter with an "earthbound" disincarnate consciousness unfolded in the fall of 1988during a weekend stay at a bed & breakfast with my first wife, Anna.

The encounter was entirely unexpected, but the facts surrounding the encounter made it completely undeniable that After-Death communication is very real. The week after it happened I wrote it up as the short story which follows.

The cold November wind blowing up from Admiralty Inlet skittered the dry leaves across the gravel parking lot as the November moon shown through forlorn tree branches surrounding the vintage house at *Crockett Farm*, a little bed and breakfast above Keystone Harbor on Whidbey Island, in Washington State.

Pebbles crunched in the chill as Anna and I approached the front door. We had come for a weekend to this pastoral retreat, hoping to re-kindle some romance after 17 years of married life. I had called ahead to tell state that we'd be arriving late after the other guests would have already retired. So, having arrived about 11 pm, the innkeeper quietly showed us to our room, whispering, **"I'll show you the rest of the house tomorrow….. You're staying two nights anyway aren't you?"**

"Yes, see you in the morning for coffee", I whispered back, as we placed our luggage into the downstairs master bedroom just off the entry hall.

"Coffee in the Library at 7:30 to 8:30. Breakfast at 9 in the dining room", he said softlyas I closed the door to our room.

Shortly, we retired to the Victorian quilts of the queen-sized bed. Anna slept near the bay window where the moonlight eerily sifting through the leafless branches moving in the night's offshore breeze. Repeatedly that night, I was re-awakened by Anna's tossing and turning.

After an imperfect rest, we awoke with the sunrise, and later, as I shaved and she worked with her curling iron sharing the single bathroom mirror, she suddenly said, **"I had the strangest dream last night. And, it kept waking me up,……. and then it kept returning when I got back to sleep……… I must have dreamed it four or five times."**….

After years with her, I knew she was sensitive to subtle vibes, and could read people's feelings from across a room. Much as I had so easily done just after the NDE. She also often had wild night visions that would portend coming events. So, my interest was now heightened anticipating what she might now reveal.

"Well……" she said, "There were two elderly men running up and down the stairs in the hall,……. and they were shooting at each other with rifles, or long guns But,

they did not know we were here in the downstairs bedroom",… she said **"The continuing violence agitated me and woke me up, again and again   but, each time I fell back asleep, then they returned again with their guns"**.

"Strange that it kept coming back", I mused   "Shall   we   get some coffee?"

In the library we met some of the other guests chatting amiably, and shortly, we were all seated in the dining room. After everyone had been served, Bob, the innkeeper, began to tell us all about the house. He was an experienced story teller with a Masters in English Literature and he easily held everyone's rapt attention.

"Colonel Walter Crockett was a Virginian who moved out here in 1852-53, along with the more famous Colonel Ebey, who homesteaded just to the north on Ebey Prairie. Crockett homesteaded the lands surrounding Crockett Lake. Colonel Ebey was killed by the Haida Indians in 1854 and they stole his head taking it with them back to the Queen Charlotte Islands (Haida Gwaii) off the west coast of British Columbia.

He continued these interesting details of local history until he came to the 1890's.when he said,

"Charlie Crockett, moved back into the farm house after he sold his homestead to the U.S. Army Coastal Artillery so they could build Fort Casey on Admiralty Head, where you see the gun

emplacements today......

I wondered about how much the government had to have paid Charlie Crockett to acquire theentire homestead as Bob continued his story.

"Colonel Crockett had left this farm house to his youngest son Walter Jr.... Apparently, neither son had ever married, and both were reclusive. Some folks said Charlie was actually an anti-social hermit type". The innkeeper continued.

"Then in 1896, a few years after Charlie had moved back into this hose with Walter Jr., **Charlie committed suicide shooting himself with a shotgun in the upstairs bedroom",** *... ... ...*

Suddenly, Anna jumped out of her chair, and screamed, *"No..., they shot at each other, both of them were running up and down the stairs..... I dreamed about it all lastnight !!!"*

The innkeeper's mouth fell open, and he stopped in mid-sentence............ Recovering, he said sternly, *"Ma'am, I don't want to hear any more about your dream"* ....

But, with that he also abruptly ended his tale. He excused himself and retired to the kitchen. He did not return to continue his narrative. Obviously, he was very upset by her response. Uncomfortably, the other guests hurriedly finished their breakfasts in silence and shortly they all left for their rooms, with no one dallying for a second cup of coffe.

Anna and I now drifted into the library without speaking......... **"So much for a romantic weekend"**, I thought to myself,....... **"Now she has gotten our host mad at us"**.

We refilled our coffee mugs and sat in silence looking at the shelved library books..... not speaking, we pretended to read........ The single night guests hurriedly checked out, paidtheir bills, and drove away leaving us in the great house alone with the proprietors.

"Oh there you are", said the innkeeper after the last guest had left. **"I must apologize for my stern reaction to your dream, and I also must explain".**

"Truthfully, Charlie's death, was only OFFICIALLY LISTED as a suicide, which is also how I choose to tell the story, but it has always been suspected by all the local historians that it was really a murder.......

"The Sheriff did not declare him dead until 24 hours later, because his brother Walter Jr. did not report the death until the day after he died

Charlie lay on the floor up

there, while his blood ran down through the floorboards into the ceiling of the bathroom off the master bedroom where you are staying.

"So, when you spoke this morning, I was not at all mad at you. My ire was instead directed at Charlie, or his ghost. I got upset because we believed that we had previously exorcised his ghost out of the house. But apparently, he was still able to influence you. You are the first sign we've had of Charlie in over two and a half years.

"Because you are staying through tomorrow you might want to check out this whole story in the local cemetery, library and museum. Later, I'll tell you more, but please keep the "haunting" a secret. I advertise this place as a peaceful pastoral setting for a romantic retreat and not as a "haunted house".

Suddenly, the weekend had reversed itself again as we now had a detective adventure to pursue together. Now, we were involved in all the intrigue of a John Grissom novel.... Excitedly, we drove toward Coupeville in search of clues.

At the cemetery we discovered that Charlie was buried at the farthest end of the family plot,as if he had been disowned, but Walter Jr. was buried right up next to Mom and Dad.

At the museum we found odd references to the "suicide" often in quotation or parenthesis, as if it were not actually a suicide. We pieced together the story that apparently, the Sheriff had chosen to declare it a suicide in order to avoid an expensive forensic investigation and trial. What would have been the point of convicting an elderly man to a life sentence when the criminal might die himself before the trial was even over. Instead of wasting tax payer's dollars, the Sheriff had simply declared it a "suicide" Case closed.

In the late afternoon we returned to the farmhouse and the innkeeper, Bob, told us a great deal more about his own experience while we sipped wine and enjoyed the sunset across theinlet.

"We have been open three years now, and when I first bought the farm", Bob said, "Wehad visions for a bed and breakfast much like you see today. But, on the first day we were here, while we were out chopping weeds, a neighbor came by and said, 'I see youbought the haunted house', at which point I knew we were in trouble".

"Since that time I have personally interviewed everyone who is still living who ever owned the house. Back in the 1970's the same psychic who had assisted the New YorkPolice with the Son of Sam murderer, came and held a séance at the farmhouse. The psychic found that Charlie was killed rather than committing suicide, and apparently did not yet know that he was dead, which is why he hasn't yet moved on.

"A couple who owned the house sometime after that, and lived here for about ten years, said that on cold evenings, if there was a fire laid in the fireplace, Charlie would often light it while they were out watching the sunset. They also said that Charlie liked to close the library door, and would often wind clocks. Their mother-in-law once sawan apparition of Charlie in the Library and ran out of their house refusing to visit them again.

"All of the prior owners tell similar stories. So, we hired the Anglican Church to come and do an exorcism in each room of the house. And, since that time we have not seen any sign of Charlie in the house. At least, that is, not until this morning when Anna toldus about her dream.

"The unsettling part of this is that, after I thought about it I realized that I never told youanything about the house, and never gave you a tour when you came in late, and neither did my wife. So, I was wondering just what did you know about Charlie before you came here?"

"We had never heard of him", I said, *"All we knew was that this was a peacefulpastoral place, and that it was a bed and breakfast on the island. We had never even heard of Colonel Crockett,… although I did know who Colonel Ebey was".*

"Just as I supposed", he said. *"So, then this almost qualifies as an actual 'sighting",he mused, "The first one since the exorcism. So, it appears Charlie is still here, we have just banished him from being inside the house, but he was still able to communicate with Anna through the bay window on the southeast of your room. It wasfascinating how sure she was that it was a killing and not a suicide".*

"The hardest thing was to get rid of the blood", Bob said, *"the ceiling of the master bathroom was a blue enamel, and when we first painted it with latex the water in the latex soaked up into the floor boards and loosened up the dried blood in the wood fibers (which had been there over 90 years), the blood colored the latex with a stain. Eventually, we had to remove the latex, paint over it with an oil based product to contain the blood stain, and then etch the surface with an acid and repaint with the latex, just to get the white ceiling you have been seeing in there".*

As he took his leave he said *"Again, please keep this quiet so as not to disturb the other guests".*

That second night there was no sign of Charlie and we left the following morning.

After we returned home, I asked the Pastor of my Lutheran congregation in Seattle, what the church said about Ghosts. He told me that the church does not have any precise doctrine on Ghosts. He said that he personally felt the often reported phenomena of Ghosts mightactually be, **"Souls of persons who had not yet discovered that they were dead".**

But, he cautioned me that anything else the church might come up with was strictly speculation, and so they carefully avoided creating a doctrine about this.

On the other hand, in my later research I found that the Hasidic Jews have been studying thisphenomena and working on this doctrine for several hundred years and have formulated some fairly firm conclusions. Here is what Rabbi Yonssan Gershom said in his 1992 book, **Beyond the Ashes** where he says that there do appear to be some common factors that hold spirits earthbound.......falling into three main categories:

1. **The spirit does not know that it is dead:** While it may seem incredible that someone could die and not realize it, this does happen. Such a soul often has no belief inlife after death, and therefore reasons that, because it still has consciousness it cannot really be dead. Also if the death happens suddenly, the transition to the afterlife can be sofast that the soul does not realize it has taken place.

    Note: My own personal NDE (1970) left me with memories of waking up with the light, but never passing through a tunnel or leaving the body (I definitely remember returning back into the body) but I had no memory of my actual death. Consequently, I can understand that a surviving consciousness could be deadand not realize it.

2. **The soul has stereotyped expectations of the next world:** Many people simply do not realize that all religious descriptions of the afterlife are only metaphors or speculations, and when they die they expect their beliefs to be fulfilled literally. For example, the absence of a Heaven with angels plucking harps, may cause some Christian souls to remain earth bound because they will not accept the help of the spirits who have come to meet them. And in some cases may believe that the helping spirits aredemons in disguise, just because that is what

they were taught to expect by their overly confident preachers who are so sure their ancient speculations are correct.

> ***Note:*** *Also, Edward C. Randall (1906) assisted numerous earthbound souls to move on during his years working with Mrs. French. He says that half of every evenings sessions for over 15 years were devoted entirely to this "mission work", assisting earthbound spirits to move on towards the light, and in several cases there were Christians literally, as Rabbi Gershom said, waiting for the savior to show up and believing that the spirits of their dead relatives were imposters.*

3. **The soul has unfinished business**: This is the most difficult type of earthbound spirit to work with, because in order for a soul to be released into the light it must want to go. As long as it feels that it has not completed its work here on earth, the soul will continue to be attached to persons, places, or things in the material world.

> ***Note****: This is the reason that most Near-Death survivors return to their physical bodies, they had unfinished business, here in the physical which they return to complete before finally moving on.*

At the time, although I knew from my own NDE that some form of afterlife existed. I also knewthat during out of body experiences NDE participants had always found it impossible to communicate directly with the living here in the normally observed physical reality. So I had assumed until then that it was not possible for a disincarnate consciousness to communicate with those still living in the physical, and also that After-Death communication must simply be imagined. Consequently, what I had experienced at Crockett Farm was something that,

"I would not have believed if I hadn't personally been through it".

In fact, if Anna had not told me about her dream *before* breakfast and prior to hearing Bob's stories, then I would not have been ***left by the circumstances with no choice but to believe it.***

Fortunately, the sequence of events left me no other explanation other than that it was actually some form of valid After-Death communication (ADC) phenomena.

1. It was obvious that Anna knew parts of the story of Charlie's murder (which occurred 96 years earlier in that house), and she knew it before anyone told herabout it.

2. Further, she told me the details of what she had seen in her dream before anyone had told either of us about the events in that house.......

For me, ***this again changed everything*** Plausible deniability was no longer one of my options I now knew that at least some form of communication from the Afterlife directly from disincarnate spirits to ordinary individuals was valid.

The result was that this unplanned episode, had forced my mind into contemplation on the issue of ***After-Death communications (ADC)***, and how that might relate to the things I had learnedin the Near-Death experience. This gnosis began to accelerate me down the path of exploration which I had begun with my NDE.

I realized at the time that either Anna was a deeply feeling person who could absorb the story through what I would later discover is called psychometry, or she had mediumistic abilities and Charlie's spirit was actually communicating with her.

At that time, as a scientist, I began to conjecture that the violence in the hallway may have forever altered the energy of the house as stored in some universal recording device (Akashic Field), in such a way that she could still detect it 96 years later, something like a steadily playingvideo.

After much additional research I would later allow the possibility that Anna might have established a p-car resonance and quantum coherence with the DNA in the dried blood which had soaked into the floor/ceiling over the bathroom, and which contains the quantum hologram of the event, which can be read magnetically, similar to an fMRI scan.

On the other hand, and now that I have myself studied to be an *Evidential Medium* what still today seems to me to be the most plausible explanation is that,....**IT ACTUALLY WAS CHARLIE'S GHOST,** a disincarnate consciousness surviving post-mortem, and still living there and whispering in Anna's ear using ESP and her intuition to send images into her dreams. This gave me the fifth clue:

5. Some surviving consciousnesses are earthbound because they have not yet figured out that they have passed on. This easily explains most of the poltergeist hauntings occurring worldwide.

So, at this point I was now fully convinced from my personal NDE and this experience that our individual consciousness survives physical death. Yet, without any objective scientific proofs to back it up, it was all a bit overwhelming. So, I continued through my working career, and the divorce which followed several years later, sending my daughter to college, etc., without ever having any personal needs to communicate with anyone on the other side.

But, when the Universe has started you on a path, you will complete your destiny. Thirteen years later, having moved on to a new relationship, and now living in San Francisco, my sweetheart and second wife Gale gifted us both with a trip to New Orleans to celebrate my Birthday. It was February 2001, just six months prior to 9/11. Late the following Tuesday eveningShe and I were enjoying decaf coffee on the square of the French Quarter, when we sawseveral psychic-mediums setting up their tables in front of the church ready to tell fortunes.

We both decided we wanted to get a Tarot reading, yet at the time those street peddlers did not appear "professional" enough to Gale, who herself reads palms and whose previously deceasedmother, Helen had often consulted with mediums during her lifetime. It was late, so we set the idea aside for the following day.

In the morning we asked around in the shops near "the Quarter" to know just who and where we could find a real "professional" medium. Several people had quickly suggested **Otis** at the "**Bottom of the Cup Tea Room**". A true professional Otis took credit cards, and so we both booked for that afternoon. February 14, 2001. Otis gave each of us a 30 minute reading, which he also tape recorded for us. We both sat in on each other's reading. Gale got a marvelous reading from Otis. But, then came the block buster.

Otis who is wonderfully off hand, quietly and carefully scrutinized my palms, then spread the Tarot several times, almost as if not believing what he was reading in the earlier spreads, he kept placing repeated layouts, and then re-shuffling, and placing them again, and yet again, as ifhe was trying to make sure of the precise reading. ...... I patiently waited nearly 10 minutes before he spoke... Finally, looking me in the eye, he calmly informed me of his interpretation that:

"You have stars on the mount of Jupiter on both hands..... "You came into the world to heal people.......

"A new cycle began with your birthday this year (I had not told him it was two days earlier) **and will continue for the next nine years** (until 2010)...... **After that you will go deep into subconscious depths where you dig and go real deep......**

"Don't worry when that time comes, you will be fine, you are just following your spiritual path......

"After that nine years are over there will be a lot of new things coming into your life, with much travel in order to follow your spiritual path....

"You have much more rationality in you than most Aquarians (obviously he knew intuitively when my birthday was) *who are usually space cadets..... People trust you because you are you, and you don't have to do anything but be you......*

"If people don't understand you it is because they are still asleep, but you are fully awake. ...... Don't waste your energy on those who don't understand the occult world, YOU ARE ALREADY A MASTER IN THIS.... YOU ALREADY HAVE ITMASTERED.....

"Obstacles will be removed, ... and you will always land on your feet. You have 'Samati' the peace of mind which all men seek, because you already possess all the things that money cannot buy....... Eyes are the window to the soul, and we (you and I, Alan) *are everybody's mirror........*

"THINK ABOUT DOING SEMINARS, IT WOULD BE A GOOD OUTLET FOR YOU.

People will talk to you because they trust your instincts. They trust your feelings,they comprehend that you are a wonderful, wonderful counselor that is fully in tune with people.......

"Here he again looked at my hands, "THE HANDS OF THE ANGEL OF MERCY" Stars on the mounds of Jupiter, increased soul, marks of concern, lines ofsympathy mark of mercy." All these quotes are transcribed from the recording Otis made.

Shaken to the core, by the import of this reading, I did not know what to do or think.... My mind quickly asked,

"Does he tell everyone that?"...... " My God, I am an engineer and a scientist not amedium and healer."....

I had never in my wildest dreams been one of my career goals to be a medium or a healer, nor to talk to the other side......

Yet, because of what Otis' predictions portend, and in my thorough confusion, I was glad that Gale the love of my life, and who is also a palm reader had also sat in on my reading with Otis, so that she also heard it live from the oracle's own mouth.

So, I went on with my life, leaving Otis' predictions in the back of my mind but not really thinking about them. Besides, he had said all that was 9 years off Plenty of time to think about it later.

Yet, looking back All of this prediction has come to pass on that same time schedule.

Yet, his use of the Tarot had been so impressive to me that I decided to study the Tarot myself, even buying a text book *Tarot for the Apprentice*, by Eileen Connolly and a deck of Tarot cards from Otis' shop And, I began studying the Tarot and meditating on it several times a week

from 2001 through 2005. Still working as a Naval Architect and traveling from shipyard to shipyard to maintain my career in the dying field of ship design. Yet, I continued to be amazed how accurate the Tarot always was both for me and when I would read Tarot for other people atNew Year's Eve parties.

Working with the Tarot, I got **the sixth clue:**

6. Belief creates people's reality.

As a tarot reader, I quickly noticed that when people believed the Tarot was real, then I would get amazingly accurate readings. On the other hand, if they believed it was a hoax, I would get erroneous readings, or just nothing of value.

Later, I would collate this finding with the observer principle of *Quantum Electro-Dynamics*, but I learned about it with the Tarot, not physics.

So, it was clear to me that (just as I would find later in mediumship) the mind of the sitter (the one receiving the reading) and not the mind of the reader (the medium or Tarot reader) determined what the quality of the reading would be...... The medium/tarot reader was just the instrument, if the sitter's heart was open and they were working from love (spirit) then the reading would be exactly on target.

But, if their heart was closed and they were working from fear (ego) nothing would work right. If they were a skeptic "testing" whether Tarot or mediumship was real, then the entire reading would short circuit. This is what Otis meant when he told me:

"If people don't understand you it is because they are still asleep, but you are fully awake. Don't waste your energy on those who don't understand the occult world"

Then in 2004 I began writing my first book, "***The Death Experience: What it is like when you die***" ©*2012*, describing my personal NDE (see Appendix 4). This writing was a long and cathartic process to get the story out, a struggle that all NDE experiencers go through with what St. Paul recalled as "inexpressible things", and so the completion took six years of re-writes and two more years to get it published.

Then, in 2006, while still working on the book, but nearing what I thought would be retirement. I decided to study mediumship "as a scientist", yet not connecting this to Otis' prediction.

My scientific rationale was that:

1. if my consciousness could survive outside my body, during my NDE, then anyone's consciousness could do the same.

2. I had seen undeniable evidence of a surviving consciousness haunting a murder scene 96 years later. Consequently, there must be other surviving consciousnesses still alive in the afterlife, and we may be able to communicate with them.

3. I had found with the Tarot, that the results of the reading depend on the sitter and noton the reader.

However, due to my having been raised by fundamentalist Baptist parents who believed that conducting a seance was "***of the devil***", I was still afraid of the Spiritualists. So, how does one become a medium without getting involved with other mediums and seances?

I cleverly researched the Internet until I found that the ***National Spiritualist Association of Churches-NSAC*** had a correspondence course in mediumship. "***Wow, a way to study Mediumship and Spiritualism without actually having to become a Spiritualist***".

So, since it looked safe enough, I signed up in March of 2006 with their

Morris Pratt Institute. It was a rigorous course which included a great deal of reading about Spiritualism, Healing and Mediumship, and of course to be a thorough scientist, I wanted to read all the "suggested furtherreading" in addition to the required reading. Therefore, I took a few extra years to complete the program. I was also an anomaly with in the NSAC, They strive to get their regular members to study the course and most simply don't, yet here was this outsider avidly studying to be a medium. I finally graduated in April 2013 receiving three graduate certificates as;

- A Spiritualist Minister,

- A Spiritualist Healer and,

- A Spiritualist Medium.

By 2010, after studying four years in the Morris Pratt Program, I had began attending an educational circle at the Golden Gate Spiritualist Church in San Francisco, but only as an occasional walk in visitor.

Yet, without realizing it I was right on schedule, this began the unfolding that Otis had forecast in2001 would begin 9 years later.

After graduating from Morris Pratt in 2013 and in order to practice my mediumship, I finally joined that Spiritualist Church, and began to demonstrate from the platform as a medium at several Spiritualist churches.

Immediately I found that I was very good at getting unknown evidence. Like the name of the unknown spirit, their personality, and details of their life, like color of their hair, etc. After my first time on the platform at Golden Gate Spiritualist Church, in May 2013, the Organist said "***Alan, you need to go to Arthur Findlay College and study Evidential Mediumship***".

During my studies with Morris Pratt Institute I had also begun daily meditations which included writing daily journal pages. Having semi-retired in 2008, in 2011, Gale and I began making ocean cruises, and on these various cruises I began to wake up between 3:00 and 4:00 ameach morning and would go up to the lido deck to meditate and read my tarot cards and writemy journal pages in my computer as I watched the sunrise. Indeed, I often completed the reading and correspondence lessons for my Morris Pratt mediumship studies on these cruises, and also completed chapters in my book. But, the 3:00 am wake up to meditate continued whether I was at sea, or at home in San Francisco.

In 2012 on Cunard's *Queen Victoria* I sailed during May to Scandinavia and St. Petersburg Russia, while I edited my book for publication later that summer. On this cruise I was doing my normal daily meditations at 3:00 am and in Stockholm part of Otis' prediction came to fruition,

> "After that (after 2010) you will go deep into subconscious depths where you dig and go real deep. <u>Don't worry when that time</u> (after 2010) <u>comes, you will be fine</u>, you are just following your spiritual path."

May 14th, 2012 as the Queen Mary 2 was arriving in Stockholm, Sweden I had a seizure at about 3:00 AM, something that had never occurred before.

Gale called the EMT's, and I clearly remember repeatedly saying to the EMT's, as they slapped my face trying to wake me up, ***"No I can't come back just now"*****.....**

They moved me to the ship's hospital. When we docked at about 8:00 AM, I was immediately discharged by ambulance to the Emergency Ward at *Karolinska University Hospital.* The hospital ran EEG's and CTI brain scans, but could find no anomalies, and finally the medical staff told me that I was fine and could continue my vacation. So, to the Ship's absoluteamazement, we arrived back to the ship by taxi and were on board *Queen Victoria* before she sailed at 4 pm, with no further complications. And no more seizures.

Later, after returning home to San Francisco, I suffered a second seizure (again occurring in themiddle of the night, while I was asleep). This time Gale, did not call the EMT's, but waited patiently till I, "got over it",.... after all, the Stockholm Hospital had found nothing wrong with me.

But, Gale did seek a reading from a local psychic-medium that she already knew, Leanne Thomas, (Trained in the tradition of Lisa Williams who is a tutor, at *Arthur Findlay College)*, to find out what was happening with me. Leanne confidently told her:

> "Oh, Alan is just going out of body to the other side to get downloads of information...... The struggle or seizure is simply because ever since his NDE he really does not want to come back to physical life, ... and so he finds it difficult to re-enter his physical body......

> "He will have two more of these seizures and then they will not recur again.....He will simply re-program himself not to resist the return to the physical body"......

This agreed precisely with what Otis had said previously:

> "Don't worry <u>when that time comes, you will be fine</u>, you are just following your spiritual path."

As Leanne pre-cognitively predicted, this is exactly what happened, there were precisely two more seizures with the last occurring in November 2012.

Note: *I later met Dr. Brian Sackett, Ph.D who had experienced a similar series of four seizures as he began to work with the other side. We commiserated that this must simply be part of the price of real mediumship, Spirit has to re-arrange your brain.*

Both, Otis' and Leanne's predictions and analysis of what was going on with me agreed, ***"You will be fine"*** and a dozen years later I am still "just fine", with no additional seizures.

So, not to worry, I continued with my life, and my practice of the early morning meditations. In the following spring of 2013 we made an additional 35 day cruise on Cunard's *Queen Elizabeth* from San Pedro to New Zealand and return. I used this voyage to complete the remaining final year of lessons for the Morris Pratt Mediumship Course, and turned in my papers for graduation when I got home in early March 2013. I received my Morris Pratt graduation certificates in April 2013. Now, I joined the congregation and began to demonstrate as a "student" medium on the platform at Golden Gate Spiritualist Church, in San Francisco.

A PREVIOUSLY UNKNOWN DECEASED GIRLFRIEND: Then, on May 1, 2013, Helen shows

up. Helen is my mother in law and Gale's mom, who had been deceased for 21 years, and whom I had personally never met in this physical life because she passed 5 years before I met and fell in love with her daughter Gale. But, suddenly now began to show up in my daily meditations……. At first I was unsure if I was imagining Helen or actually channeling her spirit.

Here I was writing journal pages, at the same time every day (3:00 AM) and this entity claiming to be the spirit of someone I have heard of but never met, wants to come through and dictate what I am going to write…… These impressions were coming in as intuitive feelings, and were difficult to tell from my own imagination…… And, although I intuitively knew it was actually Helen, on the other hand, I had never met her in this physical life…. Yet, she was adamant that she (Helen) was the *Force Majeure* that I was intuitively feeling.

Her messages always came as powerful, visceral feelings. Not originating in my intellect, but intuitively being felt through my heart.

This communication with the other side had originally begun with me actually asking questionsof Helen regarding the building she had designed and that we still live in. Gale uses me as an"in house" building engineer, and while looking at the original blue print drawings, I had noticed that the technical details did not match what had actually been built. Consequently, I would rhetorically say, ***"Helen, why did you let them build it that way?"*** But, then I would intuitively receive technical answers the following morning at 3:00 am, while writing my journal.

Sometimes the feelings were emotionally overwhelming, but I would write them all out in my journal. Shortly, it became quite clear to me that the thoughts being recorded were just not mine. They were recorded in phraseology that I often used, but were not my conclusions. Instead impressions were being transmitted to me from elsewhere, while using the images I had previously stored in my subconscious during my extensive reading.

But, a couple of weeks later, on May 18, 2013, during a Psychic Fair at the Golden Gate Spiritualist church. I chose to support the fund raiser and signed up for a private reading with a senior medium at the Church. This was the first personal reading I had experienced since the reading with Otis in New Orleans over a dozen years earlier. But, during the reading it became very clear that it was indeed Helen my mother-in-law who had been coming through.

The medium (Eunice Smith, an 85 year old lifetime psychic medium) said,

"Alan, I have a woman here who seems to be a mother figure".

This, had been designed by the communicator (Helen) precisely to throw me off track. And, it worked because I immediately thought about my own mother and my grandmothers all of whom are departed. And so I waited for a message from one of them.

But, then the medium said

"This woman also seems to have been an architect and is from Minnesota".

Bewildered, I said ***"But, neither my mother nor my grandmothers were from Minnesota, and none of them was an architect".***

So, I began to think back to my great grandmothers, but they were from New England and Virginia and they had come west through Missouri and Kansas, but not Minnesota.

The medium said, *"I will go back to her"*, and then became silent.

Finally, the medium said.

"Alan, this woman says that SHE IS NOT EXACTLY YOUR RELATIVE, BUT SHE IS A MOTHER FIGURE. … And, she is <u>not exactly</u> an architect,…… butshe did draw houses. However, she says is definitely from Minneapolis, Minnesota, and she has brown curly hair and brown or hazel eyes".

Then, suddenly all these uncannily accurate veridical facts, hit me like a ton of bricks…. The medium was communicating with Helen….. my mother-in-law. …. Who else but your mother in law is "a mother figure, but <u>not exactly</u> your relative".

And, further, Helen had been a real estate developer who had drawn the plans for severalhouses, but she was not exactly an architect…… Further, Helen had definitely been born and raised in Minneapolis, Minnesota, and she certainly had brown curly hair and hazel eyes (I have a color picture of her).

Now, I could no longer deny that the communicator talking to me every morning at 3:00 AM was, in fact, Helen, my mother-in-law who was clearly coming through to me now in this reading with the medium, who did not know anything about me and could not have researched all this information. And she must also be showing up in my daily meditations at home, just as I had at first felt it must be.

Now, it is a decade later and I have continued to be faithfully awakened by Helen between 3:00 and 4:30 am nearly every morning since then. She and I carry on a lively two way conversation in my intuition nearly every morning. And, I always share what she said with her daughter Gale every morning while we have coffee in bed. Helen is mightily concerned about her building, which Gale still owns, her daughters Gale and Bonita and her granddaughter Roxanne and her sister Genevieve. Indeed, Helen predicted Gen's demise and told Gale to drop everything at Thanksgiving (Nov. 22, 2018) to go see Gen in Minneapolis while they could still communicate on this side….. Gale went, they had that conversation which Helen had mentioned….. and then Gale came home….. Gen passed on December 7th, less that two weeks later.

Helen gives me advice from the spiritual perspective on all sorts of issues. And, she also works with me from that side when I (actually we) give readings as a psychic-medium to the public, whether Mediumship or Tarot readings.

Even now as I write, after having Helen come through steadily all these years, it still overwhelms me with awe at the power of the Universe and it makes me tear up. Recently, on a Sunday during the COVID shut downs, during a zoom church service with 86 people attending from SanFrancisco, throughout the USA including Hawaii, Oaxaca, Mexico and London England, Helen and I, as the demonstrating medium channeled spirits by name for a woman from in Maryland (we channeled Belinda), and an Icelandic Grandmother with a strange name "Runa" for a member from San Francisco.

Further, Helen has continued to come through in almost every reading I have personally had with any other medium, and whenever we practice at developmental circles and at *ArthurFindlay College-AFC* when working with other student mediums, Helen is identified by the mediums who do not know me. For example, the first time I went to AFC, Helen came through infive of the first 8 readings and I had to kindly ask her to hold back and let my other relativeshave a chance. So, apparently in a snit, Helen did not come through again for three days. Irecall a cute Danish medium to whom I was a complete stranger at Arthur Findlay College givingme a reading, and her first words were, ***"Is her name Helen?"*** as she looked over my left shoulder.

In another advanced class at AFC a couple of years later, the very experienced medium I was working with said, ***"She said she gave you a bracelet after she was deceased….How didshe do that?"***

So, I had to explain how She left the Silver and Turquoise Navajo bracelet for Gale in the safe when she died with a post it note on it saying "FOR GALE", and 21 years later when I began as a medium and Helen kept coming through, when several other mediums advised me to wear Turquoise to "break the circuit" with the people who unknowingly come to seances to feed offthe energy that mediums give off, *"Seances always make them feel so good"*. Gale had the bright idea ***"You can have Helen's bracelet"***. So, Helen gave me the bracelet from the other side 21 years after her transition. Incidentally, the turquoise works very well at breaking the circuit with the energy vampires.

Another time at a developmental circle in San Francisco, one of the mediums who knew me and also knew Helen's name and that she comes through to me said, ***"Alan I have a another women here today, I thought it would be Helen, but her name is "Dorothy"***. At which I had to literally stifle my laughter, because that is Helen's middle name, which he did not know and which she was using to sneak up on him, so his evidence would be something he did not know, even though I knew it. Such is the mirth and fun Helen has with me.

Helen also demonstrates her reality regularly by causing unmistakable things literal miracles to happen.

For example; on my birthday in February 2014, it was apparently Helen who had a birthday cardwith champagne delivered to my hotel room before I arrived at a hotel in Santa Barbara, California.

But, it was way beyond a simple coincidence......

First synergism; this was not the hotel that I had booked in advance In fact, I had

booked a different hotel...... Upon arrival at the first hotel I had been dissatisfied with the quality of the room So, I had apologized to Gale for having books such a shoddy

place and drove across town to a better hotel..... The Kimper Canary, in down town Santa Barbara. Consequently, the hotel staff did not know I was coming and could not have known it was my birthday......

Because of our recent dissatisfaction at the prior hotel, I was bit embarrassed and wanted to give Gale a better room so I asked for a junior suite.

 Due to the previous disappointment Gale, asked to see the room before we signed up. This is not our normal practice, but it seemed proper today. So, we went up and toured a junior suite, and of course they sent us to one that was already made up. Then we went back down to the desk and registered.

But, now the desk clerk had trouble booking that suite for us.

Second synergism; Unknown to us the law requires that if the innkeeper shows you a room, they can not then switch you to a different room, but must provide that room. Apparently, someone else had booked that specific junior suite and now the hotel manager he had to revise the reservations in order to give it to me, something the desk clerk could not do. But, the manager could and did.

Finally, when we went up to the room with the bellman and our luggage, there was already a chilled champagne complete with an un-opened card attached. Five minutes later the front desk called our room to apologize that the card and champagne had been 'mistakenly" left in the wrong room.....

They then said that I could go ahead and keep the champagne compliments of the hotel.

And there is the **Third synergism;;** the prior booking was for someone else's birthday. But, at this point I had not yet opened or read that card attached to the bottle. We went to dinner and then I went and gave the evening lecture I had come to Santa Barbara to present.

Finally, in the late evening, we returned to our room and decided to open our freechampagne. It was then that I found the card which said "Happy Birthday".

A skeptic will argue, that this is just a minor serendipity. But, really, free champagne and aBirthday card on my exact birthday in a room I did not reserve?....

I know that it was Helen manipulating thoughts of several people. just look at the statisticalodds:

1. The other guests booking a room with a birthday card and a champagne, Lets give that odds of 365......and with champagne 1 in 5 = 1 chance in 1,825

2. The people at the main desk sending me to a room reserved for someone else,say 1 in 5 to be conservative bumps it up to 1 in 9,125

3. Me deciding to change hotels in the first place.... For this I will give 1 in 10 odds. Thatis not something I do lightly so we have 1 in 90,125

4. Me to think I needed a junior suite to make up for booking a bad hotel, andThis cheap skate does not do that 1 in 10, bumps it up to 1 in 912,500

5. Gale to ask to see the room at that hotel, which then inadvertently caused them tohave to give us the room with the champagne Gale does not do this..... 1 in 20 leaves the odds of coincidence at 18.25 million to one

All those synchronistic events had to be manipulated to gain Helen's specific result ofsending me a Birthday Card and champagne in a room I had not reserved.

Later, that summer of 2014 at a convention of the Academy for Spiritual and Consciousness Studies in Phoenix, AZ, I met and spoke with a practicing medium Suzanne Giesemann, and she also said what I had heard before, **"Alan, you need to go to Arthur Findlay College and study Evidential Mediumship"**

So, in December 2014, I traveled to Stansted-Monfitchet in Essex England, to attend my first course at *Arthur Findlay College of Psychic Science.*

In following years 2015-2017 I finished an additional four courses there, including advanced mediumship courses. And, it was at that first course in December 2014 that I had a fantastic personal reading. and received Barbara Levines Message, as previously described in Chapter 8, which was earth shaking for me, and I could no longer deny that everyone continues to live post mortem.

To make sure I did not forget Helen has kept preforming miracles. When Gale and I vacationed to Lake Louise in mid-winter almost a year later in January of 2015, We took the overnight train from Vancouver BC to Jasper, Alberta, where we arrived on time and then drove our rental car through the snow down to *Chateau Lake Louise*. it was very cold, and we kept hearing news about delayed flights and delayed trains. The Chateau itself was nearly empty because no one was arriving due to cancelled flights and trains. But, we had a wonderful weekend in the nearly deserted Chateau and two days later we drove our car back to Jasper, Alberta (I grew up and learned to drive in high altitude Eastern, Oregon so snow driving is old hat for me). But, upon arrival in Jasper, Canadian National railroad informed us that the west bound passenger train, which they had claimed would be on time during a phone call the day before was now 17 hours late.

We quickly calculated that we could never reach our scheduled flight from Vancouver to San Francisco. So, we got a refund of our overnight train tickets for $600, and walked across the terminal to where we had just turned in our rental car. Unfortunately, our car was already spokenfor, but,

Miracle No.1, The attendant had her personal 4 wheel drive bronco, that I could rent one way to Vancouver for that same $600. The price included the additional cost of sending a driver by train down to Vancouver to pick the car up and drive it back to Jasper. But, it all made sense, so off we went through the thickening snow to Vancouver, BC, a two day drive. What arethe odds on this? I will give it a **1 in 10.**

After a long grueling drive, an overnight stay along the way, and waiting for an hour while they cleared a fatal accident of the highway in front of us. We arrived at Vancouver airport the following day just in time to check in for our flight,...... But, now with one of the worst weeks of snows in several years, and a cold snap which they called a "Polar Vortex", over 4000 flightshad been cancelled in North America alone due to the snow. But, with planes not coming in fromthe East everyone was stuck in the airport. We were simply told ***'There will be no planes to San Francisco, today".***

So, we walked to the First Class Lounge to wait. But, they said that regardless of our First ClassTickets, and regardless of it being an international flight Canada to the USA, Vancouver airport considered the first leg of our flight to Seattle to be a domestic flight. So, for us to use the First Class lounge it would be $75 each...... I grimaced and pulled out my platinum AmericanExpress to pay the $150. But,

Miracle No. 2, when they saw my credit card they said, ***"Oh you are a Platinum, this Lounge acts as a Centurion Lounge and you can go in for free"***. What if I had pulled out a master card instead? With 5 credit cards in my wallet we will give that miracle odds of **1 in 5.**

We got some snacks and took a seat in the lounge, But less than 20 minutes later we were informed that because we were Alaska First Class, there was a chance we could fly stand-by onan Alaska flight that was leaving soon for Seattle,..... So, we went out to that gate and got in thestand-by line.

But, now things really began to get even stranger.

Miracle No. 3, While we stood in the standby line other "Airport Personnel" came and got us outof the line....... How did they know who we were to be selected?...... They said that ***"US Air, Alaska and United, had collectively found an 'available plane' and were combining First Class flights onto it."*** Again what are the odds, when there are no planes and thousands of stranded passengers? Let's give it a **1 in 100,**

Now, consider that with 4000 flights cancelled how was there an *"available plane"*. But, they toldus the gate number and said they would take care of the re-route of our luggage. Looking back Ihave to ask....."***Were these airport personnel or angels.***"We walked to the appropriate gate, the United Airlines plane then loaded us all, But, now

Miracle No. 4, we were again seated in our exact same reserved seat numbers which we had booked in First Class with Alaska, and if the entire plane including tourist seats was made up of stranded First Class passengers (a 737 has 149 seats), then why did we get our same seats in the first row up in First Class and not someone else?....... odds of **1 in 149 x 2 = 298**

The plane then took off 20 minutes later. The flight also went directly to San Francisco, where our originally booked flights would have instead landed in Seattle first before continuing on to SFO.

Strangely, we touched down at SFO even before the in flight movie had finished playing, and then we taxied to United at Terminal 3, arriving about ten minutes later than we would have arrived on our original flight schedule.

Now comes the strangest part......**Miracle No. 5.** We disembarked and went to United baggageclaim where the monitor said luggage for our current fUnited light number would be on Carousel2….. At the carousel it also had our current United flight number listed….. **The red light came on and the carousel beeped, and began to turn…… but then everything stopped…..**

Next, as we stood at the carousel watching the monitor as our flight number suddenly disappeared…. I ran over to the first monitor by the base of the escalator that tells disembarking passengers which carousel to pick up luggage for which flight, and again Iwatched in amazement as our current flight number disappeared off that monitor.

Suddenly, we had no flight, and no luggage, and no ticket that said we were on that flight, andno luggage tags with which to claim our luggage….. But, we were now in San Francisco…..

But, now I remembered was that our original flight had been on Alaska airlines…. And, maybe, just maybe, our luggage could be at Terminal 1, where Alaska Airlines normally landed.

With no better plan, Gale and I trekked through the SFO covered parking lot from Terminal 3 to over to terminal 1 (where Alaska was at that time, in this continually being rebuilt airport). When we arrived at the terminal 1 baggage claim, there was our luggage sitting alone on a stopped carousel without any luggage tags, except our personal leather tags with our home address…. Lets give this odds of **1 in 2** (either United or Alaska)

We picked up our luggage and caught a cab for home. Later, I also realized that **Miracle No. 6** we had not been required to clear customs and immigration. Instead, we had been treated entirely as a domestic flight. Lets say odds of **1 in 10.**

So, now I have to ask, *"Did that extremely unusual flight really happen?"*…. Or did I imagine it all? … How did our luggage arrive at a different terminal with no tags?…. How did we avoid customs and immigration? …. And that flight arrived only 10 minutes later than we would have flown in on our original flight….. Again,… *"NO flights to San Francisco today"*

What really happened?….. You tell me….. Does consciousness work outside of time and space?….. As a scientist examining the empirical data of my own experiences, I actually no longer know. The rough odds come to **1 chance in 28.8. million**.

On the other hand, quantum physics does tell me that both time and space are just illusions which we construct to use as a frame of reference.

And, these "impossible" miracles with *no other explanation - NOE,* continue to happen, several times each year. But, those are just the miracles I can actually identify. What about the ones I don't see….. like the car wreck I was not involved in because I left early, or the flat tire that I did not have.

Indeed, both Gale and I now notice several miracles every day.

Helen always tells us to ***"Keep the faith, Hold the Joy, and witness the miracles"***. So, weask for help from the other side releasing the outcome to the universe ("Let go and let God"),and amazingly the miracles multiply.

Yeah, go ahead, call me crazy, …. but it happens. How do I ever get a departed spirit's

name? accurately right away?… I don't hear it,…. I don't see it, …. I feel it …… would you explain it to me? … Helen makes me feel it.

And, I get miracles as a side bonus.

I know it is all impossible…….. but it still happens. … … So my advice is quit being skeptical. …

"Let go and let God".

An article about my motorcycle wreck taken from May 29th 1970 Eugene Register Guard.

APPENDIX 4
MY PERSONAL NEAR-DEATH EXPERIENCE

Cyclist listed as 'critical' after accident

A motorcyclist was hospitalized in critical condition Monday afternoon after he struck the side of a moving car on West 11th Avenue near City View Street.

Injured was Alan Ross Hugenot, 21, of 2745 Emerald St., Eugene. A spokesman at Sacred Heart General Hospital in Eugene said Hugenot has head injuries and multiple fractures.

Hugenot remained in critical condition Tuesday morning, but the hospital said he had shown "some improvement."

The accident occurred about 4:30 p.m. as the cyclist was traveling east on 11th Avenue. Eugene police said a westbound car turned in front of Hugenot and Hugenot was unable to avoid colliding with the side of the car.

Officers cited Floyd Hargrove, 66, of 2256 Royal Ave., Eugene, on a charge of making an illegal left turn.

In May of 1970, and I was in Eugene, Oregon, attending evening classes at the University of Oregon and working days as a draftsman/ engineering technician, designing fire sprinkler systems. I commuted by motorcycle from the university campus to my job in West Eugene.

Until that time, I had attended Protestant services with my family on Sundays, I liked hiking and camping with the Boy Scouts. I got good grades in history, math, and science. I joined the Navy and served aboard a destroyer during the Vietnam War, before returning home to start college on the GI Bill.

My life had been mostly concerned with finding a career, getting adate, being accepted at college, etc. Any questions about what happens after death and consciousness survival were pushed aside. I easily accepted the prevailing Western cultural philosophy based on Materialism, that we live only one life, and if asked what I believed came after death, I would have said, "**According to my church we go to heaven or hell, but I'm not actually sure what really happens.**" At that stage of my life there were many more pressing problems to solve, and thoughts of the afterlife could wait.

But, everything changed on the evening of Monday, May 27, 1970. I was riding my motorcycle back to the University of Oregon campus on the way home from my design job, when I was involved in a collision with a car that turned left in front of me, and left me nowhere to go. I was severely injured and rushed by ambulance to the intensive care unit at Sacred Heart General Hospital, Eugene, Oregon, where I was hospitalized for about thirty-three days.

My right femur (thigh bone) was shattered, a portion of my right wrist (radius) was broken off and had lodged near my elbow, my right kneecap was completely crushed, and my head had experienced extremetrauma in a violent battering, due to the fact that motorcycle helmets in those days did not protect your lower face. My upper teeth had been destroyed entirely on one side of my jaw, and there were numerous fissures in my skull above the upper teeth, caused when my open mouth and skull collided with the luggage rack on the car.

When I arrived in the ER, my condition was *critical,* but I had been stabilized and was not hemorrhaging. So, they began preparing me for surgery. … … However, just prior to surgery, and about three hours afterthe accident, I became incoherent and unconscious.

My head injury had caused my brain to begin swelling, and in those days, they did not have the modern techniques which were learned in the Iraq War of cutting the skull open to let the brain have room toswell. Consequently, I went into a coma, where I remained for about twelve hours. Fearing that they might induce a permanent coma if they administered anesthesia to perform surgery, the doctors postponed my operations until after I had regained consciousness; they waited three days before performing the surgery.Basically, ***"If he is still alive on Thursday, we'll see what we can do."***

While I was in the coma, I always had a pulse EKG and an EEG, and so I was never actually pronounced dead. However, a good working definition for the Near-Death experience is a condition in which ***"if left alone, the patient would have died."*** So, I was in the ICU, in critical condition, in a coma, when the NDEtook place. Had I not been in the ICU, I would have most certainly died.

To this day, I recall nothing about the accident or arriving in the ER, although the nurses said I was actually coherent on arrival. Instead, my first recollections after the beginning of the accident were when I awoke, out-of-body, on "the other side" in communion with the *Being of Light*. I have no recollection of certain phases of leaving my body as described by other NDE survivors, but I vividly recall returning into the physical body. Surprisingly, not many NDE narrations describe the return to the body except to say, ***"Suddenly, I was back in my body."*** Yet I remember the details of this re-entry into physical matter in very clear visceral detail, which I will describe further on.

THE OTHER SIDE OF THE VEIL: The odyssey began for me when I just "woke up" on the other side, already with the *Being of Light*. The feeling was as if I had always been there. I felt completely home at last. *The Being of Light* was an old friend who had known me for eons. Time itself had ceased; there was no schedule and no hurry. Dimensional space (3-D as we know it here in physical reality) was not a concept in effect there. (*Years later, after string theory and dark energy had been developed, Iwould realize that I had move beyond this dimension and into the additional dimensions of dark energy.*)

But at the time, I just realized that borders and boundaries did not seem to exist in any concrete way wherever I was. Also, I felt loved, at peace, and as if I was being held like a babe in arms. Yet, I knewfrom deep within me that I was connected to, and an integral part of, the *Being of Light* Itself. We were notseparate beings. Instead, I was one essence with the brilliant golden white *light*. Everything was morethan okay. I knew that I had been there for quite a while prior to waking up. I was aware that I had been lovingly nurtured, and I awoke feeling "restored."

Now, slowly I became aware that I must return to physical life in time and space (i.e., move back into the physical realm of 3-D plus time). This idea, that I must go back into matter and a physical body, came to me not in words but intuitively, from the *Being of Light*. What I received was a distinct impression (ESP) that communicated:

> ***"Yet, a little while, and you can return to the Light, but for now you must return to the physical life, you have not yet fulfilled your destiny there."***

This awareness, that things were not yet finished with my prior physical life on earth, was the naturalresult of the things we (the *Being of Light* and I) had been reviewing just before my full awakening to my presence with the *Being of Light*. It was clear that this return to physical life would only be short term, andI would soon be able to return home again to the Light shortly So far, this short-term assignment has beenover fifty-four years. But, still it remains for me only a temporary assignment before I will return to my true home with the *Being of Light*. And, when you measure time in terms of eternity it is only a little while.

I noticed that the *Being of Light*, which I knew was connected with was part of the Supreme Consciousness of the Universe, yet it did not bother to identify itself as being Jesus, God, nor any other name. ... I just knew that while I was there, the *Being of Light* was part of me and of all things, and that we knew each other intimately, so there was no need for introductions or identity descriptions. We were part of each other, always had been, and what could be more simple? I had never experienced such a state of connectedness or love. Many years later in my research I would find the clearest description of this state of being a part of everything in the universe in the following passage taken from the *Gnostic Gospel of Phillip* (discovered at Nag Hammadi, Egypt, in 1945 and released to the West in 1977, these texts were written before 390 AD.):

"It is not possible for anyone to see anything of the things that actually exist unless he becomes like them. This is not the way with man in the (physical) *world: he sees the sun without being a sun; and he sees the heaven and the earth and all other things, but he is not these things. This is quite in keeping with the truth* (in the physical world).

But (when) *you saw something of that place* (eternity)*, you became those things.* (When)*you saw the Spirit, you became Spirit.* (When) *you saw Christ, you became Christ. You sawthe Father,* (and) *you shall become Father. So in this place* (physical world) *you see everything and do not see yourself, but in that place* (eternity) *you do see yourself andwhat you see you shall become."* Gospel of Phillip (Nag Hammadi Library Codex II Tractate 3 p.61)*Interpretations in parenthesis are the author's.*

This can be paraphrased as: *"You did see yourself (the **Light**) in that place and what you saw you shall become".*

MY RETURN TO THE BODY: Now, as I headed back to the physical life and reentered the feelings, pain, and suffering of a physical body, the *Being of Light* slowly began to be obscured by tendrils of reddish purple "blood," which began to wash over my view of the *Light*. The *Light* itself had now faded to an orange "sunset sky" behind a tie-dyed batik curtain of red tendrils. Slowly the red-purple tie-dyed streaks closing out the view of the golden-orange sky thickened until the *Light* was entirely obscured by the red-purple veil.

Note: I wrote down all these colors in the months following the NDE, yet I would find later in theexact same colors in the Tibetan Book of the Dead described as occurring in reverse order as one leaves the cadaver just after the death of the physical body.

In a metaphorical sense, I speak of this as a lowering of the "veil of blood and tears," believing that it represented the separation zone between the spiritual existence and the physical reality.

Many years later I would find the following passage in *A Course in Miracles,* which is clearly describing that same veil:

"In the holy instant nothing happens that has not always been. Only the veil that has been drawn across reality is lifted. Nothing has changed. Yet the awareness of changelessness comes swiftly as

the veil of time is pushed aside. No one, who has not yet experienced thelifting of the veil, and felt himself drawn irresistibly into the light behind it, can have faithin love without fear. Yet the Holy Spirit gives you this faith." A *Course in Miracles,* Chapter 5, Section VI

Being left alone again without the *Light* was now uncomfortable, and ***I truly did not want to come back here to this physical life.***

However, subjugating my "will" into the "blood" of this temporal existence, I did come back into the flesh. I reoccupied my body and this process of re-entry caused excruciating pain. I believe this pain was not from my injuries, but was entirely due to the conversion from spirit to physical. It was painful as I "slammed" back into the confinement of a body holding feelings. I could feel the dense heaviness of the body's physical mass, and the pain of having nerves, feelings, and emotions again, the literal thickness ofthe blood of existence, the hulking, dense mass of physicality. These tangible feelings and the associatedpain were all absent while I was with the *Light*; only love and knowledge remained with me there. Communing with the *Light*, only "metaphysics" existed, but when I returned to time and space, I re- entered "physics," the polarization of material existence.

During this re-entry, just prior to *slamming* into the physical, I saw myself surrounded by what I call**candle flames, or sparklers of light**. Later I would read P.M.H. Atwater, another near-death survivor, who records that:

> *"I floated ever so gently back into her body, moving as I went on **a layer of large bright sparklers** such as those used on the Fourth of July"* P.39
> *Coming Back to Life: The After-Effects of the Near-Death Experience,* P.M.H. Atwater

Apparently, from her description, she also saw the same candle flames (sparklers) that I saw. Later in my research I would find that Thoth-Hermes in the ancient Egyptian records had stated that our soul is **sheathed in flames**. I also found that the first through fourth-century Gnostic Christians, and the Hellenistic Mystery religions prior to them, all called this flame-filled reentry the "Baptism by Fire." It occurred for them after achieving enlightenment through an out-of-body spiritual communion with the *Light*. This "Baptism by Fire," marked the Gnostic level of enlightenment derived from literally "seeing the light."

> *Note: It isn't surprising that the original Gnostic Christianity often makes more sense to NDE survivors, while current versions of organized Christianity may seem to be weak, controlled, and watered-down misinterpretations. Also, particle physicist friends sometimes suggest that the flames or sparklers are merely our expanded awareness annihilating*

back into the void (zero-point field) as we return to the physical. Now, as yet we have no science on this, just speculation.

THE BRAIN SHIFT: It was just like that, lying there at peace in atonement with the *Light* and the universe, with not a care, and then suddenly *"in the twinkling of an eye"* re-entry into the intense pain and feeling of time and space.

Yet I did not come back as the same guy at all. I had undergone an extreme psychological make-over. The change that took place in my personality is described by many near-death survivors as a *brain shift*. When you return to this life, you are still a regular person; you haven't suddenly become a spiritual guruor shaman, although you may become one later. On the other hand, everything in your paradigm has shifted and you possess a rare gnosis that *Post-Mortem Consciousness Survival* is real and eternal.

It is as if your brain has been re-booted. The brain has temporarily shut down and now the read-only memory (ROM) is still there, but the random access memory, and anything held temporarily on it, has been wiped clean.

You have returned to re-energize the body's circuits (hardware) and begin to reboot the software, but itwill never be as it was before. This return to the prior life is actually a second life, and is not at all a part ofthe first life. For me, personally, it took many years to overcome the expectations of friends and relatives who still saw me as being the prior personality, and whenever I would act differently from their expectations, they would wonder what had come over me. Even to this day, they do not realize that, although I am the same *spirit*, I am a different *personality* than the one that died earlier. It is a better approximation to simply say that I was *reborn to a new life* (reincarnated) in the same body.

> *Note: NDE survivors have actually done what most Fundamentalist Christians claim to have done spiritually. The NDEr has been **"born again"** in the same body. It is a better approximation to simply say that I was reincarnated a secondtime into the same body. Also, this is **obviously what both Jesus and Saint Paul were actually talking about,** where the old person has died and a new person is living there instead.*

The previous life was over, and I now had a new life. The medical professionals may say that I revived, orhad never even died. But my memories of that prior life back in B.C. (Before Crash) are somewhat dim, and to describe them I like to say that they are recorded in black and white. To recall those memories of that first life, I have to go search them up in old files, which then have to be unzipped before I can access those dusty ROMs.

On the other hand, everything that has happened in this second life is held in RAM (random access memory) and is recalled immediately in vivid living color.

The altered worldview and the psychological changes that came back with me are these:

I have no fear of dying. While I do fear being injured or broken, I simply have no fear of death itself. I know that death is only a transition and I am fully aware that our consciousness survives that change. I have only returned here again temporarily, and so I am fully aware I can eventually return to the *Light*. I also know that to my *home-with-the-Light* is where I will go when I leave the physical existence.

1. **Material things have almost completely lost their importance to me**. I am still a very responsible worker who pays his bills and maintains good credit with the banks. But I am much more motivated by spiritual things rather than by materialism or success.

2. **I am much more feeling, psychic, able to read other's feelings and express love easily**. I have continually observed many psychic experiences merely because of my changed perspective.

3. **I realize all the world's religions don't have it right when it comes to dying**. But, also that each is founded on the honorable principle of attempting to find the truth.

4. **I no longer see any need for individual souls**. I felt a greater empathy for all souls. Later, I revisited this impression and realized that I actually see only one soul, which manifests itself in thephysical world in many different egos. Spiritually we are all part of one connected soul, although the consciousness seems to individuate on both sides of the veil.

5. **I no longer believe in retribution after death**, nor a heaven or hell as taught by most Western religions. I understood that there is only something to be learned in this physical life, and that any judgment we make after death, in our life review will be our own judgement that "it was all good."

6. **I also knew that no one leaves this physical life until their time**, which is not measured as a date, but as a condition of learning. They go when they are finished with learning. Not one second early, nor one second late.

THE TRAUMATIC AFTERMATH:

Waking up and finding myself back in the physical world, I immediately wanted to share what I had discovered about the afterlife and *Post-mortem Consciousness Survival*, and especially share with others how free that gnosis made me.

I had been gifted by the universe with the most precious piece of knowledge mankind, here in the physical plane, can ever have; the total assurance that life continues after physical death. But I quickly found that nobody wanted to hear about it! … … In fact, theyfound it disturbing.

I knew that eternal life was real, that there was no hell to pay, and that our consciousness survived in an alternative dimension. ***Oh, my God! What wonderful news is this!*** I also knew that eternal life was not something earned down at the church, but was a ***free gift for everyone***, precisely as St. Paul had declared in Ephesians:

"For it is by Grace you have been saved … it is the gift of God, not of works so that noone can boast. St. Paul's letter to the Ephesians 2:6-9 (NIV)

THE MEDICAL COMMUNITY DID NOT WANT TO HEAR ME:

Yet, when I began to describe my experience, the nurses quickly hushed me up on this subject. They seriously feared for my safety. This was back in 1970, five years before Dr. Moody's book and the near-death experience began to reach the mainstream of medicine. At the time, many nurses knew from experience about this phenomenon, but doctors trained in *Materialist* dogma were still refusing to think about it. Doctors who refused to consider it as real believed the NDE was merely a delusion. Psychiatrists wanted to condemn it as a psychotic disorder and were anxious to commit to an asylum anyone who persisted in talking about such obvious non-senes. So, I quickly learned to keep quiet about it while I remained in the hospital. I soon learned thatthe medical establishment, just like religious priests, only accept empirical evidence, or scientific evidence***And, only if it happens to agree with what they <u>already wanted to believe</u>***.

Note: I met an NDE survivor in 2014 who had her NDE in 2004 and was placed in the Mayo Clinic until she stopped talking about "that craziness." … … So, there are still medical doctors out there, in practice, who will commit people to the nuthouse for not agreeing with their chosen version of reality. This travesty of Materialist doctors denying religiousfreedom to others while forcing them to agree with their own religion of Materialism continues in the medical community even today.

MINISTERS REFUSED TO HEAR IT ALSO: After leaving the hospital, I hoped to discuss my experience with religious leaders, believing that would be a safer context and that the clergy would listen to me without trying to commit me to the asylum. ... ... But, again when I spoke with them, they also told me ima experience was merely a hallucination or a dream and simply could not be true ***because it disagreed with their particular interpretation of scripture.***

I was shocked by their desire to remain ignorant on the subject. Here, I had proof of the afterlife which thechurch had been seeking for all time. Yet, because my specific details were slightly different from their ancient speculations, they wanted to reject it out of hand. This is when I learned that the churches, just like the medical doctors, only accept empirical evidence or scientific evidence ***if it happens to agree withwhat they already choose to believe.***

My family also had great difficulties with my story. Out of loyalty to me, they wanted to believe me, but found it hard to step away from what they had believed for so long.

BIBLIOGRAPHY

THE DEATH EXPERIENCE: What it is like when you die. BY DR. ALAN HUGENOT ©2012 describes the story I have told today, The book is available in PAPERBACK or KINDLE from Amazon.

THE NEW SCIENCE OF CONSCIOUSNESS SURVIVAL: AND THE META-PARADIGM SHIFT TO A CONSCIOUS UNIVERSE **BY DR. ALAN HUGENOT** ©2016

VIDEO 1- "THE NATURE OF CONSCIOUSNESS" A December 2015 interview with Dr. Hugenot posted by Andrew Chene, https://youtu.be/yByEQfaD314

VIDEO 2 - "SCIENCE OF THE AFTERLIFE": A September 2013 Television interview with Dr. Hugenot speaking on the **Science of the Afterlife,** as delineated in his book **The DEATH EXPERIENCE, What is is like when you die,** is available at http://www.youtube.com/watch?v=sG8RAVh4VwEVIDEO 3 - "Dr. Dean Radin", Chief Scientist at Institute of Noetic Sciences (noetic.org) Discusses consciousness studies at Noetic.org VIDEO CLIP (3 minutes) is available at http://vimeo.com/113981492

ERASING DEATH – the science that is rewriting the boundaries between life and death ©2013, by Dr. Sam Parnia, M.D. with Josh Young.

QUANTUM ENIGMA – Physics Encounters Consciousness, ©2011, by Bruce Rosenblum and Fred Kuttner, Oxford University Press

CONSCIOUSNESS BEYOND LIFE – The Science of the Near Death Experience. ©2010, by Pin Von Lommel, M.D. Harper Collins

BEST EVIDENCE, 2d ©2012, by Michael Schmicker

DEMYSTIFYING the OUT-OF-BODY EXPERIENCE ©2012, by Luis Minero

BIOCENTRISM - How Life & Consciousness are Keys to Understanding the True Nature of the Universe. ©2009 , by Dr. Robert Lanza M.D. with Bruce Berman

THE BIOLOGY OF BELIEF – Unleashing the Power of Consciousness, Matter & Miracles. ©2005, by Bruce Lipton, Ph.D. Hay House, Inc.

HANDBOOK OF NEAR-DEATH STUDIES – 30 years of investigation, ©2009, By Janice Miner Holden, EdD. Bruce Greyson, M.D. and Debbie James RN/MSN, ABC-CLIO, LLC

INDUCED AFTER DEATH COMMUNICATION ©2005 & ©2014, By Dr. Allan Botkin

THE SURVIVAL OF MAN, ©1909 by Sir Oliver Lodge

RAYMOND OF LIFE AND DEATH ©1916 by Sir Oliver Lodge

THE FRENCH REVELATION ©1995, by N. Riley Heagerty:

TESTIMONY OF LIGHT ©1967, by Helen Greaves

THE AFTERLIFE REVEALED, WHAT HAPPENS AFTER WE DIE. ©2011, By Michael Tymn

Endnotes

1   Dr. Michael Sabom ©1998 p. 184, Light & Death

2   Chris Carter, ©2010, p.220, Science if the Near-Death Experience

3   Dr. Sabom discusses the Pam Reynolds case https://youtu.be/GleW0qLQUtY

4   Dr. Sam Parnia, ©2013, Erasing Death

5   Dr. Parnia discusses all this in 2019 at this URL: https://youtu.be/Hz_4FGdWVF8

6   Dr. Sam Parnia, ©2013, Erasing Death

7   Hiker Survives After Going into cardiac Arrest for Six Hours BBC NEWS, TODAY, USA TODAY, 6 DEC 2019

8   Hiker Survives After Going into cardiac Arrest for Six Hours https://youtu.be/ayyLpOtkzW8

9   Norwegian Woman Survives Lowest Body Temperature Ever Recorded www.sciencealert.com reported on 14 October 2016

10   Norwegian Woman Survives Lowest Body Temperature Ever Recorded https://www.rd.com/list/people-w 10 ho-froze-came-back-to-life/

11   https://www.sciencealert.com/this-woman-survived-the-lowest-body-temperature-ever-recorded

12   12The conclusion of volume 10 in Plato's Republic (10.614–10.621)

13   Van Lommel, Near-death experience in survivors of cardiac arrest: a prospective study in the Netherlands LANCET DOI:https:// doi.org/10.1016/S0140-6736(01)07100-8

14   Van Lommel ©2011Consciousness Beyond Life

15   Dr, Von Lommel interview youtu.be/RkF4KzWTrKA

16   Ian Stevenson, M.D ©1974 Twenty Cases Suggestive of Reincarnation, University of Virginia

17   Ian Stevenson, M.D., ©2001 Children Who Remember Previous Lives, McFarland & Company, Inc.

18   Jim B. Tucker, M.D. ©2005 Life Before Life,

19   Is There Life After Death? 50 years of Research at UVA https://youtu.be/0AtTM9hgCDw

20   Ian Stevenson, M.D. ©1997 Where Reincarnation and Biology Intersect, Praeger Westport,CT

21   Ian Stevenson, M.D ©19 74 P. 183, Twenty Cases Suggestive of Reincarnation, University of Virginia.

22   Ian Stevenson, M.D ©1974, p. 187 Twenty Cases Suggestive of Reincarnation, University of Virginia.

23   Ibid.

24   Ian Stevenson, M.D ©1974, Twenty Cases Suggestive of Reincarnation, University of Virginia.

25   https://psi-encyclopedia.spr.ac.uk/articles/marta-lorenz.

26   Robert Almeder, ©1992 ,p. 5, Death and Personal Survival, Rowman & Littlefield Publishers, Inc.

27   K.K.N. Sahay ©1927, Reincarnation: Verified Cases of Rebirth After Death, N.L. Guipta.

28   Stephen E Braude © 2003 P.183 Immortal Remains: The Evidence for Life After Death

29   https://psi-encyclopedia.spr.ac.uk/articles/bishen-chand-kapoor

30   Robert Almeder, ©1992, p.19, Death and Personal Survival, by Rowman & Littlefield Publishers, Inc, Almeder also lists numerous other publications which discuss this case uncritically.

31   https://www.carolbowman.com/dr-ian-stevenson/case-shanti-devi
32   Bruce & Andrea Leininger, © 2010 Soul Survivor, The Reincarnation of a World War II Fighter Pilot
33   ibid.
34   James Linegar https://youtu.be/h82PwADicl8
35   James Linnegar's and Barbro Karlan's https://youtu.be/9w2MCpzE8u0
36   61 children who remember past lives https://psi-encyclopedia.spr.ac.uk/articles/children-who-remember-previous-life
37   Brian Weiss, M.D, © 2001, p.7, Messages from the Masters, Warner Books
38   Brian Weiss, M.D, © 1988, p.12, Many Lives, Many Masters, Simon & Schuster
39   Brian Weiss interviewed by Ophra https://youtu.be/WMlLoPYwZ5w
40   Brian Weiss, M.D, © 1988 Many Lives, Many Masters, Simon & Schuster
41   Brian Weiss, M.D, © 2001 Messages from the Masters, Warner Books
42   Ibid.
43   Brian Weiss, M.D, © 2004, P. 8, Same Soul Many Bodies, Free press
44   Jenny Cockell ©1993, Across Time and Death,, Fireside Books, London.
45   Jenny Cockell https://youtu.be/snnmlqz_UCc
46   Peter Ramster, ©1980, The Truth About Reincarnation, Ridby, Australia,
47   Reincarnation - 1981 https://youtu.be/TrXtkYV9sk8
48   Ramster interview https://www.youtube.com/watch?v=tCmsuvbfI1E
49   Sir Oliver Lodge ©1909 The Survival of Man, Society for Psychical Research
50   Sir Oliver Lodge ©1916 Raymond or Life and Death, Methuen & Co., London
51   Deborah Blum, ©2006, P275-285, Ghost Hunters, Century
52   Brian Inglis ©1977, 1992 Natural and Supernatural: a history of the Paranormal,
53   The Cross-Correspondences are discussed by Russel Targ and Jeffery Mishlove on the video at this URL. https://youtu.be/ to7NEq0A9to
54   Cross Correspondences https://youtu.be/eZbWIdkirck
55   Jane Katra, PhD. And Russell Targ ©1999 P.87, The Heart of the Mind by, New World Library
56   HMS BARNUM & Helen Duncan https://youtu.be/yJX1hmkGgg8
57   R-101 https://youtu.be/yfTK_qjl_5Y?list=PLLB-82YMhiPFPKSm2Ke69aK0DKTftpvo0
58   Eileen Garrett & R-101 http://www.euro-tongil.org/swedish/english/er101.htm
59   R101 ENGINEERING https://youtu.be/ixxXhZVFXxQ
60   http://www.harrypricewebsite.co.uk/Seance/Garrett/leaves-r101.htm
61   Deborah Blum, ©2006, *Ghost Hunters*, Century,
62   Alan Gauld ©8319 Mediumship & Survival,
63   Deborah Blum, ©2006 *Ghost Hunters, Century*
64   Michael Tymn, ©2013 *Resurrecting Lenora Piper*
65   George Pellew https://psi-encyclopedia.spr.ac.uk/articles/leonora-piper
66   Gary E Swartz, PhD and Julie Beischel, Ph.D. ©2006, *Survival is in the Details*: Emerging Evidence for Discarnate Intention from Mediumship Research, University of Arizona
67   Ibid.
68   https://anomalien.com/has-montague-keen-really-returned-from-the-dead/
69   2012 IONS study
70   The coffin texts from the Nicropolis at Saqquara (2450 BC)